COSSACK REBELLIONS

COSSACK REBELLIONS

Social Turmoil in the
Sixteenth-Century Ukraine

Linda Gordon

University of Massachusetts, Boston

State University of New York Press   *Albany*

Published by
State University of New York Press, Albany

© 1983 State University of New York

For information, address State University of New York
Press, State University Plaza, Albany, N.Y., 12246

Library of Congress Cataloging in Publication Data

Gordon, Linda. Cossack rebellions.
Bibliography: p. 265
Includes index.
1. Cossacks—History. 2. Ukraine—History—To 1648. 3. Poland—History—Elective
monarchy, 1572–1763.
I. Title.
DK35.G68 1983   947'.7100491714   82–19705
ISBN 0–87395–654–0
ISBN 0–87395–653–2 (pbk.)

To *A. H. and the spirit of Solidarność*

Contents

Maps

Illustrations

Acknowledgments

THIS BOOK was a long time in growth. It began as a course paper under Professor Firuz Kazemzadeh at Yale in 1962. The cossacks soon became an object of fascination to me, and, eager to study them beyond the limits of material available in the United States, I went to Europe to work on them, turning the material into a dissertation, which was completed in 1969. I then put it aside entirely for a decade while I worked in quite another field—United States women's history. To my surprise, when I reread the dissertation in 1978, I was again caught up in the high adventure and complex intellectual problems offered by the cossacks. Transforming the work into a book required then several more years.

Thus it has been nearly two decades that I have been interested in the cossacks. In that time I naturally incurred many debts for intellectual, bibliographical, and other sorts of help. I worry that the long passage of time has caused many who supported me to be overlooked in these acknowledgments; if so, and if they notice the omission, I hope that they will blame a poor memory and not an ungrateful spirit.

Several professors gave me ideas and critical skills that made this work possible. They include, above all, Professor Kazemzadeh; also Professors Monroe Beardsley, Paul Beik, John Morton Blum, the late Hajo Holborn, Lawrence Lafore, and Olga Lang. The intellectual encouragement that led to this book began even earlier, with my parents, Helen and William Gordon. Skilled and imaginative archivists and librarians at many institutions—Yale University, the Library of Congress, the British Museum, the Polish Library of London, and Warsaw and Cracow universities—offered help.

Varying sorts and degrees of encouragement and help came to me from Feroz Ahmad, Len Bushkoff, David Hunt, Allen Hunter, Anne Doyle Kenney, Esther Kingston-Mann, Marta Petrusewicz,

Elizabeth Pleck, and Richard Stites. Temma Kaplan read and edited the entire manuscript at an early stage. Marta Petrusewicz and Allen Hunter found time to read and criticize sections of this manuscript. I am grateful to all these friends despite my discomfort in knowing that I have not been able to live up to their high standards.

Those who know my other scholarly work may find it odd that I have been so involved for so long with a manuscript that has no women in it. My own introspection suggests that there are connections between these different historical interests. I have particularly enjoyed the detective-like work of reconstructing a historical narrative for the first time from primary sources, a process characteristic both of this book and of the entire field of women's history today. Even more deeply, perhaps, I have been attracted to the love of freedom, however wrongheadedly it was sometimes expressed, that moved the cossacks.

Note on Transliteration

Transliteration decisions for this book concerned not only readability and the accurate rendition of the Cyrillic alphabet but two other problems: (1) that spelling was not standardized in the 16th- and even 17th-century documents that provide the information for this study, and (2) that the same names are often given sometimes in Russian, sometimes in Ukrainian, sometimes in an ill-defined Ruthenian, and sometimes in Polish. Thus, much is left to the discretion of the historian. My procedure has been as follows: The names of figures and places known to be or considering themselves Polish, or customarily rendered in Polish in the contemporary sources, are given in Polish. The names of figures and places known to be Ruthenian or Belorussian, or identified primarily with the Ukraine, I have given in transliteration from the Cyrillic. (This policy is complicated by the fact that the nationalities of some of the people in this narrative may be indeterminable, in transition, or even nonexistent.) I have adopted the spellings most recognizable to English-speaking readers. That is, I have ended names in "sky" instead of "skyi" or "skii," e.g., "Ostrozhsky." When the Cyrillic spellings are inconsistent, I have used the most common and/or the simplest. When figures have become known in modern historical writing, I have used the most well-known form of the name or place, e.g., "Kiev," not "Kiiv." Where towns have a common English version, e.g., "Cracow," I have used it.

In opting for readability and recognizability, I am aware that I am replicating a bias toward the Russian, over the Ukrainian, language. I have severe regrets about this outcome, as it is clear that Russification proceeds through linguistic and other cultural means as well as through economic and political power. However, a scholarly book should not sacrifice clarity to its author's partisan sympathies.

The problem of both Russian and Ukrainian versions of names emerges particularly in the footnotes and bibliography. Many writers have published in both languages, particularly Ukrainians and Belorussians forced at certain historical moments to publish in Russian. Again, my primary commitment has been to readers, and their ease in finding the materials to which I refer. Thus I usually give an author's name as it occurs on most of his/her publications: I list "O. M. Apanovych," who published mostly in Ukrainian, but "A. I. Baranovich," a Ukrainian who published mostly in Russian. I apologize for errors that will likely have slipped by, and wish to assure readers that no partisanship is intended by my spellings.

My transliteration system aims at readability. In the spirit of the transliteration system known as the "compromise British,"[*] I have used the Library of Congress system, with the following exceptions:

Cyrillic		*Latin*
и		i
й		i
ы		y
i	(Ukrainian)	i
ий, ый	(at end of names)	y
ъ		omitted
ь		omitted
э		e
я		ya (at beginning of words)
я		ia (elsewhere)
ая		aya
ия		ia
ыя		ya
ию		iu
кс		x

---

[*]W. K. Matthews, "The Latinization of Cyrillic Characters," *Slavonic and East European Review*, 30 (1951–52), pp. 541–45.

Introduction

THE COSSACKS are an unusually rewarding historical subject, certainly for the scholar and, I hope, also for the reader. They offer us gripping adventure stories even as they lead us to questions of great significance for the history of Europe. I have designed this book in the hope that the reader can share this double satisfaction. The book makes a complex argument about who the cossacks were, their relation to environmental, political and social conditions, and their historical influences on other events. I have tried to provide evidence to support these arguments, and to help the reader evaluate them in comparison to other previous historical arguments, without sacrificing the adventure story.

Indeed, it is part of the argument of this book that the adventure story itself is significant. Denying both romantic idealizations of the cossacks, and determinist reductions of them to mere reflections of socioeconomic forces, we show that, although constrained in many ways, the cossacks were willful, often capriciously motivated historical actors who hurled themselves into action, determined to remake their world through their "adventures." No wonder their intrigues, their defeats as well as their victories, are fascinating and somehow satisfying, like a swashbuckling adventure story. At the same time the narrative opens to scrutiny the structures of cossack society, the trajectory and power of the social changes they encountered.

On another dimension this book also attempts a double task: it is both a contribution to Ukrainian history and to the history of the Europe-wide phenomenon identified by Eric Hobsbawm as "social banditry." (See Chapter 5). There is no question but that the Zaporozhian cossacks, nucleus of the Ukrainian group, were quintessentially Ukrainian, responding to particular and unique Ukrainian conditions, and helping to form the Ukrainian people. At the same

1

time, groups of social bandits sharing significant features with the cossacks could be found in many of the less-developed parts of Europe, which were undergoing sharp social transformation, notably the spread of capitalist social relations at the expense of traditional, aristocratic–servile relations, from the sixteenth through the nineteenth centuries.

This twofold orientation structures the narrative and analysis of this book. It tells the story of a crucial decade in Ukrainian history, 1590 to 1600, a decade in which open rebellion against Polish authority first appeared to many Ukrainian residents as an option—an option which was, of course, to be acted upon a half-century later. It also tells of the formation of a coherent brotherhood of social bandits, the process of their self-organization and development as a foreign and domestic military power. In both aspects, this book adds to and challenges older interpretations. The cossacks have long been placed at the center of Ukrainian history, but there is need for a revised and critical specification of their exact relation to the development of the Ukrainian nationality. And, while Hobsbawm's concept of social banditry is useful, it only shows the need for a more complex definition of cossackdom. Their important international role as mercenaries put them in an unusual position, as did their dissident religious and national identification within the Polish Commonwealth.

Re-examining the cossacks' early rebellions raises a question vital to the understanding of both social banditry in general and Ukrainian history in particular: a question raised by this book's title. The question is, how political were the early cossack rebellions; or, how "social" was their banditry? Moreover, how did the cossacks transform themselves from social bandits in the sixteenth century to leaders of a political rebellion in the seventeenth? The rebellions of the 1590s were midway in that process, between their fifteenth-century frontier-bandit origins, and their seventeenth-century political role as the army for a Ukrainian secessionist movement.

Because of the romantic mythology and literature surrounding the cossacks, the historian's role becomes in part a debunking one, insisting upon what the cossacks were *not*. They were not a nationality, nor Orthodox Crusaders. They were not invincible warriors. They were not particularly heroic, but neither were they particularly more merciless than their opponents or other military organizations. To demystify the cossacks also requires an attempt to separate mythology from their history.

At the same time, the mythology is itself part of the historian's evidence, and the debunking process need not discard this evidence. The myths—heroic, monstrous, religious, and nationalistic—were in part made by the cossacks themselves. Myth was among their military weapons. Myth was also an important part of their self-definition and thus of their cohesion as a group. Even the legends not invented by the cossacks but applied to them by friends and enemies were at times absorbed by the cossack brotherhood and manipulated in the cossack interest. The task of the social historian is by no means to dismiss all such literary imagery as false, but to understand such cultural artifacts as potentially legitimate evidence. Like all evidence, cultural imagery must be subject to critical, evaluative scrutiny, to determine its truth and what conclusions it can support.

In this book there is, then, alongside a narrative, an argument about who the cossacks *were,* and the argument incorporates cultural as well as political-organizational material in that definition. The definition is dynamic, not static. To summarize what follows, there are three segments to the definition:

First, the cossacks were both a sui generis phenomenon and a form of social bandit.

Second, the cossacks were conditioned by many factors in their physical and human environment. The influence of *geography* can be seen in the development of similar groups across the Eurasian steppe. The particular *demography* of the Ukrainians, the numbers, distribution and social characteristics of the population, made the Zaporozhian cossacks distinct from, and much stronger than, other cossack groups. The Zaporozhian brotherhood and its behavior were further conditioned by the social, economic, and political organization of the *Polish-Lithuanian Commonwealth,* which controlled the Ukrainian lands, and also by the *old Rus* and *Tatar societies,* which had once exerted control and left their legacy. The *religious and national struggles* in the Ukraine of Orthodox, Moslem and Catholic, Ruthenian, Polish and Tatar, influenced cossack development. *International factors,* mediated through both economic and military developments, also influenced the cossacks.

Third, and weighing against the second factor, is that the cossacks also invented themselves. None of the conditions of their development were determining ones, nor were all the influences together determining. The cossacks were historical subjects. They responded of course to events structured without their will, and moved within limits they did not set, but they also made choices.

These choices, the cossacks' actions, then affected and helped cause other events and situations. Indeed, for a group of their small size they had a considerable impact on the future of their part of the world.

This definition is the argument of this book. It is summarized above at the risk of distorting it by making it abstract and static. In reality the cossacks' definition changed over time in a process beginning in the late fifteenth century. In this book I try to reproduce that process in miniature, letting the cossacks define themselves in the course of the narrative.

This dynamic and multifactor definition has rather specific implications which can be best understood in contrast to previous (implicit and explicit) definitions offered by historians. For example, from the contemporary chroniclers of the sixteenth century to today's Soviet historians, the most important stream in cossack scholarship has been the romantic one. In the Polish version, the cossacks were fundamentally alien, verging on the savage, wild, and inexplicable, representing the principle of anticivilization. Their military exploits were exaggerated, and approval and revulsion mixed together in the sensationalized descriptions of their warfare and other customs. Nationalistic Ukrainian historians, emerging mainly in the nineteenth century, represented the cossacks not as alien but as the very essence of Ukrainian character. Indeed, to the cossacks was attributed a virtually teleological definition—they were those who were to lead the Ukrainian people to freedom—a kind of chosen people of the Slavs. The Ukrainian historians also exaggerated cossack military exploits, and particularly overstated their religiosity. Russian historiography, Imperial and Soviet, presented a suspicious and mixed version of this romanticism: wishing to claim the cossacks in their capacity as Slavic adventurers but to disclaim them as Ukrainian nationalists.

In more recent historiography, romanticism has given way to a more skeptical view of the cossacks, by implication minimizing their influence and emphasizing the power of large-scale economic changes in producing the cossack phenomenon. In the last few decades substantial empirical research has been accomplished, particularly by Poles, about the east-European grain trade and other economic developments affecting the cossacks' period and region. The interpretations offered by Soviet Marxists and western economic historians about sixteenth-century eastern Europe tend to converge in an economic determinism, suggesting that forces of production or marketing, respectively, created rebels, such as the cossacks, as epiphenomena. This reductionism views not only the cossacks' but also other social, cultural and political activity as a result, never the moving force, in historical change. Both romantic and economic-determinist writings are discussed more fully in the historiographical essay at the end of this book.

My interpretation criticizes both romanticism with its exaggerated view of the cossacks, and economic determinism with its minimal evaluation of them. I am operating from a theory of history that is nondeterminist and skeptical of monocausal or teleological explanations. It is not so much that large-scale causal explanations are never true, but that in themselves, when applied to historical material, they must usually float at such a high level of generality that they illuminate little. In the story of the cossacks, events were pushed forward through the struggles of groups of people motivated by self-interests, and one might describe these interests as economic at bottom. But one must recognize that the "economic" refers not just to grain tonnages or even the amount of *corveé*, but to how the conditions of living are experienced by real, specific people. Economic conditions include, therefore, family and village organization, relations with taxing and conscripting political authorities, alternatives for servitude or freedom, and many other factors usually considered "social" or "cultural." These factors influence one another; for example, past patterns—that is, cultural norms—condition how people face present problems; and both past and present condition the formulation of future goals. These multiple influences sometimes conflict. The cossacks were frequently faced with contradictory impulses and pressures, both external and from within their brotherhood.

It is possible to try to measure the cossacks' approximate impact on events, and the degree to which they were the authors of events or merely the carriers of forces emanating outside themselves. Before measurement, however, it is necessary to identify some complex mediations in these causal patterns. There are many truths about the cossacks, not one essence. They were brutal but also calm and at times lenient; they were militarily cunning but at other times foolish, impetuous, and prideful; they were politically calculating and also spontaneous, moved by honor and ideology, and easily carried away. They had great internal coherence and a sense of brotherhood that rivaled kinship in its intensity, but they were also torn by internal dissension and jealousy. They were at times self-consciously Ukrainian even as their members came from many ethnic, religious, and even language, groups. They were a community at certain moments, but on the whole, far short of a community.

Complexity need not mean lack of synthesis or senselessness. There was long-range continuity in cossack history. The synthesis of so many factors is possible in this study—given the limitations of cossack historiography until now—because of its close focus on a relatively short and early period in cossack history. The heated, unsubtle and ideological arguments of much previous historical writing about the cossacks virtually cry out for this kind of study.

The description and narrative offered here present several advantages, I hope, for the general reader as well as the scholar. The missing pieces in the reconstruction of events are a constant reminder that this is not fiction—the free product of an author's imagination—that no matter how exotic, these events actually happened. The detail allows for a fuller understanding than has previously been available of cossack warfare on land and sea, diplomacy, political organization, sources of support, means of getting and directing this support, leadership, ritual—shaped into a kind of dynamic, narrative, ethnography. It also offers pictures of certain individual cossacks and their motivations, which in turn help to illuminate the group's coherence and conflicts. Also, the concentration on a relatively few events allows a much closer evaluation of the validity of the traditional chronicles than has previously been attempted, through close comparison of every available version of an individual event.

The implications of this study move out from its central decade—1590–1600—like concentric waves. The evidence from the rebellions of that decade affects, and requires revision in, our understanding of cossack composition, the origins of the brotherhood and its famous Zaporozhian headquarters, and its entire previous history. Similarly this study challenges some of the classic interpretations of the cossack role in later history, in the development of the hetmanate and Ukrainian national self-consciousness, and in the cession of the Ukrainian lands to Imperial Russia.

This study relies not only on microscopic analyses of two rebellions, but also on a macroscopic view of them in an international context. In the last decade there has been significant historical controversy about the economic formation of modern Europe and the international development of capitalism. Several studies have discussed the role of eastern Europe in those developments, but none has focused on the position of the Ukraine in them. This book situates not only the Ukraine but also the cossacks in these trans-European developments. At the same time it offers a methodological and theoretical look at what the study of markets and changing agricultural production implies for the historian of social movements.

A brief description of the book's organizaion may help guide the reader. In Part One, three chapters set out a basic introduction to the cossacks' environment in three categories. Chapter 1, "The Land," discusses the Ukrainian frontier and the cossacks' adaptation to their geography. Chapter 2, "The People," discusses population size, national and religious divisions, and social organization. Chapter 3, "The Rulers," describes the political control of the Ukrainian lands.

A discussion of the international economic context of cossack and Ukrainian sixteenth-century life is set out in Part Two. It contains a critical view of other interpretations and this author's own argument.

In Part Three, another three chapters describe the nature of the Zaporozhian cossack brotherhood. The chapters are divided topically—one on social organization, one on military organization, and one on relation to the Polish-Lithuanian State. Each chapter is also a small piece of history, showing how these forms developed over time, and the ways in which they were still in flux at the beginning of the actual narrative.

The rest of the book is divided into two other parts, each describing one of the rebellions of the 1590s and followed by a separate conclusion. Within each part, chapters have a dual function: they each narrate a chronological portion of the events *and* focus particularly on a theme or motif of cossack activity. Thus, in Part Four, on the first rebellion, Chapter 8 discusses the events of 1589 to 1590 and cossack–Tatar warfare. Chapter 9 covers the year 1591, and examines the relationship between personal grievances and feuds, and the cossacks' role as social rebels in the Ukraine. Chapter 10 describes the first half of 1592 and analyzes the degree to which the cossacks were functioning as popular insurgents, focusing, that is, on their relations with the non-cossack population. In Chapter 11 the crown and aristocratic defense becomes the subject, and the narrative is continued to February 1593. In Chapter 12, the story of the first rebellion is concluded with an analysis of the events immediately following the cossack "surrender" to the end of 1593, and an evaluation of who was the victor.

In the narrative of the second rebellion the themes elaborated in the previous part are not repeated—though where they reoccur, their pattern is noted. The chapters call our attention to different, and now more specific, motifs. Chapter 13 describes the emergence of the cossack leaders of the "Nalivaiko rebellion," and offers an interpretation of the nature of individual leadership and the reaction to it within the cossack brotherhood. Chapter 14 evaluates the cossacks' considerable significance, domestic and international, as mercenaries; and covers the two years between mid-1593 and August 1595. The next three chapters each cover both a particular Ukrainian province and a particular social issue and source of support for the cossacks and the social rebellion they led. Chapter 15 describes the Bratslav episodes of the rebellion between late 1594 and autumn 1595, focusing on the attitude of Ukrainian town-dwellers. Chapter 16 covers Volynia, from spring 1595 to the end of 1596, and focuses on the religious question—were the cossacks leading a protest of the Orthodox? Chapter 17 is about Belorussia, from December 1594 to February 1596, and discusses perhaps the largest issue: relations between cossacks and the masses of the peasant population. In Chapter 18 the Royal campaign against the cossacks is described, a rather significant story as a military narrative alone. Within the narrative the military behavior of the cossacks is analyzed closely with the purpose of drawing out their war aims, noticing which they were willing and able to compromise and which they were not, using their very desperation in defeat as a litmus test for a kind of final statement of what they were about.

The structure of this book was designed to allow the savor of an adventure story to pervade a closely analyzed and argued piece of social history. It would be a shame if such analysis, and the evaluation of other historical interpretations, interfered with the readers' intercourse with the subjects themselves. If not one of the major social phenomena of the modern world, the cossacks' influence was nevertheless considerable in eastern Europe. Moreover, the cossacks' historical image has been evocative beyond their immediate influence. Their determination to master an autonomous area, their pretensions and daring, their disrespectful, even naive, treatment of great political powers, combined with their own political willfulness (or "self-willedness," in a literal translation)—these qualities have had great and universal appeal. Seen as ruthless and brutal by enemies, as heroic by friends, for both sides the cossacks represented some essential quality of human aspiration, rejecting fatalism with social pridefulness. Xenophobic, authoritarian, cruel, and ignorant though they were, they nevertheless achieved some grandeur as they hurled themselves into history pursuing what they felt to be freedom and self-respect. For that alone, their story is worth preserving.

Part One
The "Wild Steppe"
and Its People

1. The Land

THE PASSIONS and willfulness, brutality and courage of the cossacks seem to fit their geographical home, aesthetically and emotionally. It is tempting to reflect that the cossacks were the human expression of the Black Sea steppe; but such an argument would be incomplete, because the cossacks also helped create the human meaning of the steppe, the very connotations of the word. In cossack history there is a dialectic between a people and their land: the qualities and quantities of their space shaped their personal lives and social structure, as the people shaped the social and political order and use of that space.

The land of the Ukraine is mostly a plain stretching from the Pruth River on the west to the Don on the east, from Kiev in the north to the Black Sea in the south. In the sixteenth century the area described as the Ukraine also included the eastern part of the Carpathian Mountains and the southern part of the forest land below the Pripet River. The cossacks often wintered even north of that, since fuel was scarce on the steppe and nothing broke the winds. But their base was the steppe.

The Ukrainian steppe is part of a large Eurasian plain that stretches from the Baltic and to the Pacific. The forest belt and tundra north of it gained historical significance relatively recently, compared to the steppe, which has supported large populations as far back as records existed. The steppe has four chief characteristics: flatness, extreme temperature variation, dryness, and treelessness. These conditions have created a relative uniformity among steppe societies, as compared to the variations in different environments. The Scyths, living on this land in the fifth century B.C., as described by Herodotus, resembled the Tatars and cossacks two thousand years later.[1]

From the point of view of military security such a plain could

11

hardly be worse. The Ukraine was not only on the direct route from the southern Asian lowlands to the heart of Europe, but was also, historically, a buffer between Occidental and Oriental civilizations. From its earliest history Ukrainian territory was the avenue for countless migrations and invasions—Sarmatians, Alans, Goths, Huns, Bulgars, Avars, Scandinavians, Mongols. In modern history, Tatars, Turks, Poles, Lithuanians, Austrians, Russians, French, and Germans have coveted the Ukraine for its agricultural and mineral riches. The Ukraine's only natural defenses are the Black Sea in the south and the Polesian marshes in the north—thus nothing breaks east–west travel.

This vulnerability, coupled with difficult climatic factors, impeded the development of agriculture. On a large part of the Eurasian plain, a kind of nomadic pastoralism remained the dominant mode of production well into the modern era. Although it was no longer dominant in the sixteenth-century Ukraine, its influence on the cossacks was great enough that a brief description of this kind of economy in its pure form seems useful. For a truly nomadic group, herds, not land, were the essential forms of wealth;[2] at times individual ownership of cattle was accompanied by collective ownership of land. In Russian, as in most European, historiography, nomadic societies have been categorized as universally and by necessity less advanced than peasant societies. This is oversimple, because in some ways the nomads had superior skills in exploiting the natural world, and they were certainly more cosmopolitan than peasants. The nomads were skilled horsemen and livestock managers. Young men quickly gained knowledge of vast amounts of territory. They used money more than most premodern or even early modern peasant communities, and often conducted a lively commerce, which was integrated with wars for booty and taxes. They were able to gather large and permanent armies. Nomadic groups, however, also had particular weaknesses, notably their inability to support large populations or to maintain stable domination over territories.[3]

In the most arid, eastern parts of the sixteenth-century Ukraine, peoples of European and Turkic origin lived, similarly, in a seminomadic herding economy somewhat close to the paradigm described above. In most of the Ukraine, in the sixteenth century, there were sedentary, agricultural populations. Indeed, parts of the Ukraine, particularly in the west along the rivers of Bratslav, Volynia and Podolia, are very fertile and by the sixteenth century had already attained a Europe-wide reputation for grain production.[4]

Nevertheless, the nomadic influence had been powerful, communicated through the rule and frequent incursions of the Mongols, Turks, and Tatars; and through a culture that revered the horseman—"kazak" in Turkish—almost as the ideal type. One could find, for example, among the cossacks a folkloric celebration of heroic virtues resembling the lore of the Asian steppe. True nomads, it was said, became camel-like, and could go for days without a drink and for weeks without food, and then consume great quantities at one sitting. They had a great respect for corpulence, as a kind of insurance. They did not hurry and appeared lazy, but could ride for days without sleeping. They were very close to horses; the nomad not only traveled but ate, slept, and held council in the saddle. They might even drink horses' milk, or make cheese of it, use horsehides for clothing and tents, horse dung and bones for fuel.[5]

The nomadic ideal persisted within a peasant–agricultural society also because of several other economic singularities of the Ukraine. The availability of virgin agricultural land created an unusually mobile peasantry, engaging in frequent moves to new lands, periodic wanderings, explorations, and armed defense. The severe winters, relative to those further east on the steppe, dictated seasonal idleness, and permitted nonfarm activities. Furthermore, some of the very features that made the Ukraine so vulnerable to attack were conducive to commercial development, notably its excellent transportation opportunities. East–west travel was available by horse in summer and by sleigh in winter, while north–south travel was available almost year-round through several river systems. The Pruth, Dniester, Bug, Dnieper, Donets, and Don rivers all flow to the Black Sea and, with tributaries and a few portages, connect Poland, the Baltic states, Muscovy and Scandinavia with Asia. This intersection of different types and speeds of movement—horses meeting boats, roving brigands and hunters meeting itinerant merchants and settled farmers—was symbolic of the "mixed economy" of the Ukraine. Thus while sixteenth-century Ukraine was not a nomadic society, it was singularly fluid for an early-modern peasant region.

These conditions contributed to the rise of cossackdom in many ways, but three factors stand out: military insecurity and the need for self-defense balanced by the promise of greater prosperity than in central Poland or Muscovy; the mixture of agriculture, animal husbandry, and extractive industry, which promoted a balance between production for subsistence and production for exchange; and varied, relatively easy, transportation and access to

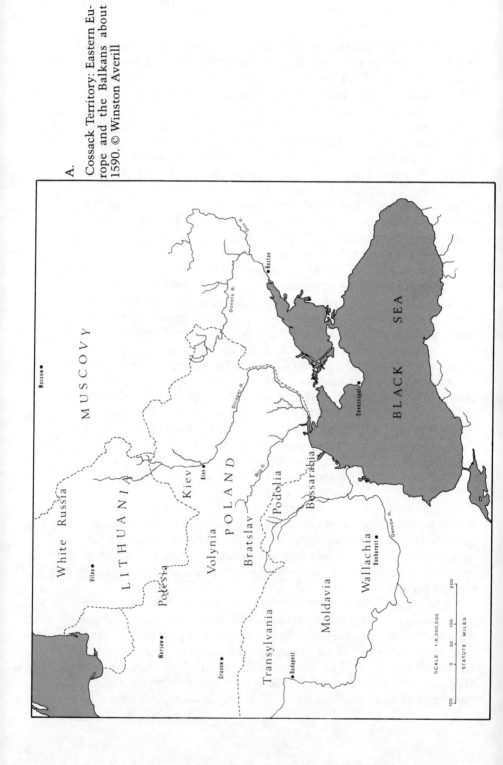

A.

Cossack Territory: Eastern Europe and the Balkans about 1590. © Winston Averill

B.

Zaporozhian Lands: The Ukraine and Environs about 1590. © Winston Averill

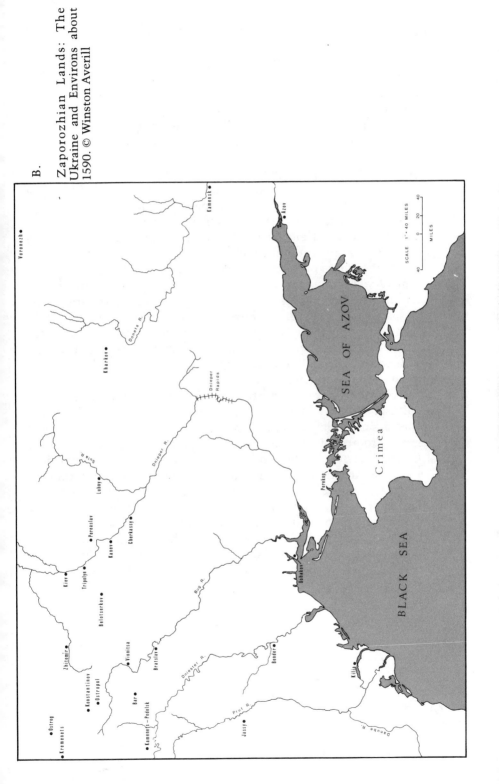

other societies with different patterns and needs. The need for defense, and the failure of any "central government" to provide it, created out of necessity a common interest between people of differing occupations—farmers, hunters, fishers, merchants, artisans, even brigands. This generalized need for protection weakened, relatively, kinship and landlord–tenant bonds in favor of dependence on a kind of popular militia, which the cossacks at times became. The frequent presence of outsiders, whether invaders or merchants—indeed, the lack of clear edges in the definition of "insiders"—kept the Ukrainian population more exposed to foreigners and thereby to the variety of social and economic possibilities that the world encompassed than the typical peasants of eastern or western Europe at that time.

Out of these influences developed a modification of the steppe-nomad style into that of the cossack: a free man, too mobile for enserfment; earning his living by some combination of agriculture, husbandry, commerce, and brigandage; defending his takings militarily and combining with others to defend his community. This heroic horseman's style also combined several specific historical influences. The military technique was learned mainly from the Tatars. The commercial routes, skills, and perhaps even contacts derived from Kievan, Byzantine, and Turkish experience. The agricultural system was brought by peasants from the forest land (and was rather inefficient, for that reason, in the Ukraine, where the sod is deep rooted and difficult to plow with the tools in common use there).[6] Individuals who combined all these activities and influences were the exception; social division of labor in the sixteenth-century Ukraine was well established. Most were exclusively or primarily farmers and husbandmen, or shepherds, or merchants, or artisans. Those for whom military activity was the primary occupation, the cossacks, were a small minority even in the unsettled Ukraine. Yet the cossack represented the ideal type for many Ukrainians, the crystalization of the possibilities of the frontier and the virtues it rewarded.

2. The People

In ADDITION TO geographical factors, historical contingencies made the Ukrainians unique in Europe in the early modern era. Two aspects of this Ukrainian exceptionalism bore with particular weight on cossack history: the definition of Ukrainian nationality, and an unusually fluid social structure.

Ukrainian nationality developed later than that of most other European groups. Moreover, the very existence of a Ukrainian nationality is still debated; both Poles and Russians have, at various times, denied the existence of a Ukrainian nationality. In the last two centuries this was the dominant point of view in Great Russian scholarship, part of an effort to justify the hegemony of Russia over the Ukraine. The chief of the Tsarist Imperial Police once announced, in the inimitable irrational fashion of the obscurantist bureaucrats of the nineteenth century, that " 'there was, is not, and cannot be, a Ukrainian people and Ukrainian language.' "[1] Ukrainian nationalists have wanted not only to assert their existence, but to give themselves the longest and most independent possible history.[2]

That the Ukrainians *are* a distinct nationality is my operational assumption in this book. They first became separated from other eastern-Slav peoples in the thirteenth and fourteenth centuries when, under the Tatars, the Galician-Volynian dukes controlled the western half of today's Ukraine; their separateness was consolidated when, in the fourteenth century, most of today's Ukraine was gathered into the Lithuanian Grand Duchy. The inhabitants of these lands were not again united with Muscovite Slavs until the mid-seventeenth century, and by that time Ukrainian national consciousness was strong enough to retain an autonomy despite efforts at Russification.

For the purpose of this study, however, it is important to bear in

17

mind that Ukrainian national consciousness became explicit primarily because of Muscovite attacks on it. Before that, in the sixteenth century, the Ukrainians' self-concept was being created in resistance to another set of rulers, Poles, Lithuanians and Polonized Ruthenians, mainly Roman Catholic. In that era, residents of the Ukrainian lands who defined themselves ethnically felt close to the Muscovites, who were also part of "Rus."

In the sixteenth century the word "Ukrainian" remained, for the most part, a geographical, not an ethnic, term; it referred to the borderland, the frontier. It was an old term, used in the Kievan chronicle of 1187, and was just returning to popular usage in the late sixteenth century.[3] The Ukraine then contained people of different nationalities—Poles, Belorussians, Lithuanians, Jews—all of whom might be called Ukrainian. The ethnic term properly describing the new nationality-in-formation is "Ruthenian," derived from the medieval Latin name for Rus, the lands of the first Kievan state. The word "Rus" originally included lands later belonging to Muscovy and the Ukraine. Later a distinction was made in most Slavic languages between a *"rusin,"* an inhabitant of Rus, and a *"rossiyanin,"* a Muscovite. Unfortunately, in many instances both words were translated as "Russian," creating a confusion in the West. In the sixteenth century the term "Rus" was applied only to the Ukrainian lands and people, never to the Muscovite.[4]

In relation to its resources, the Ukraine was thinly populated,[5] and it was easy for peasants to seize new lands and to leave old situations in which they were discontent. Ukrainians were unusually mobile. Furthermore, the population was unevenly distributed between the more densely settled west and the thinly settled south and east. In mid-sixteenth century, there were population conglomerations along the Bug and Dniester rivers, the former mainly a part of Lithuanian Volynia, the latter belonging to Polish Podolia. In the former area royal forts had been built at Vinnitsa and Bratslav, but the local landowners were expected to maintain them. To the south and east the steppe was virtually immune from Polish-Lithuanian law enforcement and offered freedom and land for those willing to deal directly with the Tatars.

In the mid-sixteenth century agriculture was less significant in the Ukraine than hunting, fishing, and a small local and international trade.[6] The Dniester and secondarily the Bug rivers provided

---

*In this study the distinction between "Ukrainian" and "Ruthenian" will be observed, the former used to describe geography, the latter, ethnicity.

some of the best travel routes in the area, routes established since ancient times. In Kamenets, capital of Podolia, on the Dniester, merchants handled goods from Lvov, Warsaw, Vilno, Kiev, Muscovy, Sweden and Denmark, sending them to Asia and importing Asian goods. Sixteenth-century Kamenets-Podolsk was thus a cosmopolitan town with significant populations of Jews, Armenians, and Greeks.[7] The Ukraine's small grain production already, by the early sixteenth century, produced an export.[8] The eastern Ukraine, by contrast, had less agriculture. Its main products were meat, fish, honey, and furs. In Kiev there was some production of wood products and some mining for iron, nitrate, salt, and clay. But there was little trade and what there was was primarily barter; little money was in circulation. Almost all the merchants here were foreigners, except a few itinerants who brought salt from the Black Sea. The slave trade became important here in the sixteenth century, and one of the primary Ukrainian grievances against the Tatars was their kidnapping of Ukrainian women for the lucrative Turkish slave markets.[9]

The uneven development of the Ukraine produced very different types of towns. All the towns, like those of medieval western Europe, served both as markets and fortresses. In the former role they were less important in the sixteenth century than they had been in Kievan Rus, or than they were in the West. Western Ukrainian towns had thriving markets and many prosperous and confident burghers. The further out onto the steppe the towns were located, the more relatively important became their fortress function. In these towns there were few true burghers, for the specialization of labor was less developed; most townspeople here also farmed, or hunted, or, as we shall see, were cossacks.

As in the towns, so in the countryside, the further out onto the frontier one went, the less decisive were class divisions, especially by comparison to the social structure of Poland. In the early sixteenth century, and even later as one moved further south and east, there were many freeholding peasants, often using the traditional communal landowning organization common among Slavs.[10] Even as the Polish and Lithuanian landowners followed, seizing the land through conquest, royal grants, or purchase, they had difficulty forcing the peasants to pay rents since so many were absentee landlords. Hired overseers were common, but they too often proved unreliable for the landowners.[11] Even among the nonlandowning, Polish-Lithuanian law in midcentury acknowledged three groups: (1) service people, who did no agricultural work but rather military, hunting, clerical, or other service duties; these might include those of noble birth but many ex-peasants reached this status because of the labor shortage on the frontier; (2) free peasants who paid rent in kind (and this was not necessarily a demeaning obligation, for many gentry service people might also be required to make payments in kind in lieu of service); and (3) bound, rent-paying peasants.[12]

Thus the Ukraine in the mid-sixteenth century did not have a developed serf system. Indeed, the Ukraine was the last place in eastern Europe where serfdom was established. Polish peasants, by contrast, had been restricted from the beginning of the fifteenth century, and jurisdiction over them transferred from state officials and courts to the nobility. Polish agriculture had been transformed into a latifundia system, the small landowners as well as the free peasants squeezed out by the great magnates. The Ukraine resisted these tendencies for several centuries because of its population scarcity, social and physical dangers, and distance from administrative centers and desirable living places for the nobility. As the population grew in the sixteenth century, jurisdiction over new lands was determined largely by possession, the rule of squatters. The myth spread among peasant communities in Poland and Lithuania that the Ukraine was a divinely protected zone of freedom. "The Cherkass* people plow their fields, anyone where he wishes," it was said.[13] The rumors were exaggerated, of course, and always lagged behind developments, for the nobles followed the squatters, usurped the land, and forced freedom-seeking peasants ever further onto the frontier. But their control was never so complete and their imposition never so oppressive as in Poland.

Furthermore, the varied conditions within the Ukraine itself contributed to the relative freedom of the peasants, both because they had a steppe to flee into and because steppe life provided them with a myth of freedom. Until at least the mid-seventeenth century the situation of the Ukrainian peasantry remained just privileged enough, in relation to that of their Polish and Muscovite neighbors, to maintain the myth. The mythology of Ukrainian freedom attracted rebellious individuals to the steppe and strengthened the resolve of Ukrainian residents to resist enserfment. In that manner the mythology became self-fulfilling, to an extent.

As an ideology, the freedom of the Ukraine materially interfered with the attempts of the Polish-Lithuanian government and nobil-

---

*A Rus word commonly applied both to Ukrainians and to cossacks in the fifteenth and sixteenth centuries; see Part Three.

ity to create a stable servile system. This ideology helps explain the irony that the Ukrainian peasants, far better off than the Polish, rebelled against serfdom far more extensively and intensively.[14] The irony, however, appears only in relation to the view that the most oppressed ought to be the most rebellious. This view contains logic and justice, but it is not supported by historical evidence. The Ukrainian peasants exemplify the prevalent pattern of peasant societies, in which rebellion comes from strength and raised expectations.

Another source of Ukrainian strength was, of course, the relative weakness of their enemies—the social and political rulers of the Ukraine, to whom we now turn our attention.

3. The Rulers

CENTRAL GOVERNMENT was only sporadically effective in the sixteenth-century Ukraine. This relative power vacuum was a vital condition of the cossacks' activity, providing them not only with a large area of impunity but also with high expectations for independence. The vacuum was created not by disinterest in the Ukrainian region but by paralyzing conflicts of two sorts—national and class—which the cossacks cleverly exploited. Let us examine both sets of conflicts briefly.

Four states claimed the sixteenth-century Ukraine: the Rzecz Pospolita, the Polish-Lithuanian kingdom; Muscovite Russia; the Crimean (Tatar) Khanate; and the Ottoman (Turkish) Empire. To attempt to evaluate the legitimacy of their respective claims would be entirely ahistorical but we must at least examine their arguments, for the nature of these conflicting claims affected somewhat the attempts at enforcing them, which in turn greatly influenced cossack history.

The Grand Duchy of Lithuania had led, in the mid-fourteenth century, in the defeat of Tatar power in the lands that had formed the western part of Kievan Rus. Though the Lithuanian rulers were of Baltic origin, nine-tenths of their population were of Rus ethnicity. Largely due to this influence from the bottom, the Lithuanian princes converted to Orthodoxy and Rus became the official language of state. Thus in the mid-fourteenth century it appeared likely that the Rus lands would be unified under Lithuanian leadership, with Muscovy a second-running contender for dominance. Instead the increasing economic and cultural power of Poland and the Roman Catholic church drew Lithuania, especially as the former offered support against the Teutonic Order. Between 1386 and 1569

Lithuania moved into a firm and subordinate union with Poland,* and the Ukrainian lands were transferred, piece by piece, into direct Polish jurisdiction.

Muscovy too claimed the Ukraine. The tsars argued two (mythical) lines of legitimacy which justified Muscovite rule over the Ukraine: they traced their personal descent to Rurik, thus making themselves direct descendants of Kievan rulers; and they set up their branch of the Orthodox Church as the "Third Rome," following Byzantium (Constantinople) as the only home of the true church, thus making the Russian church the logical focus of loyalty for all the Orthodox. Politically, the Ukraine naturally figured prominently in Moscow's yearning to head an all-Slav empire.

The Crimean Khans also had claims to the Ukraine. They considered themselves successors to the Golden Horde, in turn the beneficiary of the conquests of the Mongols. As the successor state adjacent to the Ukrainian lands, the Crimean Khans claimed jurisdiction not only over Crimean Tatars but also over two other Tatar tribal groups who lived in Ukrainian lands: the Nogay Tatars who grazed their livestock on the plains east of the Dnieper; and the Besleni Circassians, who roamed closer to the Caucasus but occasionally roamed westwards on the steppe. In the name of this jurisdiction, the khans periodically claimed tributary payments from Poland-Lithuania and Muscovy.

The Ottoman claim to the Ukraine was, like that of Muscovy, directly imperial. As conquerors of the Old Byzantine Empire the Turks demanded hegemony over the whole Black Sea area. First they defeated the Genoese, who had been allies of the Crimeans, taking virtual control of the key Black Sea ports. Then they imposed upon the Crimeans a diplomatic realignment, which involved a treaty with Ivan II of Muscovy, and reduced the Khan to vassalage under the Sultan. In the first half of the sixteenth century Ottoman forces consolidated these gains in a steady expansion northwards and westwards. Infringing on Crimean Tatar territory, the Turks built garrisons and trade centers on the steppe and at river mouths.

The Tatars did not accept their new position as Turkish vassals readily, and Tatar-Turkish struggle continued throughout the cen-

---

*The Union of Lublin of 1569 created a commonwealth, the Rzecz Pospolita, whose ruler, with the double title of King of Poland and Grand Duke of Lithuania, was elected by a single commonwealth Diet. A common monetary system and foreign policy were established; the Diet was to meet in Warsaw, rather than Cracow, so as to be closer to Lithuania; Lithuania preserved a separate treasury, judiciary and administration, operating under the Lithuanian Statute of 1566.

1. Tatar Fortress at Perekop. Eighteenth-century engraving.

2. Gentryman of the seventeenth century. From an engraving of the 1690s, reprinted in *Istoria Ukrainskoi Kultury*, Winnipeg, 1964.

tury. But by the time of the accession of Crimean Khan Ghazi Giray II, in 1588, a bargain had been struck: the Tatars were allowed a free hand vis-à-vis Muscovy, but were to bow to greater Turkish policy towards Poland.[1] Tatar raiding parties became a normal and reliable adjunct to Turkish armies operating against Poland, the Danubian principalities, Hungary, or even the Habsburgs.[2]

This military integration was merely one aspect of the larger, economic integration of the Black Sea coast into the Ottoman Empire. Control of the Black Sea gave the Ottomans great commercial strength, not only from their own export-import trade but as a transit point through which flowed grain from Egypt to Western Europe, silk and spices from the East to Europe. The hinterland of the Black Sea—particularly the Ukrainian lands—was a source of surplus requisitioned for provisioning the Empire. Not only slaves, but also grain, butter, furs, salt, fish and caviar, saltpeter and livestock came into the Empire from the Ukraine. An increase in Constantinople's population, from 100,000 in 1453 to between 500,000 and 800,000 in 1600, was sustained in large part by products of the labor of Danubian and Ukrainian peasants, hunters, fishermen and merchants.[3]

The slave trade, however, had particularly important consequences for Ottoman-Ukrainian relations. The Tatars took on a new and particular role as procurers of slaves for the Ottoman wealthy. Prior to about 1474 it appears that the Tatars had managed a comparatively peaceful *modus vivendi* with the Slavic Ukrainians, and many had even settled down to agriculture. After that year, under Turkish influence, the Tatars reversed their patterns and began a series of raids, often on a large scale, into the steppe, burning, murdering and stealing, and kidnapping. In 1502 rulers of other groups of the Great Horde, then based near the Volga, had been forced to submit to the Crimean, or Giray, Khan. This coup created a migration of more Tatars into the Crimea and its adjacent steppe, which created further pressure against the Ukraine. Before 1586 there were 84 major attacks, excluding countless "border incidents." (The latter involved only hundreds of Tatars, while the major attacks involved thousands.)[4] These attacks were extremely destructive. In 1567, it was estimated—albeit by Slavic sources—Tatars took over 6000 peasants prisoner, pillaged 351 villages and drove off 250,000 head of cattle. In 1575, one of the worst years, Tatars ravaged along the Dniester for two months, taking 55,000 prisoners, 150,000 cattle, and 200,000 sheep.[5] Even allowing generously for the exaggeration commonly employed by the contemporary chroniclers, it remains obvious that the damage and terror inflicted were a major obstacle to normal life in the Ukraine.

One source of weakness in the resistance to this Tatar-Turkish pressure was that eastern and central European powers were divided by the Reformation and Habsburg-Valois hostilities. Throughout most of the sixteenth century Poland's fear and suspicion of Habsburg policy imposed upon her the necessity of maintaining peace with Turkey at nearly any cost. Poland's internal weakness left her reluctant and sometimes unable to pay for frontier fortification and defense. Poland, therefore, was not in a position to perceive the internal decline of Turkish power after the death of Suleiman.[6] Muscovy's expansionist impulses were directed elsewhere at this time, towards the Caspian rather than the Black Sea. This left the Poles without serious opposition to their claim to be Christian sovereign over the Ukraine, but it also left them to face the Crimean-Turkish axis alone.

Polish policy towards the Ukraine was also timid for internal reasons. Numerous domestic social struggles sometimes slowed down or even paralyzed offical reactions to outlawry or social rebellion. As elsewhere in Europe, both east and west, the Polish monarchs were engaged in political and economic contests with a nobility. External military and diplomatic threats exacerbated internal class struggles, foreign powers even allying with dissident groups inside Poland, and encouraging groups out of power in Poland to search for foreign support. Meanwhile, the cossacks, as we shall see below, entered and exploited both foreign and domestic disputes.

By the end of the seventeenth century, most European monarchs had defeated the "seigneurial reactions" that were so widespread in the fifteenth and sixteenth centuries, either by definitively subordinating the aristocracies or by creating stable political compromises with them. In Poland, by contrast, the seventeenth century saw a significant defeat delivered to the monarchy, its prerogatives reduced significantly by a victorious nobility and, partly as a result, its internal coherence and sovereignty weakened. These events have influenced many historians to try to project this process backward in time, exaggerating its progress in earlier periods. Thus one historian has arged that Poland's very successes in the general European economic and demographic crisis of the late Middle Ages—Poland, for example, escaped the Black Death and thrived economically in the fourteenth century—and its prosperity from increased commerce in the fifteenth and sixteenth century, deprived it of the necessity to develop a strong central government.[7] There is in this logic an unwarranted projection backward, blaming future weaknesses on past strength, but also a kind of idealist assumption about causality, as if state strength was created by the will to it. Since the cossacks were an active factor in this weakening of the monarchy, the intellectual temptation to that error is present in our discussion of the Ukrainian situation, and we must be wary. We need to identify the roots and prefigurings of the decline of the monarchy when they are present in the sixteenth-century Ukraine, without depicting as manifest things which lay in the future.

In 1370 the Piast dynasty ended and a foreigner, Louis of Anjou, King of Hungary, gained the Polish crown. One could make an argument for the weakening of the Polish monarchy from this date, since as a foreigner Louis' political base in Poland was thin, and his foreign connections and foreign residence opened an initial space for conspiracies against the crown within Poland to appear as patriotic. On the other hand, Louis was also a decisive and powerful ruler, and the strength of the Jagellonian dynasty which he established was sufficient to remain in place for nearly two centuries. If there is ambiguity about the overall legacy of the Jagellonian rule, there is none, however, after its demise in 1573. From that time on the evidence that the Polish monarchy was having difficulty maintaining its control becomes incontrovertible. As the price for the election of Henry Valois in 1573, the "Henrician Articles" set the precedent for the *"pacta conventa,"* agreements between king and "society" making of Poland a contractual state. The political theory, in other words, was that obligations between king and the nobility, as representatives of the society, were mutual. These contracts were at the same time personal; they expired with the death of a king. The effect was to enable the Polish nobility to sell the crown for ever higher prices.[8]

The power gained by the Polish nobility as against their monarchs affected future struggles with the cossacks in four areas particularly: the jurisdiction of the Diet, local government, military organization, and perhaps most importantly, the spread of serfdom. We will look now at the first three of these areas. The fourth, serfdom, requires a fuller treatment which it will receive in the next chapter.

In 1505 the Polish monarchy had been deprived of the right to legislate without the consent of the Estates, as represented in the Diet. But these "estates" were not conceived as in western Europe. The Diet had three elements, or votes: A House of Deputies, elected by the gentry in its local Diets; a Senate consisting of the high clergy and governmental officials; and the king. The king was functionally a part of, or head of, the Senate, so that the Diet was essentially bicameral, representing exclusively the nobility. Any real duality represented the higher nobility's conflicts with the gentry; but the Henrician Articles required unanimity for substantive legislation (out of which requirement was to come, in the seventeenth century, the notorious *liberum veto* by which a single adverse vote not only defeated a proposal but dissolved the Diet). Thus constructed, it was difficult for this Polish legislature to act on a conception of the realm as anything beyond the interests of a class. The inertia of the General Crown Diet, shunted many tasks increasingly onto the local Diets, or Dietines, of which there were over seventy. Their power over the actual assessment of taxes and maintenance of the army further decentralized political power in Poland.

The Union of Lublin had divided the Ukrainian territory (except Chernigov, which remained in Muscovy until the early seventeenth century) into six provinces *(voevodstva):* Belz, Rus, Podolia, Bratslav, Kiev and Volynia. The latter three were governed according to the old Lithuanian Statute and used the Ruthenian language in administration; the former three were governed according to Polish law and in Polish.[9] Each province was headed by a *voevoda* (translated in this book as "governor"), appointed but unremovable (thus explaining the dependence of the king on the Senate), usually the leading landowner of the region. The provinces were further divided into districts *(poveti)*, each headed by a sheriff *(starosta).* Another powerful group of royal officials were the castellans, or marshals, responsible for the maintenance of royal castles and other military fortifications, and for calling the local nobility to arms when danger threatened. Many Ukrainian magnates held several such offices, often combining in their persons or their families authority over administration, justice, and defense. (These powers were also integrated with their economic power, but not in the feudal manner, as we shall see in the next chapter.) Thus Polish local government was exceptionally independent of central control. In some western European countries, for example, the monarchs were able to counter aristocratic autonomy and to enrich themselves simultaneously by selling offices. Perhaps because of the lesser development of merchants and a money economy in the east, this pattern is not encountered in eastern Europe. But in Muscovy, by contrast with Poland, the crown had been able to increase the proportion of landowners whose holdings were dependent on service to the central government; in Poland land ownership was absolute, and the central government was dependent on the cooperation of local officials to a great extent.

These weaknesses were transmitted to Poland's military organization. Indeed, they were transmitted particularly to military efforts against the cossacks, because the latter by no means threatened crown and aristocracy equally. As in most European seigneurial regimes, Polish military capacity had rested in the Middle Ages on a general levy of the gentry. The chief military commander, the crown or great hetman, had the titular authority to invoke this militia. The crown's weakness in relation to the nobility led to attempts, from Batory's time onward, to create a permanent professional army. These attempts were unsuccessful, partly because the crown was dependent on the noble-controlled diets for the funds with which to maintain this army. At most the standing army in this period numbered a few thousand.[10] Furthermore, the weakness steadily worsened. By the late sixteenth century lack of a crown army or militia in the Ukraine to meet the periodic external and internal disturbances had led to the creation of near-permanent, large private military retinues under the great landowners, governors, and sheriffs of the six Ukrainian provinces. And these private armies, in turn, further reduced the nobility's need to support a central army.

Thus far we have discussed a political struggle between monarchy and nobility as if it were a two-sided war, the nobility a unified group. Although there were moments of such unity, particularly in negotiations with monarchical candidates, the incoherence of the *szlachta* was also greater than that of other European landed classes. The Polish nobility was large, numbering 700,000, or 7 to 8 percent of the population in the sixteenth century. It had virtually no legal stratification within it; the Lithuanian-Ruthenian use of "prince," to designate claimed descendance from Gedymin or Rurik, had no legal force.[11] At the same time, the economic stratification of the *szlachta* was considerable and growing rapidly. Particularly in the sixteenth-century Ukraine, magnates accumulated gigantic estates, and turned many of the lesser *szlachta* into retainers. It is true that in the Lithuanian territories the nobles maintained something of the Rus appanage-princely tradition, especially a strong sense of absolute control over their lands; and this tradition influenced the nobles settling the Ukraine. However, even here stratification placed some gentry in the service of other, greater gentry, and these dependent relationships were self-reenforcing. The magnates gained power from their retainers, counting not only on their military service but also on their votes in the local diets, their loyalty when appointed to local governmental office, or when drawn into domestic political partisanship. These relationships of super- and subordination deeply affected the cossacks, who numbered numerous gentrymen, great and small, among their members, supporters and enemies.[12]

Part Two
The Time of Troubles

4. The Sixteenth-Century Crisis

T HE UKRAINE in the sixteenth century was a place of rapid physical, social and economic mobility. Previously we described the cossacks' world in static terms, as in a frozen frame from a motion picture. Now we must start the motion again.

The cossacks were produced by many changes in the Ukraine: shifts in agricultural production, class tensions, religious tensions, ethnic developments and politics. Furthermore, the cossacks were not only "produced"; they also produced themselves. They were influenced by events and also acted to influence events. In this chapter we will spell out both the changes that gave rise to the cossacks *and* the reasons for arguing that the cossacks were not mere epiphenomena of external events.[1] However, the main evidence for the second contention—that the cossacks were initiators, historical subjects, not just objects—is located in the historical narrative that follows. Ultimately the relation between the cossacks and their environment is most clearly revealed in their actions.

The necessity for setting out these causal arguments here in abstract terms stems not from history but from historiography. The complexity of what will be argued here contrasts with simpler explanations for the rise of the cossacks which have dominated most writing about them. (See the historiographical essay.) Most histories have presented the cossacks as an epiphenomenon of some "larger" forces. Nineteenth-century Slavic historians often emphasized the Slavic "destiny" to control the steppes, and the cossacks were the vanguard of that destiny. Others emphasized Orthodoxy and its destiny to reconquer the Roman Empire as the meaning of Ukrainian southward expansion, in struggle against both Catholics and Moslems. Great Russians have claimed the cossacks as the instrument for the (again, destined) reunification of the eastern Slav peoples under Russian leadership, after the Tatar "yoke" separated

35

them. In all these interpretations the cossacks figured as a representative of some grander destiny or mass.

In twentieth-century historiography, economic interpretations became more common. Because these are the most dominant intellectual influences today, these are the ones we discuss, and contest. The leading intepretation focuses on the agricultural potential of the Ukraine, and its international significance in a Europe increasingly dependent on commercial food production.[2] In this interpretation, the settlement of the Ukraine was stimulated by demand for its produce and the profits thus obtainable from its sale. This profit incentive in turn created a demand for labor power, and this demand was met by enserfment of the peasantry. The cossacks represent peasant resistance to enserfment.

This economic explanation hypothesizes that international European trade in grain was the means by which the landowners could make the vast fertile tracts of the Ukraine profitable.[3] Another claim is that the international grain trade caused a "second serfdom," a drastic worsening of the conditions of the peasantry in the sixteenth century. This hypothesis interprets Ukrainian events in broad European terms. An increasing division of labor within Europe assigned the Ukraine, along with much of the rest of eastern Europe, an agricultural function, as more of western Europe turned to cattle and sheep rearing, specialized crops, manufacturing, or commercial pursuits, becoming unable to supply its own food and dependent upon purchase.[4] This chapter will refer to this hypothesis as the foreign-trade or foreign-market argument.

The foreign-trade hypothesis deserves attention because of its influence on early-modern European historiography today, and because its flaws illustrate some larger problems of conceptualizing the history of the cossacks (and other social movements). In demonstrating its inadequacy as an explanation of Ukrainian events, we will challenge its adequacy as general explanation of sixteenth century European events. The foreign-trade argument is part of a general explanation of the rise of capitalism in the West, and the different path taken by the East. The concentration on trade is part of a general economic determinism that is increasingly influential, particularly in the study of large-scale historical patterns, of "jumbo history."[5] Determinism means here the view that people's destiny is fixed by pre-existing and "external" conditions—external, that is, to the will of the people caught up in the processes.[6] This economic determinism is often erroneously identified with Marxism: as we shall see below, there are controversies among Marxists about this very issue; since the foreign-trade hypothesis emphasizes commerce rather than relations of production, one might as well label it non-Marxist.

Instead we offer a nondeterminist view. The Ukrainians, and particularly the cossacks, influenced the future not only of the Ukraine but also of the political structure of Poland and Russia, and thereby the entire political and social order of Europe. We do not diminish the economic factors, nor disregard the effects of external events on the Ukraine. But the Ukrainians were not merely or even mainly the objects of more fundamental and dynamic forces emanating from the West. The Ukraine also had autonomous dynamics from which western Europe was often remote. A multiplicity of ancient and recent, distant and close events affected the cossacks, and they with their Ukrainian supporters (and opponents) acted forcefully on their environment, according to their desires, sometimes succeeding in substantially modifying external pressures and traditional patterns.

The model criticized here—the foreign-trade hypothesis specifically, economic determinism more generally—has not yet been applied to Ukrainian history. The model was developed with focus on and data from other parts of eastern Europe—particularly central Poland. Economic data from the sixteenth-century Ukraine is scarce. Furthermore, historiography of the Ukraine is theoretically undeveloped, in part because of its extreme politicization and polarization between Russian and Ukrainian nationalisms, Soviet Marxism and anti-communism.[7] We apply the model to the Ukraine, and then criticize it, as a means to organize and clarify the ensuing discussion of social and economic causes of the cossack rebellions.

The Impact of the Foreign Grain Trade

One advantage of the new historical interest in the economic crisis of early-modern Europe[8] is that it forces a look at Ukrainian events in a larger context. Placing the Ukraine in a European social-historical context can yield conclusions emphasizing either similarities or differences between the Ukraine and other parts of Europe. Consider, as a starting point, the cossack rebellions themselves. The cossacks were unique; their rebellions were not paralleled by anything in the West. Other rebellions in the West have no parallels in the East: for example, during the German peasant wars of the early sixteenth century, the Polish-Lithuanian lands were relatively free of uprisings.

Yet when historian William McNeill took eastern European events as his starting point, he found that 1595–96, the year of the second cossack-led rebellion to be discussed in this book, was the peak year for rebellions throughout early-modern Europe. The year 1648, another peak time for European rebellions, also corresponded, of course, to a great cossack uprising. Peasants and townspeople in 1595 and 1596 took up arms in England, France, Austria, Finland and Hungary—as well as Poland, Lithuania and the Ukraine. The Russians have an expressive name for the political and social turmoil that enveloped Muscovy in the early seventeenth century—"the time of troubles." In fact, most of eastern Europe and Turkey underwent a "time of troubles" then, and the first Ukrainian cossack uprisings were part of that general turmoil. These "times of troubles" shared certain characteristics. Inflation in prices and land values, devaluation of coinage, increase in the price of labor and in share-cropping and decline in popular living standards occurred almost everywhere. Every insurrection contained conflicts between monarchs and landed elites.[9]

Ironically, explanations for both similarities and differences in the sixteenth-century events focus on a drastic differentiation taking place between western and eastern Europe. The argument has three parts, although they are often merged. First, just as feudal serfdom was disintegrating in the West, a new serfdom, sometimes called the "second serfdom," arose in the East.[10] Second, there was a market relation between the growing free-labor system of the West and the bondage of the East. An increased market for agricultural goods in western Europe created a demand for the importation of grain, and several eastern European landowning classes seized upon this opportunity. The grain, however, could materialize only through their increased exploitation of land and labor force. Thus the same economic events which in the West strengthened the absolutist state and its ally, the new commercial bourgeoisie, at the expense of the aristocracy, produced a victorious seigneurial reaction and serfdom in the East. This "neo-serfdom" was not a return to any older form but a new, capitalist-caused system of productive relations.[11]

A third part of the argument concerns the social unrest of this period. The late-sixteenth-century uprisings were forms of plebeian resistance to economic ruin and enserfment. In the Ukraine the cossacks often led the peasant rebels, and many cossacks *were* peasant rebels. Thus the cossacks were the product of encroaching serfdom combined with the unique opportunities of the steppe frontier.

Although incomplete, this three-part argument has compelling evidence. By reviewing economic and socio-political change in the Ukraine in the light of the second serfdom, the foreign grain trade, and the attack on plebeian living conditions, we can simultaneously consider the argument's merit and summarize the major relevant changes in the sixteenth-century Ukraine. These changes can be grouped into nine categories, which we will review separately: rapid colonization, magnate power over the gentry, magnate power over the state, rationalization of land tenure, increasing landlord power over and exploitation of the peasantry, widespread peasant plight, changes in agricultural production, reduction of the autonomy and power of the towns and townspeople, and increased exports and inflation.

The Ukraine was rapidly settled in the sixteenth century and the colonization was overwhelmingly private (rather than state-sponsored), suggesting that private land-hunger was the dominant motive. Peasants squatted and homesteaded there; artisans and traders followed. The high nobility, or magnates, coaxed enormous land grants out of the kings. By 1600 even Kiev, in the wildest part of the Ukraine, had four thousand residents.[12] By 1629 the Ukraine's population was between 1.6 and 2 million out of a total of somewhat over ten million in the Commonwealth.[13] Settlers braved the "wild steppe," their settlements frequently challenged by Tatar settlers, nomads and invaders. The Ukrainian "pioneers" took substantial risks, suggesting that they had strong incentives.

A separate stratum of magnates strengthened its position vis-à-vis the gentry from mid-century on.[14] The Union of Lublin had promised the opposite: the extension to the Ruthenian nobles of the Polish system of "democracy among the gentry." In reality, the Ukrainian gentry often owned only small plots of land and were too poor to fulfill their military service requirements. By requiring equal service of all titled men, the Lublin Union's theoretical equality among the aristocracy ironically furthered stratification: only by entering the service of magnates could the smaller gentry meet their obligations to the state. As vassals, they forfeited the right to leave their lords at will, were sworn to obedience, lost the right to sue their lords for injuries, and became liable to punishment for insubordination.[15]

Differentiation between magnates and gentry was more pronounced in the Ukraine than elsewhere in the Commonwealth.[16]

The growth of exceptionally large estates distinguished eastern from western Europe at this time, and the Ukraine contained some of the very largest. The colonization of empty lands accelerated this process. Private owners founded approximately one hundred towns during the second half of the sixteenth century.[17] Konstantin-Vasili Ostrozhsky, governor of Kiev province and marshal of Volynia, became the most powerful man in the Ukraine by 1590. He owned approximately thirteen hundred villages, one hundred towns, forty castles, and six hundred churches with a thousand priests. Each of these churches was said to have a private, golden confessional for the Ostrozhsky family's exclusive use.[18] Ostrozhsky regularly employed a private army of two thousand in a period when the royal standing army might at best include four thousand men. Like other magnates, he controlled key manufacturing industries and consumer services such as mills, distilleries, taverns, ferries, bridges, salt mines, and forges as well as agricultural estates. Nobles extracted monopoly rights from the crown, which prevented others from opening such installations within certain areas. Inhabitants were thus obliged to use only the facilities of the magnates and to pay whatever fees were set. These revenues added greatly to direct rents and agricultural profits.

No magnates matched the power and wealth of the Ostrozhskys in the sixteenth century, but a few came close. The Vishnevetsky family owned nearly the entire left bank of the Dnieper, and claimed 230,000 subjects by the early seventeenth century.[19] In 1629, in Volynia, the most settled province, thirteen nobles (the Danilovich, Leshchinsky, Sangushko, Radziwill, Czartoryski, Zamojski, Zbarazhsky, Liubomirsky, Koretsky, Ostrozhsky-Khodkevich, Zaslavsky, Vishnevetsky families) owned more than two thousand households and controlled 56.9 percent of the land. The Zaslavsky family alone owned 19 percent of the Volynian lands.[20]

In defending and exploiting such vast resources, the magnates shifted the balance of power between themselves and the state. Previously the crown had important central powers. Military service was owed to the crown, not to an immediate lord. Public offices were neither hereditary nor attached to landowning.[21] Few nobles had judicial powers and even bound peasants were theoretically entitled to hearings in a royal court, until late in the sixteenth century. Land tenure was by and large absolute, not conditional.[22]

Throughout Poland in the sixteenth century the nobility had been chipping away at the powers of the crown. In the Ukraine the magnates were exceptionally successful. As the largest landowners they dominated local government, often combining many local positions, and became quite autonomous of the central authorities. They maintained large and nearly permanent private armies and conducted foreign wars which endangered the commonwealth. They threatened and bullied the Diet, using their military strength and wealth as leverage.

As part of the process of wrestling control over the Ukraine's resources from the crown, the magnates transformed the rules of land exploitation. They used their political power to transform all land tenure into absolute, or allodial, holdings; to enclose lands traditionally used in common by the peasantry; and to enserf the peasantry. These gains accrued through many separate reforms and private agreements with the crown. The 1557 Lithuanian agrarian reform law hurried and smoothed this process in several ways.[23] It provided for a land survey and the division of the land into parcels of 19 *desiatinas* or 51.3 acres (a *desiatina* is 2.7 acres) each. This survey occasioned a repartition of the lands, in which the magnates took the best parcels for their demesnes, forcing the peasants to double up on the remaining inferior lands. The lords also seized non-arable resources such as pastures, forests and streams that had been commons and required the peasants to pay for their use, or lose access entirely. These enclosures and land re-divisions often broke up communally farmed plots, thus depriving many peasants of the use of communally owned tools.[24]

In the second half of the sixteenth century the magnates conducted what one Polish historian has described, without exaggeration, as a "violent offensive" against the peasants.[25] Conditioned by a drastic shortage of labor, the landowners won the abolition of the personal freedom of the peasants. Many peasants in central Poland had been enserfed since the early fifteenth century. In the Lithuanian lands, however, centuries of sparse population, changing sovereignties and virtual self-rule by small communities had preserved a pluralist system with many landholding forms. There were numerous and intricate combinations of legal and traditional rights and disabilities attaching to many different peasant groups, although there were three general categories—free small holders, slaves, and half free peasants who worked under contracts which limited their movements to specific times. Beginning particularly with the agricultural reform of 1557, the second half of the century saw strenuous and rapid efforts to liquidate all these categories and force all peasants into serfdom.

The 1557 reform denied peasant property rights in real estate, and preserved such rights exclusively for the gentry and clergy. The "right of transfer" was gradually restricted, the process culminating in the 1588 Third Codification of the Lithuanian Statute. This reform introduced full bondage: it revoked all rights of transfer, and categorized all peasants who had lived with one landowner for ten years as "unremoveable."

Peasant obligations were drastically increased. In Lithuania in the early fifteenth century the labor requirement had averaged fourteen days per year. By the mid-sixteenth century peasants frequently had to give two or more days per week.[26] A full half the week was common a few decades later, and occasional landlords tried to get five and even six days per week.[27] Landlords frequently imposed various "supplementary" days and tasks, of which the most common was a cartage obligation (showing the importance of the market). Others included construction, milling, wood-cutting, fishing and road building. Women and children, formerly exempt, began to be included in these obligations.[28]

The squeeze on the peasants proceeded not only in the organization of agricultural production, but also in the areas of agricultural processing, commerce and military organization. The magnates extracted from the crown privileges of monopoly on such services as mills, distilleries, and taverns. Peasants became forced to pay for services and goods they had once produced themselves. The magnates also escalated demands for quartering. Quartering nobles, their retinues, and their animals was a traditional peasant obligation but had seldom been collected. Magnates now began to send large personal armies to be quartered for entire winters, as their land hunger sent them on missions of exploration, enclosure, survey and conquest into the Ukrainian steppe. These undisciplined private soldiers could be counted on to rob the peasants while living off their hospitality.[29]

Throughout Poland and particularly in the Ukraine, magnate agriculture suffered primarily from a shortage of labor power. To some extent, there was a pan-European rise in the price of labor against which the landowning class was struggling.[30] In eastern Europe the major tactic in this struggle was the transformation of peasant obligations from money or in-kind payments to labor requirements (from *obrok* to *barshchina*). This transformation began with the poorest peasants, paupers, who were unable to produce enough on their lands to pay rents; as early as 1563 there are records of such peasants being required to work two days a week on the magnates' demesne land.[31] This process spiralled, as the labor requirements prevented the peasants from adequately cultivating their own plots and rendered them ever more unable to pay money rents.[32] Inflation also stimulated the landlords' demands for labor rents, since money payments had to be steadily increased to make up for the devaluation of the coinage and provoked peasant resistance.[33] Thus in the 1570s and 1580s labor requirements grew more widespread and sometimes reached the level of five days a week.[34]

But the economic situation also caught the landowners in a squeeze. The heavier the obligations they laid on the peasantry, the more the number of indigent peasants grew who were unable to provide exploitable labor. The indigent included not only the landless but also some who were too poor to own the tools essential for Ukrainian farming—oxen or other beasts of burden, sledges, plows, for example.[35] Furthermore, peasants' land allotments were generally shrinking. Before the 1557 land redivision, the Rus lands had had a standard sized peasant plot which varied from place to place but was often quite large.[36] After the repartition, the standard allotment (known as an *uvolok*) diminished from the original parcel size and the decline continued into the mid-eighteenth century.[37] Ultimately this ruin of the peasantry destroyed the domestic market and ruined artisans' production as well as the smaller landowners' ability to produce on a large scale for external markets.[38]

All these tendencies were less severe in the Ukraine than elsewhere in the Lithuanian lands. In fact, economic conditions for the Ukrainian peasants in the sixteenth century were probably better than anywhere else in the Commonwealth.[39] Ironically, the very labor shortage which stimulated the acceleration of peasant exploitation elsewhere limited it in the Ukraine. Here landlords had to beware the relatively easy flight of peasants to the "virgin" unclaimed lands on the frontier. As a result, only a minority of Ukrainian peasants were effectively enserfed in the sixteenth century, although the threat of enserfment was, as we shall see, a major influence throughout the peasant class.

But the better conditions near the Ukrainian frontier deeply affected peasants in the more settled parts of the Commonwealth, producing widespread flight into the Ukraine from the north and from the more to the less settled Ukrainian lands. Landlords complained to local courts, offered rewards for return of fugitives, secured Diet prohibitions on the harboring of runaways, and required that peasants must carry written permission from their owners to be travelling. They established private specialized police forces dedicated to chasing fugitives.[40] Usually individuals and families left, but sometimes entire villages disappeared.[41] The magnates were not only the victims of these losses but also their perpetrators, kidnapping each other's serfs in their competition for labor power.[42] (One Polish historian noted the absence in fifteenth-century Poland of the kind of "feudal gangsterism" that characterized western Europe at that time; but exactly such gangsterism was common in late-sixteenth-century Ukraine.[43]) This competition becomes more understandable when one compares Ukrainian population density—three persons per square kilometer—to the West, where in France, for example, the average was forty.[44]

Ukrainian agriculture changed considerably in the sixteenth century.[45] There are some indications of a shift in the kind of grain produced. In the fifteenth century, oats accounted for approximately 40% of grain production, rye for 35%, barley 15% and wheat 10%. These proportions reflect actual cost, in resources and labor power, of production, wheat being the most expensive, relative to the amount of food harvested. By the late sixteenth century, nevertheless, wheat and rye each accounted for about 30% of the production, oats 20%, barley 10%, with another 10% accounted for by buckwheat, millet, and a few other cereals.[46] This new division of grain–producing lands, which emphasized the luxury grain, wheat, indicates an orientation toward export. There were large-scale attempts to increase the area of grain cultivation.[47] From 1583 in the western Ukraine, there were increased grain exports along the Bug River.[48]

Significant changes in the power of towns and the urban population took place in the Ukraine in the sixteenth century. In the late Galician and Lithuanian periods (approximately 1200-1500) many towns acquired rights of self-government on the basis of charters from the crown: most Ukrainian towns had such privileges by the time of the Lublin Union.[49] The frontier towns were even more privileged. Their strategic importance as forts and garrisons permitted their burghers to win additional concessions from the crown, such as trading privileges, tax exemptions, and positions in the army higher than their social status would dictate.[50] In the fifteenth century some burgher representatives had been admitted to local diets, an extraordinary breach in aristocratic rule.[51]

From the mid-sixteenth century, however, the towns began to lose ground. The magnates exempted themselves from customs duties and taxes imposed by town councils and from regulations imposed by guilds. Magnates bypassed burgher institutions to deal directly with foreign merchants. Indeed the magnates replaced the guilds with their own rule, fixing price ceilings, for example. Extorting grants of monopolistic rights from the crown for themselves, the magnates appropriated manufacturing and processing rights, and banned townsmen from landownership. In their struggle for an agricultural labor force they imposed heavy penalties on burghers for harboring fugitive peasants.[52]

Ultimately the nobility imposed direct seigneurial obligations on many townspeople. Ukrainian burghers remained personally free, but lost their rights of self-government and fell under the jurisdiction of the *szlachta* officials. Magnates forced townspeople to supply them with military material and quartering. Indeed, having exempted themselves from taxation the magnates reversed the old order and laid taxes in money and labor not only upon the town markets, but upon the residents themselves. By 1580, in Bar district in Bratslav, for example, town dwellers had to pay a tax in cattle, oxen or sheep; a tithe in bees and honey (the major local source of sugar); a tax on bread; and other miscellaneous duties. In addition they owed numerous indirect taxes, such as tolls and internal customs, as well as charges for services, such as distilleries and mills, monopolized by the nobility. Between 1550 and 1580 magnates increased the average labor dues laid on the Bar townspeople from one to six days. Although the absolute amount of such obligations was less than that borne by peasants, town dwellers paid more because they had smaller households.[53]

Finally, the movement of grain and grain prices in Poland suggests the effect of a foreign grain market. Polish grain exports grew after Poland regained Danzig in 1454,[54] indicating the importance of this main port for the Western trade. The towns along the main route to the Baltic grew particularly rapidly, and those areas with less access to the sea displayed different patterns of change. Grain prices at Danzig were usually higher than in inland commercial centers such as Prague, Vienna, and Lyublyana.[55] The share of grain as a proportion of all Polish exports increased,[56] as did Polish imports from the West.[57] Furthermore, the general price rises in Poland followed the same pattern as those in western Europe, increasing approximately 75 percent between the second and third quarters of the sixteenth century, further corroborating a connection between the western and eastern economic developments. The velocity of increase was greatest in the second half of the sixteenth century, slowing down in the seventeenth.[58] This timing corresponds, with an appropriate lag between economic incentive and social response, to the previously described social changes that indicated increased exploitation of land and labor in grain agriculture.

Class Struggle and Economic Indeterminism

In the sixteenth century Polish-Lithuanian magnates accelerated their exploitation of labor-power, their control over material resources, and their political struggle for power. Their efforts transformed relations among the social classes of the Commonwealth—magnates, gentry, peasants and townspeople—and the Crown. In the foregoing we tried to make sense of those changes by presenting them in a form that makes the best case for the influence of the foreign grain trade. That is, the argument runs, the opportunity for new and increased profits through foreign exports was the stimulus for the magnates' actions, and the other classes and political structures responded defensively.

Now we must criticize that argument. It has both factual and theoretical problems. Factually, we will see that a great deal of the evidence that would be needed to support it is not, or not yet, available, and that some data cannot be explained by the foreign trade argument. Theoretically, we will suggest that a monocausal hypothesis such as this one is extremely unlikely to be an adequate historical explanation of phenomena so intense and vast as the changes we have just described.

First, some of the evidence about the imposition of serfdom and the grain trade applies to Poland in general, or to other parts of the Commonwealth, but not to the Ukraine. Lack of data from sixteenth-century Ukrainian estates prevents checking many generalizations.[59] Regional differences in the Commonwealth were great.[60] It is true that of five Polish cities—Cracow, Warsaw, Danzig, Lublin and Lvov—prices increased in the sixteenth century most rapidly in the last, which was closest to the Ukraine.[61] But Lvov did not necessarily command most of the Ukraine's grain exports.

The southeastern Ukraine likely had its own trade networks, one with Muscovy, Denmark and Sweden, and another with Persia, India, Arabia and Syria.[62] Much Ukrainian grain probably did not go through Danzig at all. The southeastern Ukraine may have been commercially oriented eastwards rather than westwards, an orientation consistent with Kievan-Rus history. The Ukraine's trade orientation eastwards is also consistent with the argument of Immanuel

Wallerstein in his recent study of early capitalist agriculture, that Poland was part of a European world-economy, Muscovy and the Ottoman Empire outside it.[63] The Ukraine, situated amid those three powers, was a border case, its economic orientation not unified, its small exports going in several different directions.

Furthermore, serfdom, as we saw above, was not fully established in the Ukraine in the sixteenth century. Not only did freeholding continue in these frontier lands, but squatting intensified in the late sixteenth century, and peasants in service continued to labor under a multiplicity of different tenant relationships.[64] This variety does not seem consistent with large-scale agriculture for distant markets.

Serfdom and the increase in commercial agriculture made maximum impact on the Ukraine through the flight of the peasants. A high proportion of the new Ukrainian population was composed of fugitives, and their needs and self-consciousness helped make the Ukraine unique: for example, in its people's yearnings for freeholding, their mobility, anti-authoritarianism, anti-Catholicism and anti-Semitism.[65] Their flight, while perhaps a symptom of Poland's integration into the European world commercial network, effectively kept the Ukraine out of it. The impact of foreign trade on the Ukraine would seem to have been indirect, at most, in the sixteenth century.

Second, there are chronological inconsistencies in the foreign-trade explanation. It could be argued that awareness of a foreign market in northern and western Poland demonstrated the potential for Ukrainian grain, and that the Ukrainian magnates were acting with an eye to the future, not actual profits. But even in the rest of Poland, servile obligations increased before the foreign demand for grain was felt, from the beginning of the fifteenth century. There seems to have been a labor shortage prior to the impact of the Baltic trade.[66] Furthermore, the foreign-trade hypothesis implies that great commercial estates should have appeared first in East Pomerania, nearest to Danzig. In fact, that was an area in which large-scale commercial farming came much later.[67]

Third, changes similar to those in sixteenth century Ukraine occurred in places without any connection to the European grain market. Most prominently, Muscovy experienced many of the same transformations—neo-serfdom, peasant flight, decline of urban power, rebellions—at the same time. Yet Muscovy was outside the European "world-economy." Indeed, it exported no wheat at all until the nineteenth century (when it controlled Ukrainian grain), and was primarily producing for a domestic market at the time of its "second serfdom."[68]

Fourth, nothing in the foreign-trade hypothesis explains *why* eastern Europe became the granary for the West. Why did the western European countries not develop more intensive commercial agriculture to provide their own grain? In France and in some of the German territories there was an increase in sharecropping and the level of peasant exploitation in the fifteenth and sixteenth centuries, but here the nobility did not conquer a position in control of the export trade. Marc Bloch suggested that in the West, strong monarchs protected the peasants to some extent from intensified exploitation, because they needed the peasant surplus as a source of revenue for the crown. But the Polish historian Marian Małowist has shown the limitations of this hypothesis: in Muscovy, for example, powerful monarchs used their influence in the other direction, virtually handing over the peasantry to the nobles in return for political supremacy; while in England, the crown was forced to act in behalf of the landowning class.[69]

Instead, what we see in Poland, as Małowist has eloquently argued, is the influence of foreign markets acting upon intense and complex dynamics of domestic social struggle. The magnates' economic and political victory over not only the peasants but also the gentry, the burghers, and the crown was not determined by a new source of profit, but by a long history of domestic events relatively autonomous from a foreign market.[70] Indeed, the magnate-peasant struggle was affected by, for example, the weakness of the crown. These examples only begin to suggest the manifold interrelations in different aspects of the class struggle.

In addition, there are indeterminate factors concerning the magnates' actions themselves. The foreign market might have been a stimulus, but the actions produced by those stimuli were not predictable. For example: why did the magnates decide to increase grain production by plowing virgin lands and grabbing serfs, instead of making technological changes which could have increased productivity on the older arable lands?[71] Why did the Polish magnates fail to move into the grain trade by securing East Prussia from the Germans, by creating a merchant navy, by investing in ports, shipyards and forts on the Baltic? Instead they were fascinated by the drive to the Black Sea, which suggests the importance of territorial, cultural and military concerns apart from commercial considerations.[72]

Nor can the existence of a foreign market as a motive explain who won in these social struggles. In England, by contrast, after the Black Death landlords also tried enserfment in response to labor scarcity, but they failed.[73] Foreign trade cannot explain the rapid and drastic weakening of the Polish crown and state; nor the victory of the Polish seigneurial reaction in comparison to other such aristocratic attempts at power, elsewhere in Europe. It certainly cannot explain the relative weakness of the resistence of the Polish peasantry, burghers and gentry.

Indeed, the Ukraine may have contributed to weakening the resistance of peasants in central Poland, by offering lands as an escape hatch for the most militant and adventurous. Certainly the frontier helped prevent direct conflict between peasants and their landowners. Similarly the uneven status of the Lithuanian peasantry attentuated the class struggle, for there were some prosperous peasants who themselves benefitted from the magnate–imposed intensified system of exploration.[74]

The influence of western European commercial demand can at most account for the incentives behind certain social initiatives, not for their outcomes. Like most attempted monocausal explanations, this hypothesis defines a necessary, not a sufficient, condition for events in the Ukraine. It is partial, and as a result is not an explanation at all.

Nor should we expect it to provide an explanation. The objections summarized above point to larger theoretical problems in offering foreign markets as an explanation of eastern European events. Some of our objections flow from the tactic of using markets, that is, social relations of distribution, rather than relations of production, as the chief causal factor.[75] Serfdom is of course a form of the organization of agricultural production, not uniquely related to any specific form of distribution. Furthermore, what turned eastern Europe into an agricultural exporter to the West was Western urbanization, which required imports—in other words, it was a transformation of relations of production in the West. New market relations developed in consequence, not as a cause.

Other objections point to the inadequacy of an economic explanation that does not take social struggle into consideration. The foreign-market hypothesis is partly social, since it focuses a great deal of attention on the behavior of the landowning classes of eastern Europe. But it almost entirely neglects the aspirations and activities of other classes. It describes the behavior of peasants, burghers, gentry and rebel groups as mere reactions; it denies them any strategy or initiative; it excludes a priori the possibilities of victories by these groups against the magnates. The determinism of this economic "explanation" in fact re-requires the exclusion of complex social struggles, because such real struggles do not have predetermined outcomes.

Furthermore, the foreign-market explanation excludes factors not usually categorized as economic, while consideration of actual social conflict just as necessarily requires their inclusion. No actual social struggles have occurred on the basis of purely economic divisions. In the Ukraine, ignoring religion, frontier culture and psychology, diplomatic relations and military patterns would leave the cossack rebellions mysterious and impenetrable. Moreover, "economics" is an unusually abstract concept even among other categories such as the above. People rarely experience pure economic motives. Few of the antagonists in the Ukrainian cossack uprisings would have defined their motives in recognizably economic terms. Rather their "economic" passions, even passions for making money, were primarily felt and expressed in particular cultural forms, through the symbolism of moral and religious systems, kinship obligations, and in the persons of individual friends and enemies.

As a preliminary guide to such particulars that will assume great significance in the narrative that follows, we will sketch here the dynamics of several factors often entirely left out in the economic interpretations: ethnic, "national," and religious identities, particularly Orthodoxy in the era of the Counter-Reformation, and the culture and traditions of cossackdom itself. These factors were *part* of economic conflicts, not separately experienced. Economic pressures do not disappear in the discussion of cultural factors, but they show themselves in a more realistic form—in complex, specific and mediated ways.

Religious Schisms

In the late sixteenth century several events exacerbated cultural divisions within the Ukraine. The Union of Lublin created incentives for the upper class and the upwardly mobile Ruthenians to Polonize themselves. Such incentives were lacking for the majority of the peasantry and the townspeople. Moreover some individuals responded to the temptation of seeking success through Polonization by resistance, becoming more zealous in their commitment to Orthodoxy. Polonization was not, furthermore, a private matter.

The Polonized landlords and officials began to use Polish as the language of government, to emulate the more sophisticated culture of the western-looking Catholics, and to pressure their subjects into a new religion and allegiance.

Another contributing event was the Counter-Reformation. Ukrainians did not distinguish sharply between ethnic, national and religious identifications. Being Ruthenian included being Orthodox; being Catholic meant being Polish; and those ethnic terms were not associated with nation-states so much as they are today. Thus the influence of the Counter-Reformation in the Ukraine was largely fused with the Polonization process. Until the Counter-Reformation the schism had not created much social conflict in the Commonwealth. (It is one of the ironic injustices of history that the Orthodox, only peripherally involved in the Reformation, should have been treated so harshly by the Counter–Reformation.) The Reformation, which met with great and rapid successes in Poland, had strengthened the forces of tolerance by increasing the variety of religious forms in the Commonwealth, and thereby helped to effect the 1569 Union between Catholic Poland and Orthodox Lithuania.[76]

An ironic reversal followed: Increased tolerance helped create the Lublin Union, but the Union promoted the intolerance which eventually helped destroy Polish unity. The Polonization of Lithuania stimulated the conversion of Orthodox Lithuanian and Ruthenian nobles to Catholicism. The oldest Ruthenian families, even those who considered themselves descendants of Kievan appanage princes, began to convert in droves, including the Sapiehas, Vishnevetskys, Pronskys, Semashkos, Slutskys, Zbarazhskys, and Sangushkos.[77] The lesser nobility tended to remain Orthodox. Before the Union most Ruthenian Orthodox peasants had had Orthodox lords. Most now had Catholic Lords, whom the Jesuits urged to convert their wards, by force if necessary. King Sigismund Augustus had been deeply influenced by Protestantism, and had resisted the spread of religious persecution. But immediately following his death, during the first interregnum, the Diet ruled that lords had the right to force their subjects to their faith. This decision was, of course, quite in line with that agreed to by the Lutherans in the Peace of Augsburg.

At the end of the sixteenth century an official attempt at conversion was engineered by parts of the Orthodox clergy itself. The Brest Union of 1596 created a third, "compromise" church, known as the Uniate, in an attempt to win over the recalcitrant Orthodox. The motives behind this Union varied: Some of the

Orthodox clergy wanted it as a reform measure directed against a corrupt, ignorant and demoralized hierarchy. The Polish-Lithuanian crown and its officials viewed the new Union diplomatically, as a weapon against Muscovite appeal to the Orthodox commoners disowned by their rulers.[78] Furthermore, as Poland was preparing for war with Turkey in the 1590s, the allegiance of the Ukrainian clergy to the patriarch of Constantinople seemed uncomfortable. Many Ukrainian magnates joined the Uniate Church and they were able to bring with them most of the Ukrainian clergy, who were dependent on the magnates for their positions.[79] The old man Konstantin–Vasili Ostrozhsky remained adamantly outside the Union,[80] but his eldest son went over. The Union had been negotiated secretly and announced suddenly in an effort to forestall resistance.[81] That effort failed, however. The Brest Union catalyzed the 1596 cossack rebellion, stimulated popular interest in Muscovite protection and united Orthodox peasants and townspeople.[82]

3. Lvov Brotherhood church, 1591. From Hrushevsky, *Pro Stari Chasy na Ukraini*, 1907.

By and large the Brest Union reinforced the correspondence of religious to class divisions in the Ukraine. The grievances of commoners against the *szlachta* as a class gained a religious dimension—or, one might say, the grievances of the Orthodox against the Vatican took on, domestically, a class character.

The Brest Union also sparked an Orthodox cultural renascence in several Ukrainian towns. Several Orthodox magnates, such as Ostrozhsky and Khodkevich, supported printing presses and seminaries. The leading influence and energy, however, came from the Orthodox Brotherhoods, a primarily urban phenomenon. These were religious, charitable, social and fraternal organizations whose origins are now obscure. They held celebrations, provided burial and funeral insurance and services, and performed numerous welfare and educational functions. In the seventeenth century these Brotherhoods established direct and supportive relations with the cossacks. In the late sixteenth century many of these self-conscious Orthodox zealots looked sympathetically upon the cossacks, although their contacts were mainly mediated by influential Orthodox magnates.

The Brotherhood-cossack combination represented a strong potential alliance against the Polish lords. However, that potential for class conflict was checked by an opposite set of class relations: the unity among Ruthenian/Ukrainian magnates, gentry, townspeople, peasants and cossacks in the defense of Orthodoxy. Here is an example of the indeterminate nature of such social conflicts, for with these countervailing tendencies the outcome was surely unpredictable.

Anti-Semitism

In an equally complicated manner, another religious–ethnic conflict merged into the class struggle: anti-Semitism. The increase in the Jewish population of the Rzecz Pospolita, their increasingly important economic functions, and the increasing hostility towards them, are phenomena also attributable to the turn towards commercial agriculture, and thus, the foreign–trade explanation. However, in this matter too, we must avoid oversimplification.

Jews had lived in Ukrainian lands long before this period. By 1500 they could already be found in twenty-three different towns there and constituted one-third of all Jews in the Polish kingdom.

Starting in the last quarter of the sixteenth century, however, when urbanization in the Ukraine accelerated rapidly, a further intensive Jewish migration occurred there.[83] The expulsion of Jews from western countries contributed to this movement, as did the aggressions of western Polish burghers against the Jews. By contrast, in the Ukrainian areas, the Lithuanian region, colonization was primarily spearheaded by the gentry and nobility; and these found the Jews useful,[84] as we shall see below. Ironically, while the Lithuanian class structure at this time created a more secure social and economic role for the Jews, legal guarantees of Jews' rights came primarily from the Polish king. Thus the Union of Lublin stimulated Jewish migration into the Ukraine by providing Jews with the Polish king's protection in what had previously been Lithuanian lands.[85] Jews were most numerous in the West Ukraine, where agriculture and commerce were also most developed. In 1587 there were an estimated twenty-three thousand five hundred Jews in Rus and Belz provinces, six thousand in Podolia, and five thousand in Volynia. By 1629 fourteen percent of Volynian urban households were Jewish; in 1604 in Vinnitsa, a frontier town, nine percent of households were Jewish.[86] By the turn of the century, there were already one hundred twenty thousand Jews, a significant minority, in the Ukraine.[87]

Barred from landowning and the professions, the majority of the Jews in Poland engaged in humble urban occupations. A few became wealthy money-lenders and merchants. In their struggle for success in these commercial enterprises, the Jews were aided by special royal privileges. They had originally been regarded by Polish law as "*servi camerae*," a group directly and exclusively subordinate to the king. They collectively paid a separate tax, the capitation, which was normally higher than that levied on their Christian counterparts.[88] But they were entitled to govern themselves, by special royal decrees called Jewish Privileges, dating from as early as 1264. In 1495 King Alexander had established Jewish diets called by the Poles the *Kahal*, with jurisdiction over schools, welfare and the lower judiciary and religion.[89]

Indeed, like many other European burghers, the Polish Jews by the mid-sixteenth century had come to consider the monarchs their protectors. The kings often employed Jews as lesser civil servants, particularly as tax collectors, and rewarded their loyalty.[90] Sigismund I, Sigismund Augustus, and Stefan Batory resisted the anti-Semitic moves of nobles who feared this new tool of royal power, reasserting their exclusive royal jurisdiction over the Jews.

The isolation of the Jews within Polish-Lithuanian society was reinforced by their tenacity in holding to their separate customs, their resistance to intermarriage and their extremely low rate of conversion to Christianity. Forced by original discriminations into a unique social position, the Jews on the whole responded to further discrimination by reasserting their isolation, enthusiastically clinging to what was later to become an extremely vulnerable social position.

Because of the special nature of Jewish occupations and autonomy, it was at first the townsfolk, rather than peasants, who were the Jews' chief enemies.[91] In the Polish and Lithuanian towns there were intermittent battles between municipal governments, in which Jews had no voice, and autonomous Jewish bodies supported by monarchical writs. The Christian burghers fought their rivals primarily by trying to impose legal disabilities on them. Frequently they petitioned the king for, and sometimes received, the right *"de non-tolerandis Judaeis,"* to exclude Jews from their towns. At other times they restricted areas of residence (creating ghettos), prohibited Jews from the retail trade, or confined them to trade in certain commodities.[92]

From the mid-sixteenth century, several changes were evident. Jews grew more active economically; hostility to them increased; and the hostility was more encountered among the peasantry as well as townsfolk. Throughout eastern Europe and the Danube region an accelerated grain trade provided work for a growing number of merchants, money-lenders, money-changers and other commercial intermediaries, many of whom were Jews.[93] In the Ukraine Jews were particularly likely to take work as the stewards of estates, an expanding job category as nobles accumulated lands far from their homes and from administrative centers. Jews were good for such positions because they were not allowed to own land themselves and thus could not use their stewardships to accumulate their own estates, and because they were often literate and skilled at commerce. Since they were ethnically and culturally alien to the peasants they supervised, the Jews were unlikely to collude with them. The last qualification was important because the stewards were often the direct oppressors of the peasants. They acted as "sponges to convey the wealth of the country and the toil of its inhabitants into pockets of the lords."[94] They were frequently empowered with disciplinary authority over the peasants as well. A typical contract of stewardship would give an entire estate, including town and castle, to a Jew for a number of years, for a rent such as 12,000 *zlotys.* The steward had the right to judge peasants, who were often deprived of any right of appeal back to the noble, and the right to impose punishment, including death.[95] Many Jews acted in other capacities as well: as business agents, operators and managers of inns, dairies, mills, distilleries, and lumber yards, for example.[96] Jews came to control the Ukrainian liquor traffic, the "cap and cornerstone of the whole rural economy of Poland and one of the most important items in the budget of the kingdom."[97] (Since the Jews, unlike their Christian customers, did not drink much, their sobriety only added to the resentful perception of them as aliens.)

Thus in the sixteenth century many Jews became indispensable to the nobility, as earlier their commercial activity had made them useful to their monarchs. The different positions of these rural and urban Jews were recognized by royal decrees distinguishing Royal and Noble Jews.[98] Christian townsfolk remained continuously hostile to Jewish interests.

Anti-Semitism was stimulated in the Counter-Reformation. Sigismund II, influenced by the Jesuits, reversed the crown's earlier position, and began to exert pressure against Jewish privileges. Anti-Semitic Jesuit teachings in the towns may have been correlated with an increase in violence against Jews in Poland in the 1590s. In that decade there were anti-Semitic outbreaks in Posen, Lublin, Cracow, Vilna and Kiev.[99] These attacks appear to have been limited to large towns, were carried out by burghers, and peasants remained uninvolved.

The Ukraine was not at this time an area of concentration of these pogroms, nor were cossacks involved. Indeed, there were Jews among the Zaporozhian cossacks, although many of them had converted to Christianity.[100] This participation, however, should not be interpreted as a sign of tolerance or integration. The Jewish cossacks were limited to stereotypical roles at cossack headquarters: they were money-lenders, business agents, or negotiators with potential employers of the cossacks. Cossack and peasant anti-Semitism in the Ukraine appeared to grow together, the first outburst several decades later, in the cossack uprising of 1637.[101] From then on, Ukrainian anti-Semitism quickly became an uncontrollable monster. The pogrom led by cossack hetman Bohdan Khmelnitsky in 1648 slaughtered hundreds of thousands, possibly as much as 90 percent of the Ukrainian Jewish population.[102]

In both "stages" of Ukrainian anti-Semitism—the urban and the peasant stage—opposition to the Jews was integrated into a larger, complex social struggle. The social struggle in the late-sixteenth-century Ukraine gained ferocity because social divisions were many-layered, with class, ethnic, religious and geographical levels. The enemy was anti-Christ, a devil tearing away one's traditional right to livelihood, stealing land, tools, money and independence. Orthodoxy became the religion of the oppressed.

Religious passion was not a mere epiphenomenon of inhuman economic forces. The land-hungry magnates were real men, individuals, involved in politics and religious struggles larger than their own greed. Military, diplomatic, religious and class factors along with personal desires weighed in their decisions.

International diplomacy further subverted the possibilities for peace between the Ukrainians and their overlords. In the frontier conditions of the Ukraine only one factor might have counteracted Orthodox enmity towards Catholics and Jews: united opposition to the "infidel." To occupy the land all the way to the Black Sea, to capture the Danube ports and ultimately Constantinople itself, had been a common dream of many European settlers. In the early sixteenth century European expansion defined the primary antagonism of the European "pioneers" (or invaders, depending on one's perspective) in the steppe. By the end of the century, however, that antagonism was qualified not only by divisions among the settlers but also by diplomatic realignments of heads of state and powerful nobles. The Polish kings had to check not one but many foreign rivals—the Habsburgs, Muscovites and Swedes—and the traitorous dealings of the Polish *szlachta* abroad. The crown thus had to maintain a shifting foreign policy, including at times alliance with or at least neutrality towards the Ottoman Empire and its Tatar vassal. That diplomatic requirement prohibited the development of a strong and consistent anti-Moslem ideology or alignment.

Finally, we return to the cossacks themselves as a factor in the transformation of the Ukraine. Even if none of the other complexities—religious, geographical, ethnic—of the Ukraine's situation had been present, the existence and previous history of the cossacks made it unique. No land without these extraordinary adventurers would have or could have responded to the immediate economic pressures in the same way.

Part Three
The Cossacks

4. *The Cossacks Write a Letter to the Sultan*, painting by Repin, nineteenth-century Russian artist, depicting a seventeenth-century apochryphal event.

5. Frontiersmen: The Opportunities of the Steppe

T HE OBSCURITY of the origins of the cossacks is reflected in the obscure origins of their name. Most likely "cossack" came from the Turkish *kasak* or *qazzaq*, meaning free warrior or vagrant.[1] Indeed, the first people to be systematically called cossacks were Tatars, renegades from the Khan's armies, who in the fifteenth century were hired by Lithuanian and Muscovite rulers, or who robbed and pillaged independently.[2] Yet by 1493 the Crimean Khan used the term to apply to Ruthenians who, in the service of Prince Bogdan Glinsky, a Lithuanian provincial governor, attacked a Turkish fortress.[3] In the years following, Lithuanian sources also referred to military servitors of Ukrainian provincial officials as cossacks.[4] Simultaneously Muscovite sources called these frontier warriors *cherkassy*, and the Khan also sometimes used that word.[5] That the Turkish term "cossack" finally dominated suggests the dominance of Turkish influence in the cossack image.

The ambiguity of the early terminology shows that attaching a sharp definition to these warrior groups at too early a date would be ahistorical. Observers of the fifteenth and early sixteenth centuries were describing a decentralized social phenomenon that was both widespread—in the Danubian lands, the Crimea, the Ukraine and Muscovy—and novel. A new word appeared to describe this *sui generis* phenomenon.

The Cossacks Defined

Recently, however, historian Eric Hobsbawm has drawn comparisons between various groups of "social bandits," and his work shows that the cossacks do have analogues in other countries.

61

Hobsbawm's argument is that the pre-industrial era produced social banditry as a characteristic type of disorder. Social banditry is by no means an unambiguous concept. Generally, social bandits are robbers who in public opinion are not considered ordinary, indefensible criminals but remain within a community moral sense of right. Hobsbawm located social bandits in a period in which the impact of the market disrupted traditional forms of peasant social organization. They are not political rebels because their program falls short of envisioning or strategizing towards a new political order; hence, Hobsbawm's other name for them, "primitive rebels."[6]

The above is not so much a definition as a cluster of generalizations that can be made about several outlaw groups. Many apply to the cossacks. They were, as we shall see, robbers—indeed, robbery was a principal source of their livelihood. But they were not seen as ordinary criminals, certainly not by Ruthenians, even those victimized by the cossacks, and probably not even by their Moslem victims, to whom their robbery was part of warfare. One critic of Hobsbawm's social-banditry thesis argues that the difference between social bandits and ordinary bandits is exclusively in the mind of the observer, in other words, a myth, and that in the actual behavior of the outlaw groups there was no difference. Hobsbawm retorts that the "myth cannot be entirely divorced from the reality of banditry."[7] In the case of the cossacks, Hobsbawm is surely right, and he is also generally right, for what actions have any meaning at all outside their context? There is no robbery the meaning of which cannot be modified by the need of the robber, or the guilt of the victim, or the nature of the loot.

Like many modern economic determinists, Hobsbawm focussed on the impact of the market as the cause of rural social banditry. While there can be no definitive conclusion about the role of markets in the sixteenth-century Ukraine, there is no doubt that traditional peasant organization was being disrupted. The cossacks failed to create a vision of an alternative political order in the sixteenth century, thus meeting Hobsbawm's criteria on this point too. That they were, nevertheless, rebels, and not only bandits, will be amply demonstrated in what follows. Hobsbawm's desire to modify the label "rebel" with "primitive", however, does not have much specific content. It assumes the existence of a phenomenon that might be called "mature" rebellion, presumably occurring at the end of a certain process of capitalist development—a determinist, somewhat teleological assumption. Without such an assumption about "mature" rebels the meaning of "primitive" rebels entirely dissipates. The cossacks themselves explode this primitive/mature dichotomization since barely fifty years after the period of this book, without the development of capitalism in eastern Europe, the cossacks did develop a vision of a new political order for the Ukraine and a strategy for getting it. I refer, of course, to the 1648 cossack rebellion led by Bohdan Khmelnitsky which led to the Muscovite annexation of the Ukraine.

Still, Hobsbawm's conceptualization of social banditry has many benefits for the study of the cossacks and of rural history in general. It calls attention to the meanings of various violent and unlawful actions which would be badly misunderstood if they were classified merely as criminal. It calls attention to the fact that the cossack phenomenon, odd and uncategorizable to the twentieth-century, urban student, was by no means alien to many rural communities. Thus in the description that follows, Hobsbawm's ideas should help us to strike a balance in emphasis between the uniqueness of the cossacks and their similarities to other rural outlaw dissidents.

The cossacks were first evident to observers as frontier fighters. In this role they are somewhat analogous to the U.S. "cowboys," "pioneers" and adventurers who "opened" the western lands of North America to Europeans. In all this language, as that of cossacks "defending" or "reclaiming" the Ukrainian lands, there are hidden Eurocentric notions of "manifest destiny." These connotations are ironic since the earliest cossacks were probably Tatars, although often engaged in fighting Tatars. Beginning with the sack of Kiev in 1482, the Crimean Tatars had launched an offensive into the Ukraine, and eastwards up the Don and Volga, to reclaim lands which they considered theirs. Their nearly annual attacks reached as far as Moscow, Belorussia, and Polish Podlashia. The Muscovite tsars built a chain of forts and used these early cossacks as guards; but other frontiersmen, called by the same name, conducted private raids and became free-lance servitors of various princes, bodyguards and guides for messengers and merchants venturing onto the steppe. As more Slavic settlers moved southwards, Slavs began by the mid-sixteenth century to outnumber Tatars among these cossacks.

Contemporary Polish chroniclers tended to lionize these groups somewhat: "those who since ancient times considered themselves warriors, who learned to carry a sword and did not recognize the yoke of slavery . . ."[8] This view of the cossacks was part of an ideological justification for Slavic control of the steppe, just as it later became part of the Ukrainian nationalist resistance to both

Imperial and Soviet Russian cultural imperialism. In this view, too, it was seen as important that cossack groups across the steppe, from the Balkans to the Caspian Sea, were similar in military style, economy, self-government, mythology and self-image. Furthermore, there were communications, a sense of identity and even occasional cooperation between different groups. Some Ukrainian and other pan-Slav historians argued that the cossacks evolved out of self-governing village communes that had retained traditions of self-government from the days of Kiev Rus.[9] In a stronger form, this theory implies that the cossacks inherited a democratic style of and will to self-government that was fundamentally opposed to the values and interests of Muscovite autocratic, Lithuanian princely, or Polish aristocratic power.[10] It is of course possible that the cossacks retained and used some Rus traditions; for example, the law handed down by cossack judges, when such emerged (after the period of this study), was based not on the Lithuanian Statute but on old Rus law.[11] But these traditions did not create the cossacks, nor were they the dominant influence on them. For example, there was no free election of hetmans in the first half of the sixteenth century, and cossack leaders were usually called merely "Prince," or by another personal title. Furthermore, the cossacks' role in "defending" territory against the Tatars was formed primarily through a service relation to provincial nobility and government officials.

The view of the cossacks as carriers of an old Rus tradition and destiny also underemphasizes the significant differences between Ukrainian and other cossacks.[12] The Ukrainian part of the steppe was more quickly settled by Slavs and the cossacks there grew more numerous than elsewhere. Polish administration there became effective sooner than Muscovite in the eastern steppe, and as a result the Ukrainian cossacks were thrown into an adversary relation to "their" government earlier. The Ukrainian cossacks conducted larger military campaigns than other groups; in particular they developed powerful marine campaigns. The Ukrainians, as a result of their greater numbers and military strength, also developed more stable agricultural communities and commerce than their brethren to the east. In connection with this development, the Ukrainians produced "town cossacks" as well as peasant supporters, thereby developing a broader and more complex integration into the entire Ukrainian population.

Attributing a national-cultural content to the cossack phenomenon also ignores striking similarities between the social and military organization of the cossacks and that of their Tatar neighbors. Cossack military style was, as we shall see in the next chapter, very like that of the Tatars—a similarity produced by emulation and by adaptation to the same terrain. The Crimean Tatars had left their nomadic origins in the Great Horde and in the sixteenth century conducted agriculture and husbandry, raising horses and sheep, keeping bees, growing grain. Military service was compulsory and the Tatar armies, like the cossack, were renowned for their ability to mobilize speedily from among men in scattered villages, bringing their own food and equipment.[13]

Furthermore, both cossacks and Tatars emerged as the servitors of powerful princes. This fact requires emphasis. It represents a limit to the applicability of Hobsbawm's social-bandit/primitive-rebel category to the cossacks, since the latter developed as retainers of the ruling class, not as representatives of the oppressed. It is interesting to note here that one critic of Hobsbawm alleges that *most* social bandits were retainers of the rich who functioned primarily to suppress the peasantry.[14]

In their relation to the nobility we see, however, a fundamental difference between cossacks and Tatars. The latter served nobles who were effectively subordinated to a powerful central government. The relative weakness of Polish-Lithuanian government in the Ukraine meant that the cossacks were able to parlay their positions as retainers into positions of autonomy from which they could become mercenaries, and could operate as a free and independent warrior brotherhood. The Tatars remained always loyal soldiers.

The first Ruthenian cossacks were men of the Kiev provincial governors, or Prince Bogdan Glinsky, sheriff of Cherkassy, or of his brother Vasili Glinsky, also a Lithuanian provincial official. The first "hetmans," as the cossacks later called their leaders, were royal sheriffs: Evstafy Dashkovich (Daszkiewicz), Pretslav Lianskoronsky (Lanckoronski), Mikhail and Dmitri Vishnevetsky (Wisniowiecki), Evstafy Ruzhinsky (Rozinski), Bernat Pretvich (Pretficz).[15] With rank-and-file cossacks, these gentry leaders organized the construction and maintenance of forts, systems of sentries and advance warning systems. The hetmans also led their men on raids against the Tatars and Turks, often allegedly retaliatory or defensive, always producing or intended to produce large quantities of booty, which was distributed as reward among the rank and file. Towards the end of the sixteenth century, the cossacks' military abilities brought them invitations to serve not only the Polish but other sovereigns, as we shall see below.

From very early on, cossack military "service"—particularly when it was abroad—was not distinguished from piracy and banditry. Hobsbawm's concept "social banditry" enables us to see how, and why, the cossack bandits were tolerated and even encouraged by Slavic steppe settlers. Some social bandits, in Hobsbawm's meaning, are Robin Hoods, stealing to give to others; but not the cossacks. What is "social" about their banditry was—until the outbreak of cossack-led revolts at the end of the century—largely symbolic and exclusively oppositional. Even in industrial society, people have been known to cheer on gangsters for their success in defying resented authority. In pre-industrial society, where social divisions are more rigid and individual mobility uncommon, criminality was a not uncommon form of individual rebellion. As Hobsbawm wrote, ". . . they are not so much political or social rebels . . . as [people] who refuse to submit, and in doing so stand out from their fellows, or even more simply men who find themselves excluded from the usual career of their kind . . ."[16] Their criminality then becomes a model of self-help for escaping caste and status restrictions. A critical part of their appeal, then, was their success—in causing loss and distress to hated authority, in remaining free and at large in the face of campaigns to suppress and enchain them. By the end of the sixteenth century, their appeal had become at once narrowed and strengthened, by class and ethnic considerations, until they were the heroes of the largest social group of the Ukraine.

Hobsbawm subdivides social bandits into three types. One sort, "noble robbers," were altruistic; their robbery was a form of popular expropriation, designed to alleviate economic injustice. The cossacks do not fit this category. They robbed the poor as they conducted their raids; they kidnapped women to sell as slaves and to use as prostitutes for themselves; they never gave away their loot. The cossack leaders were, however, often "noble" in the other sense—of the aristocratic class. The two meanings of the word "noble" have, furthermore, a substantive relationship. In their relation to their followers, the *szlachta* hetmans appeared to be acting out of *noblesse oblige* in their acceptance of brotherhood with common cossacks. It is part of the typical traditionalism of social banditry that the cossacks did not reject but unfailingly respected social rank, and the theory that it brought with it honor. They neither conceived of themselves, nor acted, in opposition to the nobility as a class; and intra-class conflicts among the *szlachta* threw discontented and rebellious individual nobles out of respectable society and politics to seek adventure, riches and sometimes revenge through cossackdom.[17]

The cossacks also behaved as avengers, Hobsbawm's second type of social bandits. At times they practiced such widespread and extreme destructiveness that terror became an essential and cherished part of their image and self-definition. The cossacks' terroristic side dominated most when they were stirred up by religious chauvinism—against Moslems and Jews—and by class hatred; the latter was most manifest when the cossacks became, in time of rebellion, leaders and champions of an oppressed peasantry.

It was also in the context of religious and class struggle that the cossacks sometimes assumed the behavior of Hobsbawm's third type of social bandit, resistance fighters. Although rarely possessing an articulated ideology, such bandit resisters fought to defend not just individual freedoms but the autonomy and freedom of whole communities. In this behavior social bandits reach their most political moment; the cossacks began to show signs of such behavior in the last decade of the sixteenth century (another sign of the importance of that decade), and developed further in that direction in the seventeenth century. As "resistance fighters" the cossacks identified with a religious and class cause, transforming their demands from protests and grievances to positive aims, and accordingly transforming their warfare from the punitive, retaliatory *"jacquerie"* to a strategic defense of territory and institutions.

In their roles as "avengers" and "resistance fighters," the cossacks were able to separate themselves from their aristocratic employers. Indeed, this separation is key to the whole of cossack history and possibly to that of many "social bandit" groups. Hobsbawm neglects the origin of such groups as servitors of the powerful and describes primarily their later role as heroes to the oppressed. The transition has been neglected, and the transition is the crucial dynamic. The feudal patronage of a landowning and warrior class was essential to the rise of the cossacks; the relative weakness of that aristocracy's control was essential to the cossacks' movement into a mass leadership role.

Composition and Development

The earliest cossacks, as we have seen, were quasi-nomadic. They were hostile to agriculture, and for good reason: the improvement of land and the availability of farm labor power would only have made the land more attractive to the expansionist magnates. Stock raising was not well developed among cossacks until the eighteenth century, since animals were vulnerable to Tatar rustling. But commerce was relatively highly developed in the sixteenth century: as in all bandit communities, the loot had to be exchanged.[18] The cossacks used money more than their neighboring peasants, and often had gold, jewelry, slaves and animals to sell. In addition they gathered and prepared from their own region such commodities as salt fish, honey and furs.

As cossack wealth and commerce grew, their headquarters were transformed.* Originally hidden, secret lairs, cossack settlements began to attract many travellers. Itinerant merchants came from

5. Ukrainian Cossack. From Hrushevsky, *Pro Stari Chasy na Ukraini,* 1907.

*"Zaporozhian sich" literally means clearing beyond the rapids; sich later became the name for any Ukrainian cossack headquarters. Some historians have searched for the definitively first sich.[19] This emphasis on the "original" sich was produced in part by an interpretation of it as the nucleus of the Ukrainian nation-state, a state lost with the fall of the old Kievan principality.[20] Thus ideologically motivated, the question—where was the first sich—is wrong. There were many spontaneously developing cossack groups with separate headquarters; only in the second half of the sixteenth century did the Ukrainian cossacks become centralized enough to have one recognized headquarters; and, as we shall see in Part Five below, in rebellions, separate autonomous cossack groups were to emerge again.

great distances—Muscovites, Persians, Greeks, Armenians and Jews. Emissaries from various governments came to investigate, and to bargain. The headquarters of the Zaporozhians, the "sich," came to have a permanent commercial suburb; and the cossacks developed strong commercial ties with burghers of various Ukrainian towns.

Still, the cossacks themselves rarely became primarily merchants. Their warrior functions were always at least as strong as their thievery. And as their commercial activity tended to build connections with burghers, their military activity continued to be connected with disaffected gentry. Indeed, one of the complexities of sixteenth-century cossackdom is that it appeared to be removed from the Ukrainian class struggle, to the extent that cossacks were heroes to all the classes. This universal appeal was made possible by the fact that most cossack warfare at this time was directed against Turks and Tatars.

Yet by the last decade of the century the cossacks were chal-

6. Zaporozhian. From Podhorodecki, *Sicz Zaporoska*, Warsaw, 1978.

7. Zaporozhian sich. From Hrushevsky, *Pro Stari Chasy na Ukraini*, 1907.

8. Representative of the cossack elders. Illustration From map of the Ukraine by Beauplan.

9. Zaporozhian winter village. *Istoria Ukrainskoi Kultury,* Winnipeg, 1964.

10. Cossack boats in battle. From Podhorodecki, *Sicz Zaporoska,* Warsaw, 1978

lenging aristocratic rule in the Ukraine; and this challenge did not emerge suddenly. In fact cossackdom had always been a part of class tensions in the Ukraine. The understanding of the cossacks' exact role has been clouded by two opposing, and both erroneous, tendencies in cossack historiography: depicting them exclusively as nationalist leaders, and exclusively as peasant rebels, respectively.[21] The cossacks as a whole were not of course a class, and their participation in "class struggle" was highly individualistic: they were consistently loyal only to their own brotherhood, and had shifting and opportunistic relations to all other social groups. Even the peasants had no clear class consciousness, and often expressed their collective interests in religious and ethnic terms. The cossacks' ability to maintain good relations with both nobles and peasants was conditioned by the fact that agricultural exploitation required a stability of settlement which the Ukraine did not yet have in the sixteenth century. The landlords needed lands and a labor force secure from invasion, and in that respect their interests coincided with those of other Ukrainian settlers. Landlords, peasants and townspeople all in different ways used and supported the cossacks as a kind of security force, allowing them, in some sort of implicit bargain, to brigandize the Moslems.[22] The frontier and its dangers—i.e., its Moslem claimants—tended to unite European settlers across class lines. This solidarity was historically momentary, not only because conflicts of interest among the Europeans developed, but also because the Moslem groups were drawn into intra-European state conflicts. In the early sixteenth century, however, the potential for Slavic solidarity in the Ukraine was a key factor permitting the development of cossack organization.

The relative emptiness of the Ukraine also subdued class conflict, because geographical mobility was a possible escape from enserfment or other exploitation by the landowning class. This mobility not only allowed the cossacks to occupy their anomalous and autonomous place, but also provided them with constant replenishment of their membership. The cossack "liberties" were less the ancient freedoms of Kiev than the conditions of frontier life. The fact that the boundary between cossack and non-cossack was fuzzy reflects the frontier's fluidity, and demonstrates that the cossacks themselves functioned as part of an "escape valve" which allowed individual rebels to flee from Polish aristocratic rule without struggling against it.

From the middle of the sixteenth century, systematic pressure checked this fluidity, threatening cossack autonomy and involving them in a growing Ukrainian class struggle that pitted peasants and townspeople against an aggressive nobility. The pressure was felt in the Ukraine in two ways. First, the magnates advanced into the Ukraine, gobbling up the land and casting nets to catch peasants to work it. Their pace accelerated sharply in 1590, when the nobles forced the king to parcel out among them many Ukrainian lands classified as "empty,"[23] which included lands where peasants had been operating as freeholders. Second, masses of fugitive peasants and townsfolk from Poland and Lithuania migrated to the Ukraine, and many joined the cossacks when the Ukraine itself became no longer safe from serfdom. The Zaporozhian cossacks were so heavily composed of fugitives that they renamed all their members upon entry into the sich to avoid pursuers.[24] Between the encroaching landlords and the fleeing peasants a spiral of resistance arose. The more the fugitives came, the more the landlords saw the cossack groups themselves as a threat; the higher the percentage of recent fugitives among the cossacks, the more they were determined to protect their ability to offer asylum from Polish law.

Not all the fugitives were peasants. The gains of the magnates also victimized many of the lesser gentry, squeezed out of their lands. This intraclass conflict may have increased the number of personal feuds, which in turn led some *szlachta* to crime and disgrace. The cossacks were attractive to these people who "had behaved indecorously or belligerently in Poland," as one 1594 observer put it.[25] As the cossacks grew in military notoriety and prestige, they attracted even more noble adventurers; the sich became a "school for young warriors," as the Bishop of Kiev wrote.[26] These upper-class cossacks were not just the hetmans; they usually occupied the upper ranks of cossack officers, and they numbered in the hundreds.[27] They were a minority but an influential one.

Other cossacks came from among the townsfolk. In the early sixteenth-century Ukraine the most successful merchants were often also the gatherers of the wares they sold—the hunters, trappers, and fishers who braved the steppe and made expeditions down the Dnieper into Tatar territory, thus becoming cossacks.[28] As the population grew, many itinerant merchants were able to maintain settled commerce within one town. As the frontier moved further south and east, the hunters and gatherers of the northern and western parts of the steppe were surrounded by settlements and grew disaccustomed to nomadism. But even these true burghers often fled to the sich in response to the attempt of the Polish nobility to check their independence. There were always more burghers than nobles among the Zaporozhians. By 1570 the ties and aid of townspeople to the cossacks were worrisome enough that the crown ordered the Kievan burghers not to sell saltpeter, gunpowder, or lead to the cossacks.[29] Early in the seventeenth century authorities began to demand the removal of artisans, merchants, alehouse keepers, bailiffs and even burgomasters from among the cossacks.[30] In 1590 flight from the towns became so great that the Diet legislated against it. In 1616, during a cossack rebellion, the majority of the residents of Belotserkov, Cherkassy and Kanev were supporters of the cossacks—that is, they considered themselves subject only to cossack authority. In Kanev the royal tax collector listed sixteen "loyal" households and 1,346 cossack households.[31]

Indeed, sixteenth-century observers did not identify the cossacks with peasants. The burghers were originally much more closely identified with cossacks than any other group; in some documents from early in the century the words "cossacks" and "townspeople" were used interchangeably, both also denoting freemen.[32] At other times the reputation of the cossacks was that of an army of upper-class mavericks. Papal nuncio Carlo Gamberini, who negotiated with the cossacks in the 1580s, described them as an aristocratic army.[33] Yet by the turn of the century this image had been revolutionized, and, within the Rzecz Pospolita at least, the cossacks were seen primarily as peasant insurgents. Polish Commander-in-Chief Zolkiewski wrote to the Kievan nobility:

> Their unrest will give you no peace; . . . because this
> peasantry, which is by nature hostile to the nobility, can grow
> bolder and take even more dangerous steps if we do not heed
> them.[34]

This transformation of the cossack image was not a result of a shift in membership. There is no evidence that the average proportion of cossacks who had been peasants was higher in the 1590s and after than in the 1570s and 1580s. It seems rather that the military and political activities of the cossacks in the 1590s placed their peasant members in positions of much greater influence than they had been before.

An important factor making possible the greater influence of peasant and other lower-class cossacks during the 1590s crises was that not all cossacks lived at the sich. Many peasants, and later merchants and artisans, brought their families and established farms and communities deep in the wild steppe, in areas immediately protected by the sich. They became part-time cossacks. Many spend summers at the sich and wintered in Bratslav or Kiev.[35] The Zaporozhians considered these peasant or burgher cossacks a dependable part of their force. They often included them in estimating their numbers, telling visitors that they had, say, several thousand at the sich, but a readily available expeditionary force of several times that number.[36] This meant that, at the Zaporozhian sich particularly, the "standing army" was usually under the influence and control of noble elders; but when the army expanded during campaigns, the accretion of part-time cossacks made commoners the dominant force.

When the cossacks' campaigns took them above the rapids, whether they were attacking local landowners or merely moving through the Ukrainian provinces on their way to adventures abroad, they attracted large numbers of new "cossacks" from among the discontented of the estates and towns. A cossack brigade moving through the Ukraine was like a snowball. This phenomenon produced a still greater transformation of the cossacks' social orientation: the lower-class forces came with their own caste and class grievances and angers, and without loyalty to the cossack organization itself. The newcomers had absorbed no cossack traditions and they lacked the security of the knowledge of potential retreat beyond the rapids. They were much more likely to risk all to win their freedom *within* the Ukrainian provinces. To the extent that the cossacks became leaders of mass movements, they simultaneously lost moderation and control over their troops. Thus in times of rebellion their subversiveness increased not arithmetically but geometrically with their numerical growth.

Another aspect of the cossacks' identity was psychological. The Ukraine, like other frontiers, attracted certain kinds of personalities. Despite the heaviest oppression, only exceptional people, and usually not the poorest, leave their homelands for the unknown. In sixteenth-century eastern Europe such breaks were even more disorienting than in the modern world: they often meant leaving the security of communities where families had lived for generations longer than memory, and setting out for a borderland known in the folk tales for its bloodthirsty infidels, the cruelty of its winters, the loneliness of its vast plains. On the other hand the Ukraine was also legendary for its fertility; the attraction of potential prosperity explains why the archetypical cossack personality had two sides: fearless and hopeful, free-spirited and ambitious, independent and self-serving, anti-authoritarian and aggressive. Furthermore, before these people arrived at the sich, a double process of elimination had taken place: the first selection brought the most aggressive to the Ukraine; a second brought the most aggressive of those from the settled Ukraine to the wild steppe. The natural "creaming" that took place was self-perpetuating: the more the cossacks threatened the established order, the more attractive they became to other rebellious personalities; the more new rebels joined them, the more aggressively they challenged the conventional order.

Equally important to the cossacks' social role was their ethnic composition. The Polish government always claimed, in its effort to avoid responsibility for the piracy and vandalism of the cossacks, that they were a multi-national group, including Germans, Frenchmen, Spaniards and Italians.[37] In the early sixteenth century many Tatars became cossacks; even later in the century runaway or kidnapped galley-slaves from Turkish ships sometimes joined the Zaporozhians.[38] In 1570 Sultan Suleiman complained that the cossacks had been stealing whole Tatar families and bringing them to Kievan towns where the women and children were settled, the men employed by the cossacks.[39] In the official cossack register of 1581 a few Moldavian and Wallachians, one Serb, two Tatars, 13 Muscovites, and two Lithuanians could be recognized.[40] One must expect that there were many more foreigners whose names did not distinguish them.

The relatively heterogenous character of the cossacks would seem to be indicated also by their relative tolerance in the sixteenth century. An important part of their style and effectiveness was openness to newcomers. Reputedly any stranger, except a Jew, was welcome to their hospitality. And they were reported to be religiously tolerant: "yet they would not listen to sermons or religious exhortations of any kind; and the diversity of faith among them was not productive of any serious dispute."[41]

The register of 1581 and all other evidence, however, indicates that the great preponderance of the cossacks was then Slavic. Among these it is somewhat difficult to distinguish Poles from Ruthenians or Muscovites, though they were often given cossack names such as Moskal, or Moskvichin.[42] Many cossacks had false names which disguised their origins; records might use either Cyrillic or Latin orthography depending only on the record-taker or purpose of the document. Despite these qualifications, there is no doubt that the majority of cossacks was Ruthenian, with Belorussians the largest minority.[43]

Until the end of the sixteenth century, however, the hetmans were almost always Polish or Polonized Ruthenians. At first, as we pointed out above, the "hetmans" were government provincial officials. These clearly dominated until the 1570s. Then for the first time we see evidence of the cossacks electing their hetmans, but these were still usually Polish nobles, seeking adventure in the Ukraine, perhaps out of favor with the court. From the time of Sigismund III no respected Polish magnate or noble ruled the cossacks, and by the seventeenth century Polish dominance of the cossack leadership was ended. In the seventeenth century a cossack elder who spoke Polish was a rarity; out of thirteen colonels who led the cossacks at Khotin in 1621, only one was a Pole.[44]

The meaning of this ethnic shift is unmistakable: the cossacks were becoming more exclusively identified with the Ukrainian people. The rebellions of the 1590s strengthened this identification. But the forces behind it should already be clear from our previous discussion of the "time of troubles." The agrarian crisis and the increasing pressure on both peasantry and townsfolk it produced, coupled with the persecution of the Orthodox, combined to make social tensions in the Ukraine correspond to a large extent with national distinction. The cossacks' composition reflected the way the lines were being drawn in their habitat.

6. Warriors: Military Organization and Technique

T HE WORD "ZAPOROZHIAN" comes from the Ruthenian *za porohi*, beyonds the rapids. It refers to a series of rapids on the Dnieper about 45 miles south of today's Dniepopetrovsk where the river has forced its way through a granite offshoot of the Carpathian mountains (which also interrupts the course of the Dniester and the Bug rivers). These rapids continue for approximately 25 miles south; the drop of the river in that distance is 155 feet, forming a serious obstacle to navigation. Indeed, the river was navigable to the practiced Zaporozhian cossacks only for a few weeks of the flood season, and not at all to the foreigner. In this section the river divides into many arms forming many islands, which provided secure locations for forts, and many grassy and fertile plains suitable for farming and pasturing. On these islands an early cossack headquarters arose.

Using every advantage offered by their environs, these cossacks developed two kinds of military travel and attack—land and sea.

On the land, the cossacks' military technique began as that of the Tatars, their most frequent early opponents. It was a technique dictated by the steppe: employing sturdy horses, travelling very light, relying on relay communications systems, living off the land. Their earliest raids and battles were against the Tatars, who almost always outnumbered them. (By the mid-seventeenth century the khan could put over 80,000 men into the field.)[1] On a Tatar raid there were usually three horses per man, which gave them extraordinary speed and ability to travel far from their base. Thus cossack defense forces were rarely able to confront the Tatars before the latter had advanced quite deeply into the Ukraine. There the cossacks tried several methods: to ambush the Tatars at river crossings, where they were slow and vulnerable; to attack while the Tatar army was separated into small groups, as when in camp; and with raiding and scouting parties sent out separately.

But above all, the cossacks preferred offense, even in defense. Both groups of warriors moved and attacked often at night, and relied on quick retreat, often hiding booty to be collected later. The cossacks usually dispersed when retreating, reassembling at the sich. The chronicles which so frequently claim that cossacks or Tatars destroyed, or razed, or burned down, a town or fort, are usually exaggerations or tall tales; more likely they attacked once, killing and looting as much as possible, and left as quickly as they came.

Both cossacks and Tatars relied heavily on psychological warfare techniques, deliberately and effectively. Terror was their strongest weapon. They could travel silently, emerging as a nightmare out of the dark, shrieking and ululating as they charged. They built themselves reputations of cruelty (largely deserved, but reaching more people through rumor than through experience). They also built a reputation of great military prowess, functioning as a fraternity that, again more in reputation than in fact, admitted only those who could pass the most stringent tests.

As the Zaporozhian forces grew, and undertook more ambitious campaigns (into the Danubian lands, for example), they had to develop means of transporting more supplies than each man could carry on horseback, and techniques for standing up to stationary battles. Their firearms improved in the course of the sixteenth-century—they learned to use the heavy artillery which they could capture from the Turkish forts. In the use of firearms they were ahead of the Tatars, who consistently preferred bows in this century. They also became "dextrous at casting up earth, and intrenching," as a contemporary chronicler wrote.[2] They developed a unique form of transport which was at the same time a mobile defense: Having developed a very light but strong and speedy horse-drawn cart, they arranged these in a circle or rectangle and travelled with their carts surrounding them, in a formation they called a *tabor.*

> . . . they travel in the middle of their carts, which march in two files on their flanks, eight or ten of them in the front and as many in the rear: they themselves are in the middle with forelocks, and half-pikes and scythes upon long poles; the best mounted among them about their taborts, with a centinel [sic] a quarter of a league before them, another at the same distance behind, and one upon each flank. . . . I have often met . . . [Tatars] in the field at least five hundred together, who assaulted us in our tabort; and though I had but fifty or sixty Cossacks with me, they could do us no harm, nor could we

gain any advantage over them, for they would not come within the reach of our arms . . .

As to their manner of making war by land, . . . they are extremely dextrous at . . . another kind of ambulatory way of intrenching, which they perform by a handsome and orderly manner of disposing their Chariots . . . a thousand Cossacks thus defended with their Chariots, will make head against six thousand of those Infidels, who seldom alight from their Hordes, so that a Ditch or a small baricado is able to stop them, it would be very difficult in any other Countrey to make an Army march thus in the middle of Chariots, there being few Countreys in the world so flat and even as that.[3]

The cossack navy adapted some of the same military principles to the river and the sea. They built light boats *(chaiki),* sometimes constructed out of the single trunk of the linden, hollowed out, coated with pitch, and lined with skins. Outside the boats were covered with small floats which broke the force of waves, lightened the vessels, and made them steady—thus adapting a river boat for service on the Black Sea. The boats were normally about sixty feet long and ten to twelve feet wide. They had both sails and fifteen to twenty-five oars. Their most extraordinary feature was that, although they could hold forty to sixty men, they rode only two and one-half feet above the water line, so that the cossacks could approach very close to an enemy before being noticed. The construction of one such boat normally took sixty cossacks about two weeks. Yet early sixteenth-century witnesses claimed the cossacks were assembling naval expeditions of five to six thousand men, and could prepare eighty to one hundred boats in three weeks.[4]

They usually moved at night, and after gliding silently in these "war canoes" down to the mouth of the Dnieper, waited for the new moon before venturing out into the sea.[5] If the Turks heard of their intentions, they stationed galleys at the mouth of the River to prevent their exit.

To form some idea of the boldness and reckless daring of these marauders, it may be remarked that the Turks possessed forts at the mouth of the Dnieper and along the two opposite banks, Kissikerman and Tavangorod; and that the passage was defended by strong iron chains, stretched across under the cannon of both fortresses. The Cossacks, previous to their arrival at this spot, usually felled an enormous tree, which they drive before them on the surface of the stream with prodigious force: the chains were burst asunder, and, at the alarm thus given, the cannon were discharged. But the cossacks . . . in utter contempt of the Turkish fire now opened upon them, pushed forward into the Black Sea . . .

At sea, they directed their course without the aid of any nautical instruments, and by the sole guidance of the stars; and this with a regularity and precision difficult to be conceived—presaging winds, calms, and tempests, with mathematical exactness.[6]

When the cossacks slipped out into the Sea the Turks often sent messengers carrying the warning to Anatolia and the Danube. But the cossacks could reach Anatolia in only thirty-six to forty hours.[7] There they would attack the Turkish towns at night, on foot, pillaging, kidnapping women and children, massacring men, and disappearing before morning, or before a defense could be organized. They even penetrated into the center of Anatolia.

The Turks frequently attempted by the same technique to prevent the cossacks from returning into the Dnieper. The cossacks would hide themselves in shallows and sheltered creeks and slip through at night; their boats drew so little water that they could return by navigating up the small streams that the Turks could not enter; sometimes they even returned by way of the Don.[8]

The military prowess of the Zaporozhians was the basis of the rest of their power and influence, and their social organization was largely determined by their military functions. However, as a group the cossacks were also a self-conscious fraternity, a form of organization, not simply a direct product of military activity. Fraternal organizations were not uncommon in medieval and early modern Europe and while they have often been written about, few historians have discussed their fraternal character.[9] Hobsbawm's analysis, for example, does not emphasize the fraternal qualities of many groups of social bandits.

Fraternal associations use kinship as the model of the tie among individuals, specifically brotherhood. "Brotherhood" in this sense does not have its modern, post-French-Revolution, egalitarian meanings; early-modern fraternal groups were usually extremely hierarchical. By using kinship as a metaphor for loyalty, these groups were able to demand powerful committments from their members. Where military activity was involved, loyalty could require extreme risk-taking. The cossack brotherhood met this challenge with varying means of enforcing and reinforcing absolute loyalty to its cohesiveness. There were harsh and public punishments for virtually all infractions. There was a dense culture of secret ceremonies and rituals encouraging the internalization of loyalty and a sense of the value of belonging: initiation ceremonies, secret symbols of rank known only to some, taboos and fetishes, and a great deal of rather highly organized leisure activity, often providing simultaneously for training, such as competitive active games.[10] This density of ritual is characteristic of fraternal organization.

As a fraternity, the cossack host was extremely misogynist. This was expressed not only in folklore but in the energetic exclusion of women from the sich. The strictness of this prohibition can perhaps be measured by the brutality of the punishments for its infraction: women violators could be stoned to death, or hung by the feet and suffocated by smoke from a fire, or buried up to their necks and shot.[11] Although many cossacks maintained families in the adjacent Ukraine, the male specialness of the cossack group was vital to maintaining its intensity as a community, undivided in moments of need by family loyalties. Thus fraternalism as a form of fictive kinship was to a large extent antagonistic to actual kinship.

Within the cossack bands, and in the sich in particular, there was also something of the communism of a fraternity. It is dangerous to accept literally some of the tales about the selflessness of the cossacks in relation to each other, for these tales exaggerate in order to perform a mythic and a prescriptive function. Reputedly the cossacks possessed everything in common; their huts were left unlocked; lost articles were displayed in public places to be reclaimed by their owner. The stringent enforcement of rules against thievery suggests simultaneously the falsity of these tales of communism and the importance of the ideal of sharing; thieves were tied to a post in the center of the sich with a bottle of brandy and a stick nearby and every passerby had a right to sip the brandy and beat the culprit. The murderer of a cossack was tortured to death.[12]

Such intense fraternalism was the more striking given the fact that the cossacks originated as individual hired men of nobles, with no horizontal connections. These were entirely constructed by the cossacks. Early cossack bands had not the emphasis on fraternal loyalties, but rather formed themselves under individual, tyrannical leaders who behaved in relation to the men much as their original princely employers. The emphasis was on vertical loyalties and rather traditional social and military values. Cossack leaders were respected for their horsemanship, marksmanship, strength, stamina and bravery—but also for their class rank, wealth (as, for example, in quantity and quality of horses) and confidence.

The shift towards emphasizing horizontal, fraternal, bonds occurred gradually with the growth in size, independence and influence of the cossack groups. Notably, they developed decision-making forms quite different from those of Polish government and society, or from the Tatars whom they resembled in military technique. These forms, particularly their general meetings, called *radas*, were significantly more democratic than any neighboring institutions; and they have been the evidence for the argument that the cossacks carried an inherently democratic tradition from old Rus. Although there may have been some traditional influence, the primary determinants of cossack organization were their immediate work and membership.

The rada was in essence a military council. Later Ukrainians made it a legislative institution of a putative nation, but in the sixteenth century its deliberations were about military matters. The cossacks participated in it as soldiers, not as citizens, and debated such issues as an offer of employment from an outside source, military tactics and routes, the distribution of booty.

The council was necessary because of the mercenary structure of the cossack groups. Unlike a state or a state army, and in mitigation of the fraternal bonding, the cossack community left each man free to leave the brotherhood, temporarily or permanently, at any time. Similarly, if the Polish or other government offered to hire them, every man would be free to accept or reject the offer, and it would be appropriate therefore for all the soldiers, not just officers, to hear and discuss the proposal. The rada, therefore, stemmed less from an implicit or embryonic democratic principle than from an individualistic, anti-statist (or historically pre-nation-state) principle.

Another way of understanding the military basis of cossack organization is to look at the Zaporozhians' leadership. At first they had only military offices. Increasingly these began to take on other, civilian, functions, as they attempted to administer rebellious areas of the Ukraine, and as they asserted the autonomy of the Zaporozhe as a self-ruling district. The cossack leader was always called "hetman," the Polish term for general, sometimes given in Ruthenian as *ataman* or *otaman*. These leaders were at first Polish officials, as we have seen, and "hetman" was the title they would naturally assume in their fantasies of glory as heroes of the frontier. Only at the very end of the sixteenth century did the Zaporozhians occasionally choose a hetman different from the one the Poles had appointed for them, and they never gave their leader any other title. Similarly, the lesser officers used Polish or Ruthenian military terms: *polkovnik*, colonel; *sotnik*, captain or centurion; *obozny*, artillery officer; *pisar*, clerk. Their attempt to duplicate as exactly as they could the style and structure of an army was a constant in cossack history.

When the cossacks controlled sections of the non-cossack Ukrainian population they made no attempts to extend the privilege of self-government beyond themselves. They ruled as the Poles ruled, and the Lithuanians before them, and the Tatars before them. They collected tribute (which might be called taxes or rents or provisions) and demanded loyalty (obedience) without the consent of the governed. It was being a cossack, and that alone, which conferred the privilege of self-government.

Fraternal relations of this kind have political potential, but do not become overtly political unless they are generalized. Far from extending their fraternal attitudes towards all men, the cossacks, like many such small societies, considered most outsiders with extreme suspicion, and sometimes belligerence. They emphasized their separation from their surrounding society, permitting them to

11. A cossack rada, with elders in center. From Hrushevsky, *Pro Stari Chasy na Ukraini*, 1907.

induct new members as was necessary without breaking down or weakening their claim to exclusiveness.

Equally significant was the exclusion of women from the sich. So long as the cossack brotherhood was to exclude women it could not pretend to be a self-sufficient society, or even a societal model. As a military fraternity it was rather an anti-society, an institution that could only exist in a parasitic and subversive relation to a larger society.

By the end of the sixteenth century, many cossack officers were landowners.[13] By that time, too, property was becoming more valuable in the Ukraine and one of the enticements of cossack life was the possibility of obtaining land.[14] Throughout most of the sixteenth century the cossacks had been of many classes, led usually by noble officials, and united by their inclination to withdraw from Polish society. The infectious land-hunger led to a reversal of this purpose in the lives of some noble cossacks: ceasing to think of the cossack host as an escape from the society, they began to see it as a means of increasing wealth and power within the society.

Thus the increased value of Ukrainian land produced a division within the cossack ranks, a weakening of fraternal unity, not only because of property itself but because of the need for labor to make property productive. The landowning cossacks developed an enmity towards the freedom of landless cossacks, who began to appear as potential serfs. This division did not completely split the cossacks, partly because they were forced into unity by a split among the landowning classes themselves. The lesser gentry, including cossack landowners, were threatened by the aggrandizement of the great magnates, and saw the cossack host as an ally against those magnates. But this alliance was constantly shaken by class tensions within it.

By the 1590s the cossack rada normally met in two different circles—one of officers, and one of commoners or rank and file, called the *chern*. (The last word is derogatory in modern usage, meaning "rabble," but it did not carry that connotation in the sixteenth century.) Neither of the two circles was always dominant. In one instance the rank and file feared that the officers would reject an offer of employment from a foreign sovereign, so they rushed into the officers' meeting and threatened to throw them all in the river if they did not accept. The rank and file was also able to take similar action to overthrow a hetman. Officers could not as easily impose their will on the rank and file, who were much more numerous.[15] A peculiar kind of compromise had been struck, in which the cossacks paid *de jure* allegiance to Polish class structure in the way they organized their rada, but *de facto* retained an underlying democratic practice.

A majority cannot rule consistently, however, unless it is organized to formulate and express its will. The rank-and-file cossacks had surrendered executive power to officers to exercise at their own discretion, in secrecy, and without accountability. The many small decisions that were made by the officers were cumulatively more important than the few great issues that were publicly debated. Even in the public debates, the alternatives had usually been defined in advance by the officers, who often withheld information and lied to their men.

Still, while the common cossack had accepted class *privilege* he had not accepted class *rule*. Cossacks did not acknowledge that political power should follow from a title, the right to special quarters within the sich, and a separate rada. They continued to insist upon their wishes and to impose these by a primitive democratic form, the threat of majority force.

Thus the officers ruled, but in constant insecurity, never knowing when information might leak out that would lead to their removal from office, with more severe punishments also likely. The cossacks frequently executed the leaders they had rejected—a pattern common to dictatorships. Lack of peaceful methods for resolving disputes made it unsafe for replaced leaders to remain alive. The system of cossack self-government was not democracy but dictatorship tempered by mob intervention. The cossack officers could not easily resist the periodic intrusion of this mob force because they needed to perpetuate the myth of an egalitarian cossack brotherhood. This myth served them too, by distinguishing them from the rest of Polish society and justifying their autonomy. Furthermore, the cossack military mystique strengthened the convention of the rule of the mighty. Unlike the Ukrainian magnates, the cossack officers were hardly in a position to use the law to maintain their rule when they themselves lingered at the fringes of outlawry. To maintain their legal immunity they needed the *chern*, which was their army, their only resource for bargaining with their own or any other government.

The cossack officers could only have rid themselves of dependence on their rank and file by giving up the cossack life altogether, melting back into the Polish aristocratic class, accepting its limits and enjoying its privileges. In the 1570s the monarchy made an attempt to help the cossack officers do just that. In a deliberate attempt to split the cossacks, the crown introduced a "register" which would have ennobled certain cossacks and outlawed the rest. The failure of this scheme was the victory of the rank and file, and created the conditions for the cossack uprisings of the 1590s.

7. The Register: Disciplining the Unruly Child

Iₙ ᴄʟᴀɪᴍɪɴɢ the right of self-government, the cossacks did not call themselves a nation but rather a brotherhood of knights, honorable mercenaries. In medieval and Renaissance Europe there were precedents for such a status. The cossacks believed themselves within a tradition in acknowledging the King of Poland as their sovereign but maintaining the rights to choose their employers and to define their own membership.

In sixteenth-century Poland the right of a noble to hire cossacks for his personal retinue, and the right of a cossack to accept or refuse, were not questioned. But crown officials were forced to challenge the right of the cossacks to hire themselves out to enemies of the Polish state. The security of the crown required that none of its subjects conduct a separate foreign policy, nor behave towards foreign powers in a way that would interfere with Poland's foreign policy. Cossack activities such as raiding Turkish ports and Tatar cities often had injurious effects and the crown wished to ban these activities entirely, whether they were undertaken by the cossacks independently or in service.

Other complications arose in regard to domestic matters. Since the nobles had been hiring cossacks both as private servitors and as frontier soldiers of the provincial government, it was an easy transition for the central government to begin hiring cossacks. The crown also treated the cossacks as mercenaries, negotiating with them about salary and allowing them to retain their own system of leadership. The Polish crown, in the late sixteenth century, was increasingly challenged by the aristocracy's assertion of similar privileges—in the extreme, the privilege of arming against the crown whenever it found royal policy offensive, and at the least, the privilege of refusing military service. The crown could hardly look favorably on the extension of such privileges to an armed force so useful to the magnates. Yet, while the government perceived the danger in recognition of the cossacks as an independent mercenary force, it needed to hire cossacks against external enemies, because the regular army was too weak to defend its borders.

The crown's attempted solution was to create an *exclusive* relation with the cossacks, that is, to make them part of the regular army, rather than hire them as mercenaries, thereby prohibiting them from offering their services elsewhere. The government's inability to enforce these provisions left it weaker yet: angering the cossacks by attempting to impose limitations on them, and then failing to make good their threats. This was the story of the worsening relations between cossacks and the crown in the sixteenth century.

There were three stages in the development of the government's "cossack policy," overlapping and shading into one another, but distinct in their differing content. The first was the period of the employment of cossacks by the provincial governors. The earliest such recorded case was between 1511 and 1518, when the Diet endorsed the use of cossacks by magnate Prince Lianskoronsky.[1] In 1524 King Sigismund I ordered frontier officials to collect a cossack force to chase Tatars. After the success of this expedition, Sigismund suggested forming a permanent cossack detachment of one to two thousand, but since he could provide no money for wages his proposal was not acted upon.[2]

In a second stage of Polish cossack policy, the crown dealt directly with the cossacks. Individual acts of this sort occurred every early—as Sigismund I gave a land grant to a cossack who had served him well in 1512, and ransomed two cossacks from Turkish captivity in 1528.[3] As a general policy, however, it dates from about 1540, when Sigismund tried to enroll a group of Kievan cossacks in the Royal army, at the same time reproaching a Kievan official, Prince Koshirsky, for indulging cossack disturbances for his own profit.[4] In the mid-1540s, cossacks were employed at both Polish and Lithuanian forts in the Ukraine, including Cherkassy, Kanev, Kiev, Zhitomir, Lutsk and Vinnitsa.[5] In 1568 Sigismund Augustus was repeating his predecessors' attempts to hire cossacks to man Royal forts.[6]

Generally one of the cossacks' most important rewards of entering service, governmental or private, was exemption from the jurisdiction of landlords. The cossacks, naturally, expressed the view that they were entitled to permanent and absolute exemption from feudal obligation.[7] At most the crown acknowledged this exemption during the actual time of service, and expected the cossacks to return to subordination in time of peace—an unrealistic expectation. Even temporary exemptions were troublesome because they enabled the cossacks to exploit the lack of harmony between crown and nobility: peasants would refuse submission to the serf-hungry landowners by claiming that they were part of the royal cossacks. Furthermore, royal service was supposed to carry with it a salary and also some provision for maintenance. Usually this meant authorization for cossacks to quarter themselves and collect supplies ("seek cossack bread") on royal lands. In practice this meant that numerous cossack expeditions against the Tatars could be said to have been undertaken at royal command, even if they were opposed by the crown, and quartering and supplies demanded and taken in return.[8]

In short, royal service had emboldened the cossacks to assert a right to do what they had previously done more discreetly, and to do openly in the Ukraine what they had previously done in the safety of the Zaporozhe. For every cossack actually hired for a royal expedition, perhaps ten claimed to be royal soldiers, rode in the Ukraine "seeking bread," and settled down for the winter as free men on a royal estate—attracting peasants from all the nearby estates. This tendency was, to say the least, aggravating to the owners of those estates, and their complaints were vociferous.

Partly in response to such problems, the crown began a third stage in its cossack policy in the 1570s, with the creation of the "register." Early in that decade King Sigismund Augustus sent an emissary, Yuri Yazlovetsky, to the Ukraine to recruit some cossacks for royal service. Once hired, many of them complained of mistreatment by local officials, and in response Yazlovetsky removed them from local jurisdictions entirely and placed them directly under the Royal Army commander-in-chief. In 1572 Sigismund Augustus endorsed this new relationship with the cossacks, appointing a special royal commissioner, Jan Badovsky, to have judicial powers over them.[9] The importance of this decree was not so much in the privileges it granted to those cossacks who were hired—which were not unprecedented—as in what it meant for those cossacks who were not hired. The latter were declared to have no special standing in relation to the local administration and nobility; they were expected to cease being cossacks and to return to one of the social categories permitted in Polish aristocratic society.[10] Whereas all cossacks had previously been extra-legal, the creation of this allegedly permanent "register" of hired cossacks made most of the cossacks illegal. Presumably nobles remained free to hire their own cossacks, but that meant merely using one's bondsmen as warriors instead of ploughmen. The decree was a direct attack on Zaporozhians, and an attempt to split them since some had been recruited and some not.

The Zaporozhians might have been more resistant had the Yazlovetsky register succeeded. With his death in 1575, however, the cossack regiment apparently dissolved; and it was unlikely that it had ever enrolled more than three hundred.[11] Furthermore the Zaporozhians had found other outlets for their energies; while Yazlovetsky recruited hundreds, they drew thousands into campaigns against the infidels. In the spring of 1576, just as Batory assumed the throne, cossacks burned Tiagin, an important Tatar fort on the Dniester. They took twelve important prisoners whom they proudly sent to Batory. He, of course, was horrified—and to the astonishment of the cossacks, lamented the Tatar defeat. Like Zamojski after him, Batory took pains throughout his reign to protect the peace with Turkey. He sent an important Polish diplomat, Andrei Taranovsky, to pacify the khan. This mission was unsuccessful, however. Later that year a Tatar envoy returning from Moscow laden with rich presents was robbed by cossacks with the collusion of Kiev governor Ostrozhsky. The Tatars, under Muhammad Giray, had been headed towards Moscow at the time; hearing of the attacks, they turned aside and sought revenge by ravaging Kiev and Volynia. The following year the Zaporozhians became involved in one of the numerous Moldavian civil wars, putting up their hetman as an anti-Turkish candidate for the throne.[12] In response, the khan's complaints grew more and more vociferous and threatening, and behind him loomed the Sultan.[13]

At the same time a move to hire cossacks grew attractive to Batory for another reason: by late 1577 a war with Muscovy over Livonia threatened. First, he needed to raise an army, and was frantically hiring soldiers from many sources—Hungarian hussars, Scottish infantry, German mercenaries, and even Belgorod Tatars.[14] Second, since Batory wanted to avoid a two-front war, he urgently needed to control the cossacks and prevent them from embroiling him with the Turks. Although most of Batory's papers are lost,[15] it is evident from his policy that he perceived the new cossack register he inaugurated as performing two functions: repression and recruitment. He appointed a new hetman to replace Yazlovetsky, and ordered him to gather a permanent cossack army of six thousand. Simultaneously he reproached the frontier nobility for their cooper-

ation in cossack raids; ordered them to help Kiev governor Ostrozhsky whom he had asked to bring the bandits to justice; and
appointed Lublin governor Tarlo as overseer with full powers to
judge and sentence the outlaws. The terms on which the cossacks
were hired obligated them to "pacify, seize and exterminate all the
disobedient as enemies of the Crown."[16]

Batory's register has attracted the attention of historians more
than its predecessor because it was more pretentious. Previously the
cossacks had been promised ten florins a year and some cloth; there
was no quota and the provincial officials had been satisfied with
whatever cossacks answered their call. Batory raised the salary
during the Livonian Wars to fifteen florins and material enough for
two caftans a year. He created twelve army regiments of five
hundred men each and gave them a military hierarchy and organization similar to that of the rest of the regular army. Each received a
regimental flag and a regimental staff of thirty.

Most important, the register confirmed important privileges for
the registered: the right to elect their own elders, to be judged by
their peers, and royal confirmation of their ownership of lands they
held—which was, in a sense, a promise of *ennoblissement* for the
commoners who could lay their hands on a piece of property.[17] The
cossack army received the estate of Trekhtemirov, with two thousand horses, for an arsenal and headquarters, and a hospital for their
wounded and aged was promised there.[18]Those outside the register
who had called themselves cossacks were to return to their places of
origin, and to subjection by their rightful lords.[19]

Some historians have considered Batory's reform not only inno-
vative, but a break with the traditional, "weak" pattern of treating
the cossacks as if they were outside Polish sovereignty.[20] On the
contrary, Batory and his agents continued to treat the cossacks
deferentially and to recognize many of their claimed privileges. For
example, Batory did not establish his register by fiat but in negotiation. First he sent his envoy, Janosh Beger, to the sich with gifts, to
ask the cossacks to send plenipotentiaries to Lvov. Then he himself
went to Lvov and met with the cossack delegation.[21] It was hardly
standard procedure for all regiments to receive estates, hospitals, or
the right to trial by their peers. Nor did other mercenaries receive
such privileges.

And yet no other mercenaries contributed so little to the war
effort. Only nine hundred cossacks actually served against the
Muscovites.[22] Either few signed up, or many signed but then refused
to go, perhaps dissatisfied with the conditions. No cossacks went

beyond Cherkassy in 1579, thus contributing nothing to relieve the pressure on the Poles, who were fighting in Belorussia and northwest Muscovy. Instead the cossack regiments pillaged the areas around Chernigov and Starodub.[23]

Nor did the register create a strong royal armed force outside the control of the nobles. In practice the cossack regiments continued to serve the provincial magnates. Batory had apparently felt constrained to appoint as cossack hetman Mikhail Alexandrovich Vishnevetsky, sheriff of Cherkassy and Kanev, and greatest magnate of the left bank of the Dnieper. Like Ostrozhsky, he had already hired cossacks himself and led, or instigated, numerous cossack expeditions. Batory gave him a fancy title: *Supremus dux militum Boristhenis Nizovii doctorum.*[24] In the Muscovite campaigns, where he led the armies of the southwest-Muscovy theater, Vishnevetsky used the cossacks exactly as if they had been in his private service— except that their salaries did not come out of his pocket!

Nevertheless, the Ukrainian nobles were on the whole displeased with Batory's register. Indeed, the King's intent to usurp the ancient rights of the nobility was revealed, many nobles believed, in his cossack policy. Not only were they reluctant to see six thousand new nobles join their ranks and dilute their power, they also viewed any increase in the strength of the Royal army as a threat. Throughout the period of Polish rule in the Ukraine the nobles fought against representation of the new cossack nobility in the Diet, and refused to grant them the legal privileges that inhered in their new aristocratic status.[25]

The great magnates were, of course, less hostile to the register than the smaller gentry, because the former could use the cossacks in their own interest. But the usefulness of the cossacks would continue only so long as they were dependent upon the magnates for their protection and immunity from servile obligations. Few nobles imagined that the cossacks could become rebels against the aristocratic regime itself. Some perceived the danger of the cossack sich becoming an asylum for runaways, but they believed that they could check the growth of that danger by hiring the cossack leaders themselves. Should the cossacks be guaranteed their independence by the crown, however, the whole system's stability would be threatened. The cossacks would no longer need protection, salaries, or political influence from the magnates, and might become rivals instead of proteges.

The magnates were worried about the wrong thing. Had they been able to take a longer view of the relative strength of the Polish monarchy, they would have seen that one monarch could not significantly alter the basis of power in Poland. Had they been able to take a longer view of the strengths of the cossack phenomenon, they might have understood that neither the nobility nor the monarchy could control it. The authority of the lords, from which the registered cossacks were removed, was being replaced not by the crown but increasingly by virtual self-government among the cossacks, or "self-willedness" as the Ukrainians put it.

There were many reasons for this. First, the government rarely paid the promised salaries, and never on time. As a result the registered cossacks saw no reason to perform as ordered unless the campaign was in their own interest as well. Another result was that the unregistered were not at a disadvantage: there was no reason for them not to participate in cossack campaigns, and no reason for the registered not to welcome them. The notion of using the register to divide the cossacks against themselves was nonsense if the promised privileges were not forthcoming.

Second, the Ukrainian nobles refused to recognize many of the legal privileges promised to the cossacks by the register; the government, poor and politically weak against the nobility, was unable to enforce the registered cossacks' promised rights, so the latter had no choice but to defend themselves. In this task, again, it was only logical that they should welcome support from the unregistered cossacks. Furthermore, since the cossacks had to defend their own privileges, they naturally began to articulate those privileges in their own way. The end of this process was that the "legal" rights granted by Batory merged in the cossacks' interpretation with their traditional "cossack liberties," which implied complete autonomy, subjection to no one save their own elected officials, and no other duties than to fight frontier enemies. The government-appointed hetmans were never able to wield the authority that the noble hetmans had in earlier days. When communications were needed with the cossacks the government was unable to rely on these official hetmans, but had to send special envoys. Between 1570 and 1600 the cossacks came gradually to grant allegiance only to their own, elected hetmans.[26]

Third, the government repeatedly destroyed its own register by hiring unregistered cossacks during time of need, as we shall see below.

Batory had attempted to slip through the horns of a dilemma to reach a solution to the cossack problem. The first horn was the resistance of the nobility to the cossacks joining their class, especially under royal protection. The second horn was the resistance of the cossacks, a resistance created and constantly strengthened by myriad factors of geography, economic pressure, and religious and national differences, to being forced into the lower classes of Polish society. Batory's proposed solution was the most promising that had yet been offered. The cossacks would be made a small, limited and closed group; through emphasizing these conditions, he thought he could make the nobles accept their integration into the lesser nobility. Once that integration was begun he hoped these cossacks could be relied upon (a) to be loyal to the crown that created them, since their status would not be hereditary; and (b) to see that it was in their own interest to suppress the movements of others to band together and call themselves cossacks.

This was a scheme that could roughly be called cooptation. By accepting some cossacks into the Polish elite, Batory thought he could divide the cossacks against themselves and use their own leaders to destroy their autonomy. A similar scheme succeeded, haltingly and with many setbacks, for the Muscovite government after it took control of the cossacks' territory eighty years later. But its success for the tsar of Muscovy was based on different social conditions. In seventeenth-century Muscovy autocracy rested on what might be crudely described as a bargain between monarchy and nobility: absolute control over the peasants for the latter, in return for absolute centralization of power in the hands of the former. Batory could not achieve that bargain. Since 1410 no outside military threat had forced the Polish landowning class to share its power with the central government. In 1570 this security was shattered—by an expanding Muscovy, a powerful Swedish monarchy based on an army still composed mainly of free peasants, and devastating Tatar attacks with the threat of war with Turkey behind them. Batory saw the need for a much stronger military force, but the great magnates did not. Perhaps the new threats came too suddenly for them to understand; perhaps they were misled by initial successes, as in the Livonian wars. Certainly the magnates were opposed to the gentry democracy that an autocracy implied. In any case Poland ended the century with the repudiation of Batory's reforms. Sigismund III Vasa ruled with the consent of a cabal of magnates and Catholic prelates.[27] The gentry, oppressed and defensive, became more conservative and continued their vain efforts to hold onto the power they had once commanded. They would not give an inch to the cossacks. Batory's "cooptation" scheme was beyond their conception of self-interest.

The register was a failure in relation to the interests of the Polish-Lithuanian state. For the cossacks, ironically, or at least for the elite, it was somewhat beneficial.[28] It increased their ability to negotiate for privileges and to resist dispersal. It did not limit the growth of cossackdom, nor did it motivate some cossacks to police others, nor did it create a new armed force loyal to the crown.

The register did, however, accelerate a split within the cossack movement. This was not the distinction between registered and unregistered, but more precisely a class distinction, between landed and landless, rich and poor, privileged and unprivileged cossacks. The class distinction roughly corresponded to the legal one, both because official service could bring land as a reward, and because the landed were the first to be chosen for the register.[29] But the class distinction did not function as the legal distinction had been intended. It did not affect those cossack activities that most concerned the crown: raids against the Turks and Tatars. It turned out to be critical rather when the cossacks began, in the 1590s, a series of uprisings against the Polish social order which culminated in the removal of a large part of the Ukraine from Polish rule.*

No one had foreseen such a turn of events. In Batory's reign, the influence of the cossacks upon the peasantry had seemed to lead in the opposite direction—towards flight rather than resistance. The cossacks themselves had seemed pawns in the game between monarchy and the nobility; focussing on that contest, neither monarchy nor nobility could imagine the cossacks as an independent force.

---

*The failure to make this distinction between external, mercenary and piratical activities, and internal rebellions, has contributed to several historians' misunderstanding the impact of the register. Soviet-influenced interpreters, such as Holobutsky, wrongly consider the registered cossacks conservative on all fronts; and this view is ironically repeated by some anti-Soviet historians.[30] In other interpretations, the obviously active role of the registered, gentry, cossacks in their illegal activities is interpreted as evidence that stratification among the cossacks was not politically influential at all. In other contexts, failure to make this distinction results in dismissal of the cossacks as simply bandits.[31]

Part Four
Kosinsky and
The First Rebellion

Introduction to Part Four

Previous chapters criticized an intepretation of the cossacks that makes them a mere epiphenomenon of general economic forces. We argued instead a multifactor analysis, one that is nondeterminist: The cossacks arose and rebelled in response to immediate and unique conditions in the Ukrainian steppe. These conditions were in turn affected by pan-European social and economic changes, and by old-Rus, Lithuanian, Polish and Tatar traditions, some of them many centuries old. Cossack institutions and behavior had political and religious motives as well as economic causes. Furthermore, the cossacks were by no means merely reactive. They developed images of the kind of society they preferred, or at least of the kind of society they opposed. They were a powerful initiating force in the Ukraine and their actions were propelled at least as much by their own socio-political desires as by the actions of their enemies. They influenced Ukrainian history greatly, and ultimately the history of all eastern Europe.

The necessity for this complex, multicausal interpretation will become more obvious as we look closely at the first two substantial Zaporozhian-led rebellions. These events supply the evidence for an understanding of what cossackdom is, and also for some generalizations about this type of social banditry.

Certain general themes about the nature of cossack rebellions will emerge from the narrative, and they deserve mention here. They are not only general themes but also serve as the topics around which the story will be organized. First, the cossacks' piracy and banditry against neighboring countries, particularly those dominated by Turkey, were a provocative aspect of their insistence on autonomy from the Polish government and their subversiveness towards Polish society. Second, the social rebellions led by the cossacks were detonated by personal grievances and private feuds. Third, the cossack insurgency was in some respects like modern guerrilla warfare, as for example in their mobility and reliance on popular support for supplies and intelligence; while in other respects they functioned more like mecenaries, seeking booty, shifting allegiances readily, pursuing no lasting social alliances. Fourth, the forces of counter-insurgency were deeply divided, largely because of the fundamental incoherence and rapid transformation of Polish-Lithuanian society at this time, but also partly because of deliberate cossack exploitation of that incoherence. Fifth, the complexity and ambiguity of the cossacks' goals made the question of victory or defeat complex and ambiguous, for these rebellions were not isolated uprisings but part of a continuing process of struggle about the nature of a future Ukrainian society. The five chapters that follow each have a dual function: narrating a portion of the story of the first rebellion, and illustrating one of these themes.

8. Cossacks against Infidels: Piracy and Polish Politics

FROM THE 1570s on, the crown's primary concern about the cossacks was to prevent them from subverting Polish foreign policy. Yet the cossacks grew steadily bolder in their foreign adventures. They harassed, attacked, robbed and kidnapped Tatar and Turkish settlers. Poland's inability to control the cossacks did not, in the eyes of the khan or sultan, exempt her from retaliation for these damaging and humiliating provocations.

Jan Zamojski, Polish chancellor from 1576 to 1605, had the responsiblity for keeping the peace. His problem was worsened by threats to Poland from Austria and Muscovy, which created the danger of a two-front war should open conflict with Turkey break out. Furthermore, Zamojski was by education a man of the Renaissance, committed to the delicate task of maintaining international peace. Educated in Padua, fluent in several languages, he was also a supporter of the principles of democracy of the gentry and elective kingship, and at the beginning of his period in office he commanded great influence among the nobility.[1] Shortly thereafter, however, he became the enemy of many of that class. From their point of view, Zamojski had betrayed them. Concerned for Polish security, the chancellor believed that the state could only be strengthened by imposing restrictions on the traditional liberties of the *szlachta*. Particularly he attempted to stop the foreign intrigues of the powerful magnates, including their use of the cossacks. Zamojski did not, however, have the power to deprive the nobility of their fundamental constitutional and economic power; and his compromising attempts to convince them of the necessity of strengthening the state were unavailing. His "minor restrictions" were resisted.

The Ukrainian magnates in particular saw the cossacks as "their" men. In the Diet they successfully egged on the whole nobility to vote against funding the royal cossack register. In the

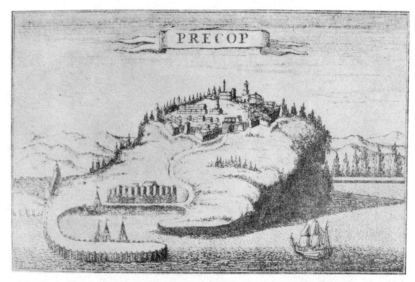

13. Tatar fortress at Perekop. Eighteenth-century engraving. From *Istoria Ukrainskoho Viyska*, Winnipeg, 1953.

14. Jan Zamojski. From a photograph, taken by Alinari, of a portrait in the Uffizi Gallery, Florence.

Ukraine they continued to hire and support unregistered cossacks in their personal retinues, and to lead the expeditions abroad that strengthened and enriched these cossacks.

Both Zamojski and the Polish nobility, however, failed to perceive the cossacks as an independent force. Nor did they understand that the very structure of Polish-Lithuanian society kept the cossacks alive. Ironically, the cossack activities which threatened Poland's external security were stimulated by Poland's system of internal security. To the extent that Polish society rested on its privileged nobility, it deprived the cossacks of freedom within it and forced them into the wild steppe, into the life of pirates and mercenaries. As the magnates moved to install the Polish class system in the Ukraine, they smothered the cossacks' "traditional liberties" and forced them into foreign territory, "to breathe freely," as the cossacks said.

Of course the "liberties" the cossacks demanded were not at all traditional, but new: a product of the frontier which the cossacks then articulated as a "right." These "liberties" included free farming, squatters' rights on land, other private property guaranteed to the first possessor or the strongest, free hunting and fishing, freedom to fight infidels for their land (Tatars still controlled some of the richest lands) and treasure, free piracy on the Black Sea, exemption from all feudal dues and royal taxes, administrative autonomy; and, when necessary, royal subsidies and free quartering on royal estates! This hodge-podge of personal privileges and collective autonomy was inconsistent in itself. It was also incompatible with a centralized state and a society based on aristocratic power, increasingly commercial agriculture and attached peasants as the main source of labor power. And it was a sharp and constant threat to Poland's international security.

In the cossacks' search to "breath freely", an enticing region was on the Danube, in the principalities of Moldavia and Wallachia. Both were under Ottoman control, but unlike the Bulgarian and Thracian regions had not been incorporated into the Turkish provincial system. Rather the Ottomans collected annual tribute but left the traditional social structure alone—with the major adjustment that the governors were now appointed by the Sultan. The result was a serious worsening of conditions for the peasantry, as the governors now ruled at the will of a foreign power whose main interest was in expropriating wealth out of the principalities.[2] The opportunity to buy governorships stimulated many coups and power struggles.

In the 1570s the balance of power in the Balkans began to shift, just as it had in the Ukraine. It may be that the Ottomans had reached the extreme radius of their possibility of control from Constantinople.[3] Whether or not that is true, the distance and remoteness of the principalities from Turkey made control and stability difficult, and the result was a kind of moving stalemate, characterized by sharply fluctuating balances of military forces.

Local potentates began to seek and receive support from foreign powers such as Austria, Poland, Crimea; or from factions within such powers, who maneuvered to use the Balkans to aggrandize their domestic power. Many Polish and Lithuanian nobles joined in the game, for there was rich booty to be collected. Others had higher ambitions—to hold the crown of Moldavia or Wallachia themselves. For their purposes the cossacks represented a ready army.[4]

In 1489, 1493, and 1508 cossacks led by Ukrainian crown officials had attacked Tatar and Turkish travellers and bases.[5] Such attacks continued throughout the sixteenth century. Cossacks sank Tatar boats in the Ukrainian rivers and Turkish galleys in the Black Sea; they robbed merchants travelling to and from the Crimea, Turkey and North Africa; they besieged and burned Tatar and Turkish towns from the Ukraine to Anatolia, from Armenia to the Balkans. Between 1575 and 1590 there were cossack attacks in every year but one.[6]

Meanwhile the military prowess of the cossacks gained them an international reputation. First, starting in the 1570s, Danubian rulers and pretenders began to hire Ukrainian cossacks as mercenaries.[7] In 1583 an outlaw Polish noble, Samuil Zborowski, served as an intermediary in negotiating for the cossacks to serve the Crimean khan in a war against Persia.[8] His plan did not succeed,[9] but it was typical of the attempts of several Polish nobles to live out their fantasies of aggrandizement and revenge through the cossacks. They erred in seeing the cossacks as their personal tools, forgetting that cossack self-interest hardly coincided with their own. Nor did they perceive that the Danubian expeditions built cossack strength and confidence, which could one day be turned against themselves.

Throughout the sixteenth century both khans and sultans behaved with intermittent forbearance and vengefulness in the face of incessant harassment from the cossacks. Constantinople, which did not desire war with Poland, sometimes acted to check the more belligerent Crimeans (whose righteous indignation was in part used to cover their own aggression and slaving). Many times the khan and sultan limited themselves to vigorous protests about cossack depredations; other times they threatened retaliation. In 1583 and 1588, after particularly large cossack attacks on Turkish fortresses, Turkey mobilized. Appeased both times, the sultan was rewarded with a severe attack on the Crimea in 1589. Poland now came closer to war with Turkey than ever before. The Turks sent eight galleys to the Ukraine, had the khan attack Podolia, and massed an army at the Polish border.[10] ". . . In truth," the Beylerbey Pasha wrote Zamojski, "we have no cause other than the cossacks, who have done us great evil. If you had restrained the said cossacks, never would the Tatars have entered into your country."[11] Zamojski wriggled out of this predicament, as he had previously, partly, because the Sultan did not really want war.

In avoiding war with Turkey, Zamojski only strengthened his domestic opposition. Zamojski had begun his political career in the chancery under King Stefan Batory, and had adopted Batory's foreign

15. Conquest of Kaffa by the cossacks. Eighteenth-century print from Podhorodecki, *Sicz Zaporoska*, Warsaw, 1978.

policy orientation toward peace with Turkey. Known as the "Paduan Turkophile,"[12] Zamojski could be represented by his noble opponents as not sufficiently pro-Christian.

At the death of Stefan Batory in 1586, the anti-Zamojski faction of the nobility had made a bid for power, putting up the Habsburg Archduke Maximilian for the Polish crown. When Zamojski engineered an electoral victory for his candidate, Sigismund Vasa of Sweden, the opposition assembled their own dissident Diet and elected Maximilian, who then raised an army and besieged Cracow. (The anti-Zamojski forces were led by the Zborowski family, whose scion Samuil had attempted to lead the cossacks into the khan's service a few years previously.) Needing an army quickly, Zamojski was forced to turn to the cossacks, immediately after having cursed and threatened them for nearly provoking a war with Turkey![13] With their help, he defeated Maximilian, but the cost to him was high: the cossacks gained spirit and strength, while Zamojski's troubles were only beginning.

Sigismund Vasa, now Sigismund III of Poland, betrayed his mentor Zamojski. Involved in a challenge to his Swedish title, Sigismund was encouraged by his family to support a Habsburg and Vatican project for a multilateral anti-Turkish league. In return, he found himself supported at the Polish court by the very nobles who had been partisans of Maximilian. Zamojski considered involvement in an anti-Turkish alliance an unnecessary danger. Poland's religious obligations to the Vatican and other Catholic states did not loom large in his world view. His concepts of Poland's national interest was largely secular and modern, and peace with Turkey seemed to him at the very heart of that national interest. He was probably sceptical about multilateral alliances in any case, and preferred unilateral diplomatic maneuvers. In his determination to keep the peace, he now had to resist not only the blandishments of papal nuncios, the intrigues of the Austrian ambassadors, and the provocations of the cossacks, but also the inclinations of his sovereign.

Throughout the spring and summer of 1589 the cossacks plundered, sinking Turkish ships and attacking first the Crimea, then Tiagin, Belgorod, and other Turkish fortress towns.[14] Sinan Pasha, the Turkish Grand Vizier, wrote that "certain theeves in the partes of Polonia called Cosacks, and other notorious persons living in the same partes ceased not to trouble and molest the subjects of our most mightie Emperour."[15] In retaliation the Crimean Horde, and then the Turks under the Beylerbey, raided Podolia as far north as

Lvov, administering what Sinan Pasha called "condigne punishment."[16] Zamojski prepared for war, but continued to try to appease. He sent a personal envoy to the Beylerbey, but nothing was achieved.[17] In a letter to Elizabeth of England of June 1590 Sinan Pasha claimed that the Sultan was not at all interested in peace but hoped "utterly to subvert and overthrowe his Kingdome [Poland]."[18] It is more likely that this was an expression of his own, and not the Sultan's, sentiments. But Sinan at that time had enough personal power to make things extremely difficult for Zamojski. He gave the Poles forty days to send a new envoy with with first installment of what was to be a yearly tribute of one hundred horses, each laden with silver, or else accept Islam! "Who has ever stood against me? Persia dreads me, the Venetians tremble before me, the Spanish plead with me, the Germans must pay what I demand. If you refuse I will send to you all the Tatar hordes, I will send the Wallachians, the Moldavians, . . . with an army of 200,000. Myself I will come with 300,000 . . . All the world trembles before me."[19]

Polish nerve was broken, at least temporarily. The nobility actually voted a head tax on themselves, with no exemptions—even the church and the royal courtiers had to pay—except the Ukrainian districts, which were excused in recognition of the damages the Tatar raids had inflicted on them. The Diet sent envoys to the Vatican, to Venice, throughout Europe, trying with little success to raise money for an anti-Turkish campaign. (The irony of the situation could not have escaped the Habsburgs, the Venetians, and the papal officials who had so recently been pleading with Zamojski to join an alliance against the Turks.) An army was quickly thrown together which may have totalled 110,000 if all its separate, feudal components were included. Of these, 20,000 were cossacks and they were ordered immediately to Wallachia to hold the Turks, if possible, while the rest were organized.[20]

The army was never put to the test. A new Polish envoy to Constantinople found several circumstances altered to his advantage: Sinan Pasha was replaced as vizier by Ferhat Pasha, whom the Poles found more reasonable—or possible more venal, as they succeeded in bribing him with twelve thousand thalers. An English ambassador in Constantinople (he had been sent, apparently, to devise some action to exploit the common Anglo-Turkish hostility towards Spain) was persuaded to intercede for Poland.[21] The sultan accepted 140 sables as payment for the damages inflicted by the cossacks and called off his retaliatory expedition.

Peace treaties were concluded with Turkey and the Crimea, one of their conditions providing that cossack attacks would be permanently suppressed.[22] It was not the first time the Polish and Lithuanian governments had made such promises, and there was less reason to expect them to be kept this time than before. Twice in rapid succession—for the battle against Maximilian in 1587 and against the Khan in 1589—the Crown had undermined its own attempts to isolate the cossacks by hiring large numbers of them, disregarding the register. Nevertheless, the stakes were higher than ever now, and Zamojski made yet another effort to discipline the cossacks, this time trying a slightly different version of the register.

Zamojski planned to establish a fort at Kremenchug, on the Bessarabian side of the Dniester, to serve as the headquarters for a frontier police that would prevent cossack attacks. The fort was to be manned by one thousand cossacks, and two emissaries were sent to collect and organize them.[23] This plan worked no better than earlier ones. No fort was built. Zamojski's chief emissary, Nikolai Yazlovetsky, sheriff of Sniatyn, appeared as the instigator of a cossack attack on the Crimea a few years later,[24] exactly the sort of attack he had been charged to prevent. His assistant led a piracy expedition into Moldavia in 1594.[25] As usual, the interests of the nobles did not coincide with those of the central government, and the cossacks exploited the division.

Meanwhile the 1590 Diet attempted to reactivate the register. The cossack brotherhood was ordered subordinated to the crown hetman. Under him cossack officers would be appointed, not elected, from among the nobility only. The cossack hetman was to enroll six thousand cossacks into the army and to keep a register, thus to prevent the constant exchange between peasants and cossacks, depending on the agricultural and military needs of the season. No one under death sentence was permitted on the register. All royal officials, and all ranks of the provincial nobility, were required to swear that they would not permit men to flee from the towns and villages to join the cossacks below the rapids. The cossacks were not to be permitted to travel through the Ukraine except with formal passports from their elders, and those who hid in the towns, castles or villages without permission were to be punished by death. The 1590 plan recognized that the Ukrainian nobility was an important part of the cossack leadership and the instigators of much of the worst mischief. Those nobles who accepted booty taken from foreign countries would be punished. Violators of the prohibition, even if they were titled, would be liable to the death penalty, like plebians; officials who were negligent in administering the plan would be prosecuted.[26]

The 1590 plan was unworkable in its very design. The provincial nobles given responsibility for administering it were the worst culprits. Immediately after the government itself had hired 20,000 cossacks to fight the Beylerbey, it expected 14,000 of them to disperse peacefully and return to plebeian status and occupations. Furthermore, the possibility of their being officially returned to the army was written into the plan, which authorized the crown hetman to hire unlimited numbers of cossacks at any time he thought necessary.[27]

The 1590 arrangements gave the cossacks both grievances and the opportunity to mobilize around them. Like previous register plans, this one, the cossacks understood, defied their most fundamental principle: the self-definition and self-government of the cossack brotherhood. Recognizing this, the cossacks could hardly have been expected to remain quiescent until the threat became a reality.

9. Personal Grievances, Social Banditry

O NE OF THE COSSACKS hired to serve at the fort at Kremenchug was Kristof Kosinsky. He was of the gentry, an experienced registered cossack.[1] Crown Hetman Zolkiewski later claimed that Kosinsky had entered into treasonous dealings with Muscovy,[2] which, if true, would suggest only that he was a typical *szlachta* cossack leader.

In 1590 Kosinsky, along with other cossacks employed for Yazlovetsky's fort-to-be, received a land grant as part of his salary.[3] (Had he been a commoner his salary would not have included land.) Kosinsky was assigned a large but unpopulated piece of land on the river Rokitna,[4] a tributary of the Ros River, which is in turn a tributary of the Dnieper. Its location was most unlucky for Kosinsky. The Rokitna estate lay within Belotserkov district, governed by Janush Ostrozhsky. Just a little further up the Ros, possibly thirty-five kilometers from Rokitna, was Volodarka, a private estate of Janush Ostrozhsky. In the other direction, about thirty kilometers downriver from Rokitna, lay Boguslav, another royal town and fortress run by Ostrozhsky.[5]

As if it were not enough to be encircled by Ostrozhsky lands, Kosinsky also had to contend with the interests of the Vishnevetsky family. Due east of Rokitna was Kanev, the seat of one of the districts of Alexander Mikailovich Vishnevetsky. Indeed, the same Alexander just nine years previously had himself been the owner of certain lands on the Rokitna River,[6] which may have included the land given to Kosinsky.[7] Even if this were not the case, Kosinsky was still surrounded by the two most skillful land-grabbers in the Ukraine, the Ostrozhsky and Vishnevetsky families. True to their reputations, they ended up in possession of Kosinsky's parcel.[8]

Given these facts about the land transfers, it seems significant that in Kosinsky's first attack, on an Ostrozhsky castle in December 1591, he stole the Rokitna deeds.[9] Right or wrong, he had a grievance about this land,[10] and being legally helpless against the magnate families, he resorted to extra-legal means to get what he wanted. A strong personal anger against the Ostrozhskys propelled Kosinsky into the leadership of this rebellion. In the series of cossack and mass attacks that constituted the "Kosinsky Uprising," a disproportionate number of those led by Kosinsky himself were aimed at Ostrozhsky property.

Elements of personal feud were present in many early cossack rebellions. Personal material grievances, frequently of gentry towards magnates, operated as the connection between long-range collective grievances and the detonation of violence. These uprisings always required both long-range structural conflicts and individual precipitating factors. The structural problems of Polish government and society delineated in the previous chapters did not in themselves produce uprisings. Long-term causes operated through individual, even accidental, mediations. If in retrospect the uprisings seem an inevitable result of the structural problems, that is so only because of the statistical likelihood that among the individuals involved, some at some point would find those conflicts crystallized in a personal loss or injustice that seemed unbearable. Kosinsky's fight for his property was such a conflict, for it symbolized to Kosinsky and his followers a host of enduring grievances; and because of its symbolic nature, it escalated the rage and determination to act among Kosinsky and his followers.

That this and other uprisings appeared first as personal feuds also affected the defense against the cossacks. Zamojski described the situation as "former friends of the Kievan governor [Konstantin-Vasili Ostrozhsky, father of Janush] and to him they caused iniquity in order to get their due revenge for his stupidity and unreasonableness."[11] Although this diagnosis was partly correct, it was also a welcome justification for royal noninterference. It spared the Kingdom expense, and it afforded Zamojski the hope of letting two of his enemies weaken each other.

The attacks were only partly personal, however. The cossack rank and file were inclined to follow Kosinsky's aggressive leadership because they had a consonant grievance: The registered cossacks, plus those who had been specially hired for the Kremenchug fort, were due to be paid their salary, in money and cloth, on June 24, 1591. The payments did not arrive. Polish officials rarely met such financial obligations graciously, and thus typically created for themselves angry groups of armed but idle soldiers. The cossacks on this occasion were patient enough to write to Yazlovetsky demanding payment, but they received no reply.[12]

Kosinsky understood the situation and attempted to exploit the cossacks' complaint, writing them in August 1591:

> To our gracious comrades . . . We have heard that the sheriff is not exactly hurrying to us with the money. Therefore do not wait but come to us immediately. Tell Pretvich* in the name of the [cossack] army that we will no longer wait for him, that we intend to take care of ourselves. Tell the vice-sheriff in Sharovka to inform his lord [Pretvich] that the army will not wait for this money. . . . Your well-wishing comrade, Kristof Kosinsky and all his knights.[13]

Many cossacks rallied to Kosinsky and they headed east, towards Kiev and the Ostrozhsky domain. Ironically, the old man Konstantin Ostrozhsky was at this moment at the Diet urging the strengthening of the Kiev and Belotserkov forts against the cossacks, but to no avail.[14] Arriving in Belotserkov, Kosinsky recruited still more men from among the unregistered cossacks wintering there. On December 29, 1591, they attacked the estate of the Belotserkov vice-sheriff, Prince Kurtsevich-Bulyga. There they stole all the movable property to be found, including the deeds to several estates among them the Rokitna lands.[15]

The cossacks remained in the Kievan lands through the spring of 1592. After the attack on Kurtsevich–Bulyga they besieged the Belotserkov castle itself and then the castle at Boguslav, both ruled by Janush Ostrozhsky. They took both castles and removed all the artillery and ammunition. They plundered royal and noble property, robbing, destroying, and murdering. Finally they burned the castles to the ground, or so the Diet's declaration on the subject claimed.[16] From here the cossacks moved upriver to Kiev where, as Ostrozhsky had predicted, they took the castle with little difficulty.[17] They captured a fourth royal castle at Tripolye and made it their headquarters for most of the spring of 1592.

For several months Kosinsky's cossacks were masters of the Kievan region. This does not necessarily mean, of course, that they had wide popular support. Most of the nobles and the royal officials probably fled before the cossacks arrived. At least one set of events suggests that the middle classes and the service people may have

---

*Jakub Pretvich, sheriff of Terebovl, often used by the crown to lead cossacks.

been hostile to the cossacks. Late in 1591 or early 1592 the cossacks had demanded one hundred fifty thousand Lithuanian *kop* (one *kop* was approximately two and one-half Polish zlotys) as tribute from the town of Pereaslav. The town refused and, when a cossack delegation arrived to insist, it was attacked and robbed by some Pereaslavians. In retaliation the cossacks attacked, killed many local officials and burned both the town and fort.[18] Not satisfied, and perhaps wishing to demonstrate their "legal" control of Kiev, the cossacks filed a suit with Kievan provincial officials against the town of Pereaslav. A commission sent in judgment—feeling quite terrified—decided against the Pereaslavians.[19] When word reached the capital of this decision, a royal writ overruled it. But the crown was powerless to help the townspeople who had had to agree to pay a tribute and were now desperately negotiating with the cossacks to reduce its amount.[20]

Cossack motivation in demanding tribute was partly punitive, but also reflected necessity. Their domestic attacks were no different from their foreign adventures in that the booty they collected from both was their sustenance. The cossacks lived off the population, and like guerrillas this presented them with problems when the population was not friendly. When their stores of supply were abundant, they required only that people not betray them to the authorities; at other times they needed money, supplies and shelter; but if the maintenance exacted was too stringent, or too forcibly taken, the populace might turn against them and betray them to their enemies. These constraints determined the strategy and success of the cossack rebellions.

In this case the cossacks had leaned too heavily on the townspeople of Pereaslavl. Or, put another way, they overestimated the strength of their position among the Kievan towns. Still, their error was an overestimation, not a complete illusion. In the two years preceding this affair, the Pereaslavians had twice rebelled against their provincial government, and their insubordination had to be forcibly suppressed.[21] In other areas of the Ukraine the cossacks were already getting consistent support from townspeople, as we shall see later. The cossacks were not an isolated band of troublemakers. At the least they were *social* bandits. Despite their miscalculation in regard to Pereaslavl, the evidence—their ultimate victory over the town, their arrogance in forcing a royal commission to accept their demands, and their demands themselves—demonstrates the contrary: that they had a significant basis among the local population.

10. The Nature of Cossack Insurgency

ALTHOUGH KOSINSKY'S PERSONAL MOTIVATION and leadership set this particular fire, it soon burned far beyond his control. Word of the Kievan attacks stimulated similar violence elsewhere—in too many places at distances too great for Kosinsky to have been responsible for them all. By the end of the summer of 1592 there had already been outbreaks in all four Ukrainian provinces, in Belorussia and in Muscovy.[1] News of these disturbances terrified landowners at great distances from the actual incidents.[2]

In both its personal and collective dimensions, this uprising sought what its participants believed was a return to tradition. This belief was in part a myth but in part accurate. It was mythical in that the Ukraine—long a sparsely-populated frontier, long the location of conflicting political claims, long without any effective government or homogeneous society—had few effective traditions. It was accurate in that the magnates, not the cossacks, were the "party of change" in the Ukraine. Cossack demands, implicit and explicit, were for a reinstitution of their semi-nomadic freedom of the days when Tatars and free peasants shared, turbulently, the Ukrainian land. The magnates were seeking to destroy the nomadic life and establish agriculture; to liquidate and enclose the small peasant farms and autonomous commercial centers; and to destroy free smallholders and free burghers as classes. It was the magnates' intentions that pushed many peasants and burghers, often the victims of cossack brutality and greed, into alignment with the cossacks in defense of their freedom and livelihood.

The defensive nature, then, of this and most cossack and peasant uprisings, conditioned their general characteristics. First, they were erratic. Not having long-term offensive goals, such as occupying territory or installing a new government, the insurgents often believed they had succeeded in repelling their enemy and therefore stopped fighting, when the latter had by no means given up. Cossack maneuvers rarely aimed at taking and holding land and property; they were willing to carry out a scorched-earth policy. Their tactics were punitive, vindictive and selfish. They burned and razed, murdered and pillaged. They rarely took prisoners,[3] even when ransomable figures fell into their hands. They rarely left a castle or manor-house without attempting to burn it to the ground.

The erratic destructiveness of these uprisings does not, however, imply that the cossacks were disorganized or innocent of planning. Their emphasis on destruction was in part calculated to terrorize a population into acquiescence. The cossack armies under Kosinsky and his successors were structured and hierarchically organized. Although not always superbly disciplined, they were able to execute ambushes and encirclements effectively. They were capable of great feats of mobility and stealth. When a stable head-quarters was useful and obtainable, the cossacks were capable of occupying and governing large areas and even towns (as we shall see below in this chapter, for example, in their 1592 occupation of Ostropol).

At times the cossack belligerence was undirected. The members of a cossack horde were always, informally, bandits—that is, they considered looting their due. They stole everything that lay in their path. Their path normally lay across the estates of the nobles,

16. A cossack tabor. From Hrushevsky, *Pro Stari Chasy na Ukraini*, 1907.

but they were not Robin Hoods, benevolent towards the poor. If their defiance symbolized and crystallized many of the interests and aspirations of the peasantry, this did not prevent them from murdering neutral villagers, raping their women and stealing their cattle.

Nevertheless there were some significant differences in cossack treatment of different populations. Noble estates were normally hit without warning, robbed, destroyed and abandoned as quickly as possible, except in those rare instances when the cossacks occupied an estate as temporary headquarters or wintering spot. The royal castles and towns were often treated somewhat more leniently: a cossack delegation would arrive demanding supplies, quarter, and sometimes money. The cossacks would attack if refused; but if the townspeople opened their doors to the cossacks they could sometimes escape with minor looting.[4]

This and other cossack rebellions have sometimes appeared exclusively directed against the nobility, and the sufferings of commoners were underestimated, because virtually all of the documentation consists of complaints from the nobility. The poor villager who happened to stand in the path of a cossack cavalry unit was unlikely to register a written complaint. Furthermore, the Ukrainian nobility had an interest in exaggerating the power and the threat of the cossacks, as they were anxiously seeking royal assistance in suppressing the unrest. Hence the language typical of their complaints: "a great threat to the Kingdom from this Ukrainian insubordination."[5]

The government readily agreed to view the uprising as an attack on the nobility, but did not accede to the Ukrainians' estimate of the size of the threat. Zamojski and Zolkiewski declined to send Ostrozhsky military aid. Instead, on January 16, 1592, the king ordered a royal commission to investigate, and directed "cossack officials" to seize and punish the rebels according to the law.[6] These cossack officials were, of course, the appointed elders of the registered cossacks who, largely because they had not been paid, had deserted their official duties in favor of Kosinsky, whose activities at least netted them some profit. Despite the obvious toothlessness of the royal order, the commission assembled and went through the motions of an investigation. The commissioners were five. There was Alexander Vishnevetsky, sheriff of Kanev, Cherkassy, Korsun, and Chigirin, the second greatest magnate of Kiev. He was joined by Jan Gulski, a military official of Bratslav, Jakub Strus, sheriff of Bratslav and Vinnitsa, Stanislav Gulski, of Bar, and Jakub Pretvich, sheriff of Terebovl and marshal of Kremenets. No Ostrozhsky was among them. This attests to the royal impression that the disturbance was primarily a vendetta against the Ostrozhskys, and that it would not do, accordingly, to place the injured party on the investigatory commission.

The commissars set off down the Dnieper and en route met Nikolai Yazlovetsky, the crown-appointed hetman of the registered cossacks.[7] As they approached Tripolye, where the cossacks were then holed up, in late February or early March of 1592, they sent out numerous communications and orders, to all of which they received no response whatever.[8]

Probably nothing could have induced the cossacks to negotiate at this point; but it is worth noting that they were not even offered a chance to spell out their grievances. Yazlovetsky, for example, did not address them as a mediator, or as part of an investigatory commission, but as a nobleman. "Despite my first writing," he wrote on March 10, "you remained disobedient, both to the King and to myself . . . if you do not now send to me immediately, but instead cling slavishly to that brigand [Kosinsky], with the help of God I and the lords will take revenge on you."[9] He was responding less to their disturbances of the king's peace than to the effrontery of their insubordination towards their lords. Resentment and fear of threatened privilege ring loudest in his futile attempt to bluff the cossacks into submission.

Meanwhile, news and complaints of cossack outrages continued to pour in from Kiev, Volynia and Bratslav, and from the Danubian principalities. In their frustration the commission issued another decree, as empty as the king's own, and went home. This second ukase, dated March 14, "punished" the cossacks by depriving them of their traditional rights.[10] No threatened punishment could have been more meaningless. The cossacks' "traditional rights" had never been recognized by the Rzecz Pospolita. The 1590 Constitution and many previous statutes had already deprived them of these "rights."[11] The decree was no more than bluster.

As the commissars left, the cossacks attacked and took the town and castle of Kiev. This, had they remained, would have put them in control of the key points of Kiev province.[12] Nevertheless they left and headed out into the steppe. Kosinsky's next target was Ostropol, one of Ostrozhsky's richest and most important Volynian estates. It held his chief stores of arms, gunpowder and supplies,[13] and its position was important because of the emptiness of the adjacent Bratslav lands. A new province in the Polish administrative system, created in 1565, and the most thinly populated,[14] Bratslav contained most of the empty land available for distribution. More than other parts of the Ukraine, Bratslav land was still in the hands of free peasants under customary rather than feudal land tenure and this made it a natural breeding ground for cossackdom.[15] At the same time several Bratslav towns, especially the two royal towns, Bratslav and Vinnitsa, had produced ambitious and aggressive commercial and artisan classes who were dissatisfied with the spread of aristocratic jurisdictions. Threatened, both peasantry and townspeople of Bratslav province often welcomed the cossacks as their protectors.[16]

Passing through Bratslav,[17] Kosinsky reached and took Ostropol by November.[18] He established his headquarters there and replaced the royal and noble administration with a cossack one.[19] He ruled "like the head of a cossack republic,"[20] maintaining peace and extending cossack jurisdiction over the entire population. This meant, for the residents, subordination to cossack officers for legal decisions; paying dues and "taxes" of various kinds to cossack authorities; performing military services, sentry duties, and numerous other jobs at the behest of the cossack commanders.

The Ostropol "liberated area" served as a spark to further unrest, and as a safe area of retreat and flight for cossack and peasant rebels from elsewhere. Cossack attacks and peasant disturbances spread, throughout Volynia, into Podolia,[21] and then Belorussia.[22] In Lutsk, capital of Volynia, court sessions and other provincial administrative operations were forced to close.[23] The cossacks inflicted considerable damage, seizing royal and noble estates, castles and towns, and causing much bloodshed and destruction.[24]

11. The Nature of Aristocratic Defense

AS COSSACK INSURGENCY spread and intensified, the alarm of the nobility grew. At least sixteen provincial diets, including some in central Poland, called upon the crown to undertake military action to suppress the cossacks.[1] But the effective response, from both crown and nobility, was slow and inadequate. The reasons for this failure were short-sightedness and weakness, both caused by the same structural contradictions in Polish society that had produced the cossack menace in the first place.

The emergence of the rebellion from specific grievances against Ostrozhsky confirmed the natural inclination of non-Ukrainian nobles and crown officials to view the troubles as spillover from a private feud. Although Zamojski understood the national danger of cossack warfare—for foreign policy and for the spread of peasant revolt elsewhere—he thought suppressing it was the responsibility of the magnates who had provoked it. Thus in the Royal Instruction to the Diet of 1592 he said:

> The Ukrainian insubordination is spreading fast and is so dangerous that God help us if your graces again fall out with the pagans, as happened before, and must raise an army in a situation of difficulty and insecurity.[2]

Zamojski not only declined to send aid to Ostrozhsky, but asked the crown commander to write Ostrozhsky and urge him not to permit war to develop,[3] i.e., implying that Ostrozhsky *could* by his own restraint prevent war.

The debates in the central and provincial diets of 1592 showed that nobles and crown officials shared this interpretation of the

123

problem. Nevertheless, the rebellion inevitably became an issue in the struggles between nobility and crown, each side demanding that the other should assume responsibility for the necessary police action. The Royal Instruction blamed the cossack problem on the miserliness of the Diet, emphasizing that the cossacks' salaries, due them for their participation in the campaign against the Wallachian gospodar, had been withheld because of insufficient funds in the treasury.[4] Senators and provincial diet members by and large demanded that the crown should supply permanent border guards to place the cossacks under constant supervision.[5] In response Vice-chancellor Tarnowski thundered against the "rebels and enemies of the fatherland, . . . infamous in the realm and banished and proscribed . . . for eternity," and again deprived the cossacks of their constitutional rights and privileges.[6]

Tarnowski's plan would have added to this empty rhetoric a threat to confiscate cossack property. Many cossacks, and especially their leaders, were nobles and considerable landowners, so that the threat might have worried them had it been enforceable. The strength that the rebellion had already shown, however, made this threat also empty. Nor could it work as long-term policy, since fear for land tenure was already a prime grievance and a prime source of enmity against the land-usurping magnates. However, even this toothless legislation was never enacted due to the Diet's paralysis.

At this same Diet Ostrozhsky also tried to exculpate himself and thereby to obtain funds to rebuild the fortresses at Kiev and Belotserkov which the cossacks had burned. Rejected, he insisted on a formal declaration absolving him, as Kiev governor, of responsibility: he wanted it on record that he had repeatedly warned that the forts were weak and needed repair.[7]

Ostrozhsky got his written absolution but no armed forces. Recognizing his isolation, he proceeded efficiently to organize his own "militia," a private, feudal army, assembling soldiers through the use of his economic power over small landowners, and by hiring mercenaries, rather than through his authority as a provincial governor. Only two other Ukrainian magnates—Pretvich and Vishnevetsky—joined. The bulk of the army was the Ukrainian Orthodox gentry, dependent on Ostrozhsky not only economically but politically as well, for his support for Orthodoxy in the Ukraine.[8] Even they came only slowly and in small numbers. Konstantin's son Janush Ostrozhsky, governor of Volynia, organized the militia. At Tarnopol, in Galicia,[9] he hired 300 infantry and 600 cavalry, and from there he sent to Hungary for additional mercenary infantry.[10] The king contributed only a letter urging the nobility to join the effort.[11] By the end of January 1593 the militia numbered only about 1,000, and it was poorly disciplined. The group included, oddly, cossacks—the personal servitors of Ostrozhsky, among them one called Nalivaiko, whom we shall meet again later. Despite being called upon to fight their "brethren," the cossacks were among the more eager and reliable fighters.[12]

While the Ostrozhsky army was building, so was Kosinsky's. He was thought to have about 5,000 men collected by this time.[13] He also had some 26 cannon—an imposing artillery for this time—which he had stolen, of course, from royal castles. He still controlled most of the fortresses of Volynia and Kiev, and he had the added security of help and supplies coming to him from Zaporozhe.[14] Kosinsky was confident. He wanted to draw Ostrozhsky into an open battle which he believed he could win, and for this purpose he moved from Ostropol to the village of Piatka, about seven miles away.[15] The surrounding population was known to be partisan to the cossacks, and to the south there was the possibility of escape into the steppe, which made it a desirable location for Kosinsky.[16]

Janush Ostrozhsky accepted Kosinsky's bid and followed him to Piatka, where he found the cossacks in their defensive encampment, the tabor. The cossacks, however, full of confidence, deserted their cautious ways and attacked, opening their tabor themselves. At first the Ostrozhsky militia, sluggish and fearful, bent with the attack.[17] Many deserted the Ostrozhsky forces,[18] and a rout seemed imminent. Then Janush Ostrozhsky took command of the troops himself, heartened them and began an offensive—or so claim the Polish chronicles, attempting to fashion Ostrozhsky into a military hero. The Hungarian mercenaries, armed with long lances and fresh, large horses, attacked. The cossacks fled but their horses were weak and small and they sank into the deep snowdrifts, and the militia chased them to the very gates of Ostropol.[19] The cossacks shut themselves in the town.

Cossack losses were apparently heavy, although the Polish sources, the only ones we have, are unreliable. Out of an army of five to six thousand Kosinsky may have lost two to three thousand and all his cannon.[20] The Ostrozhskys claimed that they lost only ten men.[21] This seems dubious since it took them eight days more to force Kosinsky and the remainder of his men out of Ostropol.[22]

Polish chroniclers later rendered this story in such a way as to make Kosinsky's defeat appear most inglorious, his army never a threat to the gentry militia.[23] Had that been true, Prince Ostrozhsky was near saintly in his forbearance, for the "surrender" document signed at Piatka was most lenient. Since this document must serve as the primary evidence of the nature of Kosinsky's defeat, and hence of the balance of forces, it is essential that we quote from it at some length:

> I, Kristof Kosinsky, at this time hetman, and we captains, officers, all the knights of the Zaporozhian army, do confess in this our writ that, despite the great virtue and kindness of our most illustrious lord Prince Konstantin Ostrozhsky, governor of Kiev, marshal of the Volynian lands, sheriff of Vladimir, which his grace at all times of his life, as befits his gracious noble power, showed to the whole army and despite his doing for each of us many special kindnesses; we, having forgotten all this, caused both him personally and his children, and his servants and subjects, many grievances and losses, and violated his kindness to us; and their graces here at Piatka, after our most humble and heartfelt entreaties and after the intercession of many notable men, through their gracious kindness as Christian gentlemen, not wishing to spill our blood, have forgiven us.
>
> Therefore we, the knights of the aforenamed army, promise and swear our oaths: no longer to have lord Kosinsky as hetman and in his place to appoint another from the Ukraine within four weeks, and then to put ourselves in obedience to the King, not breaking the peace with foreign neighbors, in the royal realm to live beyond the rapids in the appointed places, not taking provisions or quartering ourselves or doing damage to the properties and jurisdictions of their graces the princes and their friends, or of his grace the Prince Alexander Vishnevetsky, sheriff of Cherkassy, or of others, finding ourselves at this time at their mercy; also not to lure away servants from the properties and jurisdictions of their graces; not to harbor runaways, betrayers and servants of their graces but to give them up; to return the arms and whatever was taken in the castles, towns and jurisdictions of their graces, other than that from Tripolye; also to return the flags, horses, cattle and movable property taken from the estates of their graces the princes; furthermore to send away the menial servants of both sexes which we are not keeping; eternally to live with the princes in the amity of former days, never to join a single man against their graces but on the contrary to serve them. . . .

I, Kosinsky, with the authority of my own hand have
signed this paper and affixed my seal; we all have ordered
affixed to this paper the army seal and those of us who can
have signed it; we asked also their graces the magnates to do
this: his grace lord Jakub Pretvich of Gavron, marshal of
Galicia, sheriff of Terrbovl; Prince Alexander Vishnevetsky,
sheriff of Charkassy, Kanev, Korsun, Liubets, Lovsk; lord Jan
Gulski, knight of Terebovl; lord Vatslav Bogovitin, cornet of
the Volynian lands; lord Vasili Gulevich, knight of Vladimir;
their graces, at our request, have deigned to do this and, having
affixed their seals to this our writ, have deigned to sign it.

Done at Piatka, 1593, 10 February.[24]

The most important points in this document are that Kosinsky
was left free and no punishments were meted out to his followers.
None of the cossacks were deprived of their property, despite the
many threats to do so, or of their nobility. Kosinsky was removed
from the hetmanship, to be sure—certainly a minimal precaution to
take with the leadership of an insurrection. The cossacks were
ordered to choose another hetman within four weeks, and Ostrozhsky did not even attempt to appoint one himself.

The cossacks were ordered to place themselves in obedience to
the king and eternal loyalty to the princes, as in "former days." Both
these rather vague admonitions referred, in fact, to specific prohibitions. Obedience to the king meant, primarily, no piracy expeditions
into foreign countries. Zamojski had insisted upon this restriction
in his dealing with the Ukrainian senators such as Ostrozhsky,
whom he knew to be involved with and sometimes responsible for
the cossack raids. But this was the only important protection of the
royal interest that Ostrozhsky accepted. Presumably obedience to
the king also implied readiness to join a royal army when so ordered,
to defend and warn against Tatar attacks, and to be answerable to
the royal governors and officials; none of these latter obligations
were mentioned in Kosinsky's surrender. The last, subordination to
the royal administrators, the cossacks consistently refused, and
their banishment to their "appointed places" beyond the rapids
suggested that a continuation of that refusal would be tolerated and
even expected.

Ostrozhsky and his noble army were out for themselves and not
for the kingdom. They required, for example, that the cossacks
return all stolen property except that taken from Tripolye, the royal
castle. This might have been a spiteful gesture in view of the

crown's refusal to help Ostrozhsky with a royal army. More likely it was an unconscious expression of their natural assumption that Tripolye was not their concern, that a private war produced private settlements.

The document shows that Ostrozhsky thought himself engaged in disciplining unruly proteges, punishing his children for their lack of gratitude. Ostrozhsky first got from Kosinsky a long apology directed not to the crown, not even to the victorious militia, but to Ostrozhsky "personally and his children, and his servants and subjects." Kosinsky and his men promised not to damage the territories of "the princes and their friends, or of his grace the Prince Alexander Vishnevetsky, or of others." The fact that Vishnevetsky is mentioned specifically shows that, as elsewhere in the document, "the princes" refers to the two Princes Ostrozhsky, father and son, and not to the Ukrainian princes in general. The document was signed by all the notables except the Ostrozhskys—because the document was a communication *to* Ostroshskys, witnessed by their supporters.

Loyalty to the princes as in "former days" was, of course, mainly cant. Any loyalty the cossacks had shown in former days had been bought for a good price, and was extremely unstable. The traditional relationship of the cossacks to their princely patrons, if not equal, was frequently insubordinate. Nobles who came to the Zapopozhe to lead the cossacks had always to participate to some extent in the military democracy of the sich, and were overthrown and sometimes assassinated by the decision of the cossack rada.

As the cossacks grew in strength and number, and the economic situation in the Ukraine changed, the nobles could less easily tolerate the insubordination of their proteges. The scramble for land and for a labor force to cultivate it meant tighter controls were necessary. "Loyalty to the princes" took on a different meaning. It referred to a series of specific limitations the nobles wanted to impose on the cossacks: The cossacks were forbidden to seek their traditional quarter and provisions from gentry estates, or to harbor runaways or to kidnap peasants belonging to the nobles. They were ordered to send away all the peasants who were among them at the time. The rationale behind these requirements was the landowners' need to establish a stable agricultural labor force. Since the cossacks could not easily be forced into servitude, they were asked, as it were, to step aside. They would be allowed to live in their customary style—but somewhere out of the way, beyond the rapids, beyond the law. They would not be allowed to obstruct the forcing of the rest of the peasant population into the new system.

Here, then, the terms of the agreement were not lenient, but quite demanding. Elsewhere in the document, as if to compensate, were guarantees, even concessions, to the cossacks. They were to retain the right to choose their own hetman and hence, by implication, to govern themselves. They were to retain virtual sovereignty and autonomy in the area of the sich, below the rapids. They were even rewarded with some of the royal property they had stolen! The language of the document was most respectful towards the Zaporozhians: Kosinsky was always addressed with the aristocratic form, *pan;* the cossacks in general were permitted to refer to themselves as an army and as "Knights."

Precisely because the cossacks, too, had won concessions, they insisted that the document be signed by the nobles' representatives as well as by themselves.

One must conclude that the Kosinsky–Ostrozhsky agreement was not an unconditional surrender. Although written as a series of unilateral promises, in content it balanced concessions, and was probably worked out through negotiations. From this conclusion follows the questions: *why* did the victors grant concessions? It is an important question, because in answering it we must define both the attitudes of the Ukrainian nobility and the cossacks towards each other, and the relations of power between them.

Let us discuss matters of attitude first. It is doubtful that many of the Ukrainian landowners yet considered the cossacks a serious threat to their own interests. They understood, no doubt, that the cossacks were likely to create frequent harassments, and that they were lacking in humility. They did not, however, understand that the mere existence of the cossacks was a subversive force towards the social system they desired. (Vishnevetsky, as we shall see below, was an exception.) They considered, on the contrary, that they could control the cossacks, as they had always done, and use them to their own advantage. The latter consideration was particularly important. So long as Ostrozhsky and his cronies wanted to keep cossacks in their own employ, and to continue using large segments of the Zaporozhian army from time to time in their own battles for aggrandizement and forays after booty, they were anxious not to antagonize the cossacks completely—nor to liquidate them as an army.

Furthermore, the magnates did not accept responsibility for disciplining the cossacks on behalf of the Commonwealth. The alienation of the Ukrainians from the Cracow government reflected ethnic as well as personal interests. Ukrainian nobles did not consider themselves Polish. Most were still Orthodox, speaking and

writing mainly in Ruthenian. Many were descendants of the Lithuanian dynastic family,[25] and most had been Lithuanian subjects until
the Lublin Union just over twenty years previously. The cossacks
and the Ukrainian nobles, coming as they did from the same
Lithuanian-Rus origins, shared a community of interests and traditions as against the Poles. Many historical factors, as well as the
unique contemporary conditions and their expansionist aims in the
Ukraine, prevented a class solidarity between Ukrainian and Polish
nobles.

Many of the frontier nobles were even sympathetic towards the
cossacks' provocations of the Tatars. The frontier people, after all,
had to bear frequent Tatar attacks unaided; even the smaller of these
expeditions, often unnoticed in central Poland, were extraordinarily
destructive for the Ukrainians. The question of guilt—whether the
cossacks provoked and the Tatars retaliated, or vice versa—was
irrelevant to the sufferers. The cossacks were "their" people; the
Tatars and their Turkish overlords were not. Zamojski's policy of
peace with the Turks at nearby any cost was unpopular in the
Ukraine, while the cossacks' plucky piracy seemed to be a heroic
defense of Christian lands.

The Ukrainian lords were also relatively sympathetic towards
the cossacks' traditional autonomy and self-government. The autonomy of the sich and its environs seemed acceptable to a frontier
nobility accustomed to the dangers of hostile neighbors and the
difficulties of communication. As a matter of necessity many
Ukrainian nobles accepted cossack demands which the Poles found
impossible and provocative. The Ukrainian nobility not only
planned on coexistence with the cossacks but, in 1593, had not
seriously considered the possibility that coexistence would not
work.

Even if Ostrozhsky had wished to crush the cossacks, he would
have been inadequate to the task. At the time of the Piatka battle he
needed a settlement quickly because a major Tatar attack on Volynia
loomed.[26] He was aware that cossack capitulation at Ostropol meant
nothing about their future capabilities, and feared new resistance in
the case of harsh punishments being meted out.[27]

Ostrozhsky's leverage was also reduced by the insecurity of his
relations with his own allies. His militia was by no means a
homogeneous group, or even a stable alliance. The expansionism of
the magnates like Ostrozhsky was preventing the development of a
coherent class rule even in the Ukraine. There were deep conflicts of
interest among the militia, conflicts which were a microcosm of
differences among the landowning class of the Ukraine.

Let us look more closely at the militia. We mentioned above that only two magnates responded to Ostrozhsky's call: Pretvich and Vishnevetsky. Both were concerned with the affair in a royal as well as a personal capacity. Both had been members of the Royal Commission of 1592. Pretvich was marshal of Kremenets as well as sheriff of Terebovl.[28] Vishnevetsky was sheriff of Cherkassy, Kanev, Korsun and Chigirin.[29]

It is equally important to notice who did not come. The Zaslavskys, who owned approximately 19 percent of the peasant households of Volynia, sent no representative or retinue. The Khodkevich family, which owned in Lutsk about two-thirds as many peasants as the Zaslavskys, sent no one. The Sangushkos, who in Vladimir owned almost as much land as the crown, 2262 peasant households, sent no one. There were no Lubomirskys (5215 households in Kremenets) or Zbarazhskys (4812 households in Kremenets); no Ruzhinsky, Konecpolski, Kalinovsky, Seniavsky (all huge landowners) came.[30] These stayed home because they did not believe their personal interests affected. What they had been asked to do by the king's edict—to join Ostrozhsky's militia—was hardly a routine request. To oblige would have been strictly a magnanimous gesture, unlikely towards someone they mainly considered a rival.

The militia was in the main composed of small gentry personally dependent on Ostrozhsky.[31] They were nobles, but their economic position was in many cases precarious. Frequently they were losing their holdings to the magnates; in some cases they were already landless, and had engaged themselves as personal servitors to the magnates.[32] The magnates upon whom they depended now for their livelihood, protection, and social status were the very men who had deprived them of their independence by robbing them, legally and illegally, of the land. Their hatred of the magnates was all the greater as many of them were among the oldest nobles of the Ukraine, with a tenacious conviction that their rights to the land transcended those of the newly powerful magnates.

The division between gentry and magnates in the Ukraine was, at least until 1600, still widening. Most of the higher nobility was becoming Catholic, while the lesser remained stubbornly Orthodox.[33] The magnates who went to Cracow and Warsaw frequently were influenced by many aspects of Polish culture and tended to become impatient with the old Rus ways. As the Polish social structure pushed its way out into the Ukraine, the lesser Ruthenian nobility became insecure as a class. While in the Lithuanian period there had been many ranks among the gentry, each with different duties and obligations and a secure place in a complicated system of social relations, now the Polish system pressed these many groups into one legal category. Those not among the number of great landowners, with their attendant political power, were in danger of losing nearly all their status and social security.[34] The reaction of the lesser nobility was naturally ambivalent: at times they pandered to the magnates for patronage; at other times it seemed to them preferable to flee the new system entirely. And for any Ukrainian man fleeing from anything, an obvious place to go was the sich.

We have already noted the frequent appearance of nobles among the cossacks. As social stratification jelled, the noble cossacks became fewer. But this change became pronounced only in the seventeenth century, and now the sich still held many men who called themselves *pan*.[35] Even outside the cossack organization itself, intercourse and common action between cossack and nobles remained frequent. The smaller landowners looked upon the cossacks as their defenders and even avengers against the magnates. When the cossacks turned on the magnates, there was every reason for men such as Ostrozhsky to fear that the lesser nobility might join them in large numbers, no reason for him to trust his gentry servitors. Had he decided, after Piatka and Ostropol, to press the cossacks, to chase them onto the steppe, to occupy their lands and subject them to his authority, would he have had an army to follow him?

As an example of the equivocation of the nobility, the Gulevich family's adventures are instructive. This was a relatively prosperous family of the old Lithuanian nobility, now slowly losing wealth and power. In 1629 they owned 1129 peasant households in Volynia;[36] they owned even more land in 1593. Vasili Gulevich, identified as "soldier" from Vladimir, fought in the Ostrozhsky militia and was considered important enough to sign the agreement. Yet he and his relatives and ancestors had a history of participation in cossack mischief. Back in 1579 one Gulevich got into a squabble with one of his own noble servitors, Ivan Potushinsky, over a stolen pair of horses. Both raised groups of cossacks to aid them and began a series of attacks, stealing and destroying each other's goods and property.[37] In 1593, immediately after fighting Kosinsky at Piatka, Vasili feuded with his relative Mikhail Gulevich. The latter, using a group of Kosinsky's cossacks, ravaged Vasili's estate.[38]

These are special cases, it might be argued, of individual nobles using cossacks to fight their personal feuds. But that could be said equally well of the whole Kosinsky rebellion. It is risky in this period to try to distinguish personal from social struggle. In 1606, for example, Josef Lisovsky, a servitor of Prince Adam Vishnevetsky, ran away and then, with ten other cossacks, returned to attack and rob a Vishnevetsky estate.[39] In 1605 one Matsko Martynovich, a servitor of Okhrem Gruzevich, attacked his master's house with cossack comrades and beat him up badly.[40] However the motivation for such incidents is described, it is clear that the nobility was still deeply involved in so called cossack activities.[41]

There was no well demarcated class struggle here. Neither of the two parties to the struggle—cossacks and Ukrainian militia—were themselves united as a class. Their dispute was not centered about class grievances. Yet it was fully a social struggle, in that both parties were attempting to impose upon (or, as they themselves saw it, to preserve in) the fluid Ukraine a social order beneficial to themselves. This struggle took place at a time when the participants could not comprehend fully how and why the old social order had broken down. The complexities and ambiguities of a document like the Piatka surrender are in part due to the fact that both parties believed they were merely protecting their traditional rights. As the struggle developed, and the issues became defined, the documents were to become simpler.

12. The Ambiguity of Defeat

FOR A SHORT TIME after the Piatka surrender the cossacks permitted Ostrozhsky a respite, most of them disbanding to their homes and the sich.[1] At the Diet in May the Senators expressed their thanks to Ostrozhsky for his victory, as Janush Ostrozhsky arrived in Cracow with his men carrying the captured cossack banners. As a reward the king elevated Janush to marshal of Cracow, a move which only exacerbated the enmity of other nobles and further interfered with the possibility of *szlachta* solidarity.[2] The Diet then attempted to punish the cossacks by holding out a virtual license to kill them: "... henceforth, without legal procedures, they may be set upon by the soldiers in the Ukraine and each may freely take back from them his property with impunity, no matter who among them might perish."[3]

But the respite was too brief for the enforcing of such a plan of revenge. Towards the end of the Diet came news of large Tatar attacks in Volynia,[4] and Alexander Vishnevetsky wrote from Cherkassy that the new attacks were part of a Tatar–cossack plot to "ravage the kingdom and to put the Crown under the yoke of the infidels."[5] Vishnevetsky's judgement was a bit hysterical, especially for an old cossack hand, but it was well designed to force the attention of the Diet to the Ukraine. The nobles gathered in Cracow formed a good sounding board for hysterical rumors.[6]

Prior arrangement between cossacks and Tatars was unlikely; but the cossacks recognized an opportune moment for their own action. This time Kosinsky organized an expedition against Vishnevetsky at his Cherkassy lands. The cossacks could have argued that this attack was not a violation of their undertaking with Ostrozhsky because they were not now attacking his property. But they had never had any intention of abiding by an agreement which deprived them of so many basic economic needs: quarter and

135

provision, the right to move freely through the Ukraine, the right to increase their numbers by receiving fugitives. Kosinsky and his retinue had signed a paper to buy time and his life. Now they resumed the offensive, their only means to survival.

The attack on Vishnevetsky was one in a series of revenge attacks.[7] They had just accomplished two smaller attacks on the estates of two other signers of the Piatka agreement—Vasili Gulevich and Yuri Cherlensky, both proteges of Ostrozhsky.[8] By the time they appeared at Cherkassy they numbered three hundred fifty to four hundred and had another fifteen hundred men heading there from the sich.[9] Vishnevetsky was able, however, to repel them before their reinforcements arrived. Uncharacteristically, his account of his victory was terse and vague,[10] perhaps because the circumstances were somewhat less glorious than he would have liked to publicize. Kosinsky was caught with some of his men in a Cherkassy tavern, drunk and carousing. Several of Vishnevetsky's men came in, picked a quarrel, and murdered Kosinsky and the cossacks.[11] "Thus ignobly died this Kosinsky, such a fate as usually overtakes all like him," pontificated Bielski, the Polish chronicler.[12]

Kosinsky's movement was not yet suppressed, however, and cossack maneuvers in the Kievan lands continued through the summer.[13] It was not until August that an agreement between the cossacks and Vishnevetsky was reached, and judging from its terms the cossacks had been operating effectively without Kosinsky's leadership. The settlement represented a virtual capitulation to the cossacks. "Eternal peace" was established on the basis of a series of guarantees: Vishnevetsky was to return to them the property he had captured from them—horses, boats, and supplies. If any Zaporozhian recognized his property within the district of Cherkassy he could demand of the possessor proof of ownership, and failing such proof could claim it for his own. The relatives of Kosinsky and the other noble cossacks killed in the tavern by Vishnevetsky's men were to be able to seek compensation from Vishnevetsky in the courts! Vishnevetsky as sheriff forswore for himself and his subordinate officials the customary right to claim the property of the deceased cossacks. This old custom, dating at least from the beginning of the sixteenth century, had begun to be abused toward the end of the century; all kinds of minor officials used it as a justification for stealing from the cossacks. The cossacks were also guaranteed free movement from Zaporozhe in and out of Cherkassy, the only stipulation being that those who came into Cherkassy choose themselves an elder who would govern them, judge and punish them for their crimes. Finally, a general amnesty was declared for all the cossacks, including guarantees to cossacks now or formerly in Vishnevetsky's service, enabling them to go freely to Zaporozhe and return without persecution or retribution.[14]

The significance of these promises and renunciations by Vishnevetsky becomes clear when we remember that the cossacks had several times been declared outlaws and, in the eyes of the state, had no legal rights whatever. From the point of view of the Polish law, therefore, this treaty had no validity. It was a strictly private arrangement between two feuding parties. All the promises were made by an individual prince, isolated, fearing for his property. His appeal for royal help had been ignored, nor were there other Ukrainian magnates aiding him. Just as Ostrozhsky before him, Vishnevetsky was defending himself alone. He not only signed away personal and class privileges but, without authority to do so, freed the cossacks from some of the restrictions placed upon them by Polish law: He surrendered the right of others to claim the property of deceased cossacks, thus abjuring one of his official duties; he guaranteed the cossacks freedom of travel through Cherkassy as if it were his private principality, and amnesty as if their only crimes had been personal insults to him.

This settlement was reached towards the end of August, 1593. Within weeks, by September 13, the cossacks were raiding in Volynia again.[15] Vishnevetsky's concessions had done no more than Ostrozhsky's to pacify the Ukraine. By early October there were four thousand cossacks outside Kiev, with artillery, in an aggressive mood.[16]

The background to the October 1593 attack on Kiev reveals once again the complexities of the cossacks' social position. Shortly after Kosinsky's death, the Zaporozhians had sent envoys to Kiev to bring legal action against Vishnevetsky as their agreement stipulated. They demanded that a bailiff be appointed to take their evidence.[17] The Kievan municipal authorities refused, arrested the cossack envoys and tortured them. One died and all of their property was confiscated. In retaliation, the entire Zaporozhian army sailed up the Dnieper, set up their artillery and threatened to bombard the city.[18]

The Kievans' high–handed and foolish action was probably motivated by fear in the first place; now, even more frightened, they reversed themselves and tried to appease the cossacks.[19] The Kievan nobility was at this time collecting for the assizes. After consultations, probably including the more prominent burghers, they asked

Bishop Vereshchinsky and Prince Kirik Ruzhinsky to serve as mediators. Ruzhinsky was to become one of the most effective and violent opponents of the cossacks later in the decade, but now he was still thought of as half cossack himself. With his brother Mikhail he had led several cossack expeditions in the 1580s; in 1588 Muscovite Tsar Fedor had addressed him as hetman.[20] Vereshchinsky was the Catholic bishop of Kiev. He had settled in the old village of Khvastov, renaming it Novaya Vereshchina, defended it, populated it, and grown rich and powerful; his private military retinue was largely composed of Zaporozhians and he reportedly had a positive reputation at the sich.

Vereshchinsky and Ruzhinsky agreed to mediate. They simultaneously organized the defense of the city, advancing with a militia to meet the cossacks some one and a half miles from Kiev at the village of Lybeda. They were wise to do so, for their mediation attempts failed. As they first approached the cossack camp they narrowly escaped ambush by a cossack vanguard. Vereshchinsky reportedly saved himself and his men by ordering his musicians to play a psalm—David's "Cantabo Domino in Vita Mea," to be precise—which he knew the cossacks would identify with himself.[21]

The cossacks were skeptical about what they could expect of a negotiated settlement. Ultimately bloodshed was avoided less because of the bishop's prayers, we suspect, then because he correctly apprehended the cossacks' determination and persuaded the Kievans to offer concessions. According to his own narrative,

> . . . we urged the cossacks that instead of advancing into Kiev in full force they should seek justice in fewer numbers; but they did not agree, saying that what befell their envoys would also happen to a small delegation. And when the cossacks arrived at Kiev the nobility collected there, not wishing to drink with the town . . . the beer they had brewed, dispersed to their homes, and the townspeople and castle troops shut themselves up in the castle. . . . The cossacks, for their difficulties and losses, for the torture-to-death of their one envoy and the robbery of their comrades, agreed finally to accept 1200 zlotys, and they established among themselves a written eternal peace, without oaths, preserving the famous capital of the Kievan fatherland. . . . They left Kiev without shooting and without spilling of blood, doing no harm to the people other than the animals, with which they provided themselves well.[22]

Vereshchinsky afterwards asked the Polish senate to instruct the town not to behave similarly towards the cossacks in the future. "For such stupid actions one ought to exact from the town government all the losses borne by the townspeople from the cossacks, so that they would be more clever in the future; otherwise one fears that Kiev could become a wasteland."[23]

As before, the settlement was hastened by Tatar threats, and Vereshchinsky immediately entered a new fray. Assuming leadership of a detachment of 3,000 cossacks, or so he claimed, he wrote the chancellor that he had succeeded in repelling a Tatar attack.[24] Vereshchinsky claimed that the khan was so furious that he sent the bishop an Arabic book which had been trampled by horses' hooves— a symbolic demonstration of how Vereshchinsky's body would be dealt with. The khan also threatened a new attack and Vereshchinsky hastily strengthened his fortifications with a new stockade, ten cannon—and 2,000 more cossacks.[25]

Here was another of those rapid reversals of policy that constantly marred Polish cossack policy: the unruly cossacks were no sooner pacified than they were called up to rearm and fight again, summoned to do legally what they had been condemned and punished for doing illegally. Though Polish society could not assimilate the cossacks, it continued to need them.

Vereshchinsky exaggerated the size of the threats and the importance of his own efforts. His stories have the sound of tall tales, and he was enthusiastically playing the role of frontier hero, a favorite role of the Polish nobility. But such roles were possible only because of the real dangers and the fluidity of the situation. The very nobles who fought against the cossacks at Piatka were now fighting with them against the Tatars.

In 1593 there were three major confrontations with the cossacks—at Piatka, Cherkassy, and Kiev—each resolved only to be followed immediately by Tatar–Turkish threats. Although marked by many shifting alliances and skirmishes, the cossack struggles of 1592-93 constitute a single rebellion. It was conditioned by the tradition of feuds among the nobility in this decentralized country. Kosinsky exercised those privileges like dozens of dissident nobles before him.

But Kosinsky's rebellion was also different from, and greater than, its antecedents in internecine aristocratic rivalry. First, the numbers of participants in the cossack forces gave a new dimension to events. Armies of five thousand, though small by Tatar standards, were far larger than those raised by individual magnates. Further-more, the extraordinary dispersal of the men, with the scenes of action moving rapidly from Volynia through Bratslav to Kiev, hun-dreds of miles, was unlike that of a personal feud. It was not one army which travelled through the Ukraine in 1592–93, periodically returning to the sich, but many armies. In this respect Kosinsky's attacks were unlike both traditional cossack piracy expeditions and aristocratic feuds. These latter operated with a fixed number of participants, fighting for loot or salary; Kosinsky fought with *levées en masse* of the peasantry, armies capable of expanding and shrink-ing rapidly.

Second, Kosinsky's cossacks were fighting a rudimentry sort of guerrilla warfare.[26] Kosinsky's soldiers fought sometimes for loot—what they could steal from the estates and farms and towns they raided—but also from anger at the disruption of traditional status and occupations, envy of the magnates, desperation and flight from servitude. The Kosinsky rebellion followed a guerrilla fighting pat-tern—attacks followed by rapid disappearance of the forces, sudden new offensives in other places. The cossacks' defeats themselves were ambiguous, for in a decentralized army the defeat of one unit need not affect the others. The cossacks had no face to save, and hence needed no great victories. They did not fight when the odds were heavily against them, but surrendered readily, even on humili-ating terms, only to regroup and attack again.

Third, the cossacks were difficult to defeat decisively because they had no systematic war aims, and certainly no revolutionary program. Total victory would have required liquidation of all the cossack trouble-makers; permanent victory, elimination of the con-ditions which gave rise to them. The nobles had the war aims, whether they knew it or not: control over the land and peasantry of the Ukraine. The cossacks' "program" being preservation of their "traditional liberties," their tactics involved exercising these liber-ties strenuously, by resisting harassing official authority. No single victory could suffice against such tactics, for they would be contin-ued as long as there were dissident Ukrainians who called them-selves cossacks.

Prince Vishnevetsky, in his fright, imagined the worst. In Hobs-bawm's language, one might say he imagined these social bandits as political rebels. He suspected Kosinsky of conniving with both the Crimea and Muscovy to give away the Ukraine; or at other times of planning to seize the Ukraine for himself, to rule it as a cossack military republic.[27] Vishnevetsky's fearful imagination was correct in recognizing the destructive potential of the cossacks. Some of his allegations about cossack understandings with the Tatars and Muscovites may even have been true.[28]

Vishnevetsky's claim that the cossacks planned to snatch the Ukraine from Polish rule was, however, far from accurate. The cossacks were ready to make any available alliances for even the most short-range objectives, but they were not yet taking it on themselves to make plans for the future of the Ukraine. Vishnevetsky's fears were conditioned by the political as well as the social insecurity of the Ukraine. Poland's claim to it only dated back thirty-five years and was far from universally accepted. The cossacks were not loyal subjects of the Polish crown, to be sure, but this was because they did not define themselves in terms of loyalty to a state at all. Their land had long been a no-man's land and they were accustomed to shifting allegiances and hegemonies and rival claims. At the sich, the cossack brotherhood was itself the ultimate identification of most cossacks; the Zaporozhian army demanded and received the loyalty of its men far more successfully than any of the adjacent states. The allegiance they paid to Poland was more of the nature of a contractual, temporary, and voluntray homage.

But to define the cossacks as traitors to the Polish kingdom would be a distortion. Because the political jurisdictions in the Ukraine were not at issue for them, schemes to overthrow the Polish authority did not seem relevant. The cossacks fully expected that they would be able to continue to operate as an independent force, bowing for tactical reasons to the authority of whatever rulers might represent the strongest force in the Ukraine. Nor was the cossacks' sense of social injustice developed to the point where they had become revolutionary, planning, as Vishnevetsky feared, to destroy the class system. To be revolutionary a group must have a notion that it can only get what it wants by altering an entire social and political system. The cossacks believed the opposite: that they could force the recognition of their customary liberties by the existing system.

Considered in these terms, Kosinsky's tactics, and those of his immediate successors, had been successful. After striking a premature and militarily ill advised blow at Ostrozhsky at Piatka, they managed still to escape with an armistice less punitive than might have been expected. Afterwards they managed, despite Kosinsky's death, not only to win agreements promising that the Ukrainian lords would respect most of their autonomy and privileges, but also to extract a tribute of twelve hundred zlotys from the town of Kiev.

These accomplishments they owed in part to the intervention of other forces, notably the Tatars. But whatever the reasons, their non-revolutionary tactics seemed to be working. The opposition had shown itself willing to give in. This inclination to appease arose partly out of fear, but also because the lords of the Ukraine did not yet believe it necessary to smash the cossacks in order to preserve their power.

For these reasons the cossacks "won" the Kosinsky rebellion. It was only a skirmish, of course. In fact, the confidence they gained as a result of their handling of the private armies of 1593 was to hinder them in coping with royal armies a few years later. The Ukrainian nobility, though they would hardly have admitted that they were defeated in 1593, learned some lessons which they used to their advantage later. Greatest among these was their recognition of the enormous military potential of the cossacks—not only their fighting skill but their ability to mobilize large numbers of the Ukrainian population behind them. It was the latter ability that carried the most important omens, though few, not even the cossacks, understood them in 1593.

Part Five
Nalivaiko and the Second Rebellion

КОЗАЦЬКИЙ ТАБІР 1 А р. СОЛОНИЦІ [illegible]

17. Cossack tabor at Solonitsa, 1596. From a lithograph by an unknown artist, in Kiev State Historical Museum, reprinted in Rozner, *Severin Nalivaiko*, Moscow, 1961.

Introduction to Part Five

The pattern of the Kosinsky rebellion, between 1591 and 1593, has already suggested the general reason the cossacks could not easily be suppressed: they were nourished by the most fundamental, structural problems of Polish society, stemming from both history and immediate pressures. They inhabited, so to speak, the spaces in its contradictions. At least seven such contradictions were visible in the preceding narrative, each contributing to cossack leverage. First, the territory of the Ukraine by its nature presented conflicts to the Polish ruling class: it contained free land for land-hungry, expansionist magnates, but also freedom for peasants, making it difficult for the magnates to collect the labor force they needed to make the land profitable. Second, the location of the Ukraine complicated its agricultural future. On the one hand it was politically attached to Poland—which was becoming increasingly integrated into a pan-European trade system, able to sell grain profitably to western-European countries, primarily through Baltic ports. On the other hand the Ukraine was socially more dominated by Rus traditions and economically more tied to a southeastern trade orientation. Third, and closely related, were conflicts within the social and religious allegiances of the Ukrainian magnates themselves. Seeking political and economic power within the Polish kingdom, they were nevertheless ethnically and often religiously drawn towards Rus-Lithuanian traditions as appanage princes. In their Polish orientation they were placed in adversary relations with cossacks, in their Rus-Lithuanian orientation, in more friendly and respectful relations. Fourth, the economic opportunity offered by the Ukraine created conflicts within the aristocratic class. Magnates' attempts to establish profitable demesnes required not only aggressive land-grabbing but political aggrandizement as well, for example, developing military retinues to defend their lands and labor force. These efforts collided with the attempts of the majority of the Polish nobility to maintain "democracy of the gentry." Thus the Ukrainian magnates incurred the enmity of many other nobles and could not lead a unified class against the cossacks. Fifth, all sections of the Polish nobility were engaged in a political struggle with the crown, which prevented unity against the cossacks. Sixth, the crown's own

145

attempts at maintaining a consistent cossack policy were undermined by its military needs. Attempts to circumscribe the cossack brotherhood through a register were frequently undone by massive drafts of cossacks to fight Turks, Tatars and even Christian powers. Seventh, Poland had entered a particular political crisis, domestic and international, after 1586. The power vacuum after the death of Stefan Batory allowed Poland's entanglement in foreign competition for the crown, foreign wars, and religious conflicts, and the cossacks were able to exploit many of these differences to increase their autonomy.

These contradictions continued, and sharpened, during the remainder of the cossacks' "membership" in the Rzecz Pospolita. Yet the cossacks did not parlay their advantages into the creation of a political power bloc or even permanent victory for themselves. The continuousness of cossack rebellion demonstrates not only cossack strength but also weakness, their inability to achieve decisive and lasting goals. The ensuing discussion of the second rebellion, accordingly, will continue the themes above, but will introduce a new set of themes—areas of cossack failings as well as strengths, and the connections between them. Just as in the preceding narrative, chapter organization will function in a dual manner: to subdivide the story chronologically; and to illustrate, one at a time, certain analytic themes.

The previously discussed characteristics of cossack rebellion will remain evident: the provocation of foreign piracy; the spark supplied by a personal feud; the style of warfare that is both guerrilla and mercenary; the division of the forces of repression; and the ambiguity of the final outcome. In addition, each chapter will introduce a new general issue: (1) The second rebellion, although usually called the Nalivaiko Rebellion, actually had a number of important leaders who represented different cossack outlooks. These outlooks, in turn, rested on different social groups within cossackdom. This rebellion was in fact weakened by divisions among cossacks, and in these divisions the germs of the ultimate possibility of successful cooptation of the cossacks by the Muscovite state become visible. (2) The cossacks' continuing foreign piracy and mercenary work demonstrates the increasing necessity of large-scale warfare to the maintenance of the cossack host. (3) The Bratslav areas of the uprising highlights cossack relations with town dwellers. (4) The Volynia uprisings demonstrate the cossacks' commitment to Orthodoxy as one of their motives. (5) Belorussia affords an opportunity to focus on the cossacks' relations with the peasantry. (6) Finally, in the context of the royal army's campaign against the cossacks, we can evaluate the ultimate war aims of the cossacks, looking at which of their goals they were willing to compromise and which they were not, thus seeing the nucleus of what might be called their political ideology.

Throughout, the general focus of the story will be on this last question, the ultimate goals of the cossacks. More particularly we will illustrate the contrast between the naiveté, narrowness, short-sightedness and self-centeredness of those goals, and the support they were able to muster from other social groups in the Ukraine. The conclusion will show that this support came less from cossack ideology or strategy than from the initiative of the cossack suppor-ters. The cossacks were the creation not only of their circumstances and their own willful activity, but also of the needs of the Ukrain-ians in general. The cossacks became, not through any choice but almost despite themselves, representatives. Like all forms of repre-sentative government, this was not perfect; the cossacks crushed and violated some of their supporters' hopes while defending others. And of course the influence between cossacks and supporters was mutual, for the cossacks helped form the hopes and worldview of the Ukrainians as well as representing them.

13. Cossack Divisions and Conflicts of Interest

T HE KOSINSKY REBELLION was never suppressed. Kosinsky's murder was only a setback, for the cossack brotherhood quickly produced a new leadership. Peasant unrest in the Ukraine subsided somewhat in 1594, then redoubled in 1595 and continued unabated until 1596 when the cossack rebels were defeated by Polish Commander-in-Chief Zolkiewski and a royal army. The events of the entire period 1591–96 could be considered one five-year uprising; they are traditionally known as two rebellions because there were distinct periods of differing tactics and differing leadership. The 1595–96 wars are often called the Nalivaiko rebellion, after Severin Nalivaiko, the cossacks' most articulate and perhaps most militant leader. The Nalivaiko rebellion was bigger in the size of insurgent and counter-insurgent forces, larger in the land area involved, broader in the social groups involved. Furthermore, in the Nalivaiko period, cossack self-righteousness about the justice of their cause was increased by several factors, notably a religious one, discussed in Chapter 16. And in this second uprising the forces of "order"— both nobility and crown—recognized more quickly than with Kosinsky the seriousness and extent of the cossack threat.

In the Nalivaiko rebellion, too, for the first time divisions deeper than personal animosities appeared among the cossacks. These divisions were symbolized and sometimes led by different leaders, and in this rebellion cossack leaders with distinctive personalities became Ukraine-wide celebrities. The key figure, Severin Nalivaiko, was never a Zaporozhian. He had been in the service of Ostrozhsky but his primary reputation and self-image were of independence. He was a free-lance bandit, mercenary, and frontiersman. His independence from the discipline and fraternal loyalty of the Zaporozhians was an important factor in transforming his particular personal grievance more quickly and broadly than Kosinsky's into a social movement. His grievance, like Kosinsky's, was against a Ukrainian magnate, and it was again about, appropriately enough, one of the Ukraine's most important resources—land.

It was also important to the development of the rebellion that Grigori Loboda, next to Nalivaiko in importance, *was* a Zaporozhian. Indeed he might be called a typical Zaporozhian officer, playing a double role as a Polish-recognized head of the registered cossacks and as elected hetman. This rebellion had exceptional force because of an alliance between the Zaporozhian brotherhood—including the official, registered, cossacks—and the cossack "rabble," the cossackized peasantry; and that alliance could not have happened without Loboda. Heidenstein considered Loboda a representative of the old, "true," Zaporozhians,[1] indicating that in some way he met Polish expectations of what a cossack should be. Loboda's social background (unfortunately we know little of Nalivaiko's) was significant because it typified Ukrainian social mobility. He came from a town cossack family and had connections with many influential Kievans—merchants, clergy and nobles. He used his hetmanship to bring him ennoblement, buying a village in Kievan Polesia.[2] Then in the midst of the rebellion he married the daughter of another noble who brought more wealth with her. At his death Loboda was an extremely rich man.[3]

Other important cossack leaders included Sasko Fedorovich, who had also purchased entry into the nobility through marriage.[4] Loboda's second–in–command, Matvei Shaul, was also a Zaporozhian of long standing.[5] He also came from a burgher family but had relatives who were landowners in Kievan Polesia; he himself owned lands which he had mortgaged to the Pechersky monastery.[6] Another leader, Fedor Polous, became hetman over the most subversive fraction of the Zaporozhians in 1597-98, but there is no information about his background.[7]

A constant in these and other cossack leaders' backgrounds was a mixed social status. Few fell simply into one category of the Polish social structure. They represented in their persons the cossack drive to find an autonomous place and set of privileges, and they were always using their cossack "careers" to raise their status. Thus the particular grievance of one had similar meaning for many.

The process of social stratification among the cossacks worked both ways. Nobles used their social and economic prestige to win themselves leadership positions at the sich, while common-born cossacks used their military activity and standing within the brotherhood to ennoble and enrich themselves. This two-way mobility was part of a general contradiction in cossackdom: On the one hand the cossacks as a mass tended to deny and disrupt the Polish aristocratic social and economic system, explicitly by demanding a special place for their brotherhood, and implicitly through the mass uprisings they provoked which subverted the servile system. On the other hand there was a tendency for individual cossacks to try to enter the existing aristocracy, thereby renewing and strengthening it. The tension between these two opposing tendencies pervaded the entire history of the Zaporozhians under Polish rule and was especially visible in this rebellion, as we shall see below. This tension might have been used by the crown to weaken the cossacks, through the register, for example, as a means of consolidating the division between landed and commissioned cossacks and commoners. But the register remained unenforced.

In addition to these class tensions, the cossacks were also divided by loyalties to different cossack sub-groups. Though these different loyalties reflected class differences, they also had an independent force. Particularly powerful was the exclusive group identity among Zaporozhians, a group distinctly not the same as the registered cossacks and at times including men of all classes; it was an identity that grew out of shared experience, tradition, ritual, and oaths of brotherhood. It was important in this rebellion that Polous, Sasko, and Shaul were Zaporozhians, normally subordinate to Loboda, while Nalivaiko was not a true comrade to any of the others. There were, of course, conflicts among the Zaporozhians. For example, in May 1595 Loboda was overthrown and Shaul replaced him as hetman; Shaul then lost the hetmanship back to Loboda a year later.[8] But these struggles were internecine. Nalivaiko, by contrast, was an outsider. Periodically during this rebellion he operated jointly with other cossack leaders, but he always returned quickly to solo operations. Loboda at times not only disclaimed any connection with Nalivaiko but reviled him. Nalivaiko had "forgotten the fear of God and is without respect for anything in the world . . .," he wrote, though the Zaporozhians were by then robbing and destroying just as thoroughly as Nalivaiko's men.[9]

Loboda's hostility had three motives, all overlapping. First was his fraternal loyalty to the Zaporozhians, and this helped mask a second motive, resentment at Nalivaiko's challenge to his own leadership position. Third, there was social antagonism between Loboda's and Nalivaiko's forces. Zamojski's secretary Heidenstein recognized this: "Loboda exercised influence among the more important part of cossackdom, namely the Zaporozhian elders, Nalivaiko mainly among the riff-raff—mostly fugitives who having received some kind of punishment or having left their lords, fled to the cossacks seeking asylum: he [Nalivaiko] obtained glory and respect among them for his audacity and his outrages."[10] The threat to Loboda's leadership position came not just from Nalivaiko himself but from the strength of the masses he led, from the "rabble" or "riff-raff." Thus Loboda and the Zaporozhian elders felt the class antagonism in personal terms. The traditional loyalty to the Zaporozhian brotherhood could not be distinguished from their sense of superiority to the peasant masses.

Fundamental and irreconcilable divisions among the cossacks emerged during their Ukrainian attacks. In the Ukraine, willingness to compromise with magnates and later the crown generals was most often a function of status. Gentry cossacks, those with hopes of becoming gentry, and those assured of places on the register, did not share the desperate need for special guarantees of "liberties" that the cossackized peasantry and burghers did. However, these divisions were also operative during the cossacks' piratical and mercenary foreign expeditions and diplomatic negotiations. All cossack individuals and groups were happy to collect booty and other forms of "payment." But decisions between alternatives produced differences of opinion that again reflected the options available to individuals. The aspirations of some cossack leaders included becoming rulers of Balkan principalities, for example, or negotiating directly with representatives of sovereigns such as the Habsburg emperor or the pope—aspirations hardly shared by the rank and file. On the other hand, the higher the aspirations, the more the cossack hetmans depended upon the fidelity of large cossack armies. Thus in some ways foreign ambitions represented a countervailing force to stratification among the cossacks, giving the most aspiring of the adventurers a greater interest in winning freedom for the rank-and-file.

14. Mercenary Diplomacy

Aᴄᴛᴇʀ ᴛʜᴇ ᴘᴇʀɪᴏᴅ of Kosinsky's leadership, and before the great Volynian and Belorussian uprisings of the spring of 1595, the Zaporozhians directed most of their belligerence outside of Poland.* From the end of 1593 to mid-1595 they made seven military and piracy expeditions into Turkish and Tatar lands. All these forays were illegal in terms of the "agreements" that Kosinsky and his predecessors had accepted, as well as by numerous statutes and resolutions of the Diet. Many of them were extremely dangerous to Poland's international position. Yet some of them were acknowledged and even tacitly supported by the Polish government, because of vagaries of the international situation which the cossacks aggressively exploited. The tricky and shifting international circumstances, as exemplified particularly in the threat of war with Turkey, forced the Poles to deal very gingerly with the cossacks. This in turn permitted the latter to exercise, with temporary impunity, greater freedom and power in the Ukraine than ever before.

In particular the cossacks benefited from the outbreak in 1593 of a long-expected war between Turkey, aided by the Crimean Khanate, and the Holy Roman Empire. The Emperor, Rudolf II, sought allies, hoping to create an anti-Turkish league involving not only Poland but also Muscovy, Spain, the Vatican, and the Danubian principalities.[1]

The first stage of what was to be known as the "Long War"

---

*The Nalivaiko rebellion had two general periods. First, from autumn 1594 until autumn 1595, the cossacks alternated piracy on the Danube with insurrectionary activity in the Ukraine and Belorussia. From then until their defeat in summer 1595 the cossacks remained in the Ukraine. In telling this story, however, in order to avoid repetition, we will discuss all the Danubian activities of the cossacks together in this chapter. Then we will backtrack chronologically, and discuss the main domestic insurgency, one theme at a time.

between Turkey and the Holy Roman Empire occurred on the Danube, known to the Turks as the Hungarian War. It was provoked by the instability of Turkish control over the Danubian principalities. Stefan Batory, formerly prince of Transylvania, had managed to secure his family's control over that country when he became king of Poland in 1576; and until his death, Transylvania was *de facto* controlled from Cracow.[2] Upon King Stefan's death in 1586, his nephew, Sigismund, prince of Transylvania, was no longer able to maintain neutrality between the Habsburgs and Ottomans, and went into an alliance with Prague.[3] Seeking his own aggrandizement, Sigismund also managed to draw the rulers of Wallachia and Moldavia into rejection of Turkish suzerainty and alliance with the Habsburgs. This fundamentally changed the balance of power in the region.[4] Furthermore, the principalities were economically crucial to the Turkish Empire. As the English ambassador to Turkey noted, their loss would be "of infinitt damage unto the Grand Signior in as much as the chiefest partt of the victualing of Constantinople, cominge out of those two princes . . ." would be cut off.[5] Accordingly in the spring of 1595 the Turks began to strike back against Christian armies, by then controlling the mouth of the Danube; and a major European war was detonated.[6]

There were advantages for the cossacks no matter which side was winning. Throughout the war there was a steady stream of envoys of foreign rulers coming to the sich to bid for cossack support. In fact the dreamed-of anti-Turkish league did not develop stably as the European countries were divided, and mercenaries such as the cossacks were needed. The cossacks accepted some employment offers and refused others; at yet other times they claimed to be acting in the service of a foreign government when in fact they were pirating for themselves. From the foreign raids they made in this period the cossacks gained enormously—not so much in wealth, for they were frequently forced to scuttle their booty, as much as in notoriety, the awe of their victims, and their own military strength. The cossack armies that burst into the Ukraine in 1595 were far larger than those of 1592–93, and wherever they travelled in the Ukraine or the Balkans, they were swollen still further by a peasantry who knew of and delighted in their reputed exploits, and whose attraction to them was strengthened by their heroism against the infidel.

The cossacks' raids were led at times by Zaporozhian hetmans Loboda and Mikoshinsky, at other times by irregular leader Nalivaiko. They travelled with forces of one thousand and up; some chroniclers attributed twelve thousand men to them.[7] They travelled by horse across the steppe, and by boat down the Dnieper and out the Black Sea. They burned and murdered widely, but also took booty, particularly the coveted Tatar horses. On the whole the evidence suggests that, despite cossack claims to be in the service of governments, the cossack raids were self-serving, self-initiated, and unresponsive to any outside direction.[8]

There is no space here to detail all the cossacks' "diplomatic" negotiations or foreign expeditions in this period. However, for an understanding of the cossacks' international position we must examine the main incidents in their relations with three great powers who sought to use and control them: the Habsburgs, the Vatican, and the Polish kingdom itself.

Until 1592 Emperor Rudolf II had tried to draw Poland into an anti-Turkish league by supporting anti-Zamojski, pro-Habsburg dissidents within Poland, but Zamojski held to his neutrality policy. The emperor then turned to the cossacks, hoping to use them to aid his Hungarian and Danubian allies and to embroil Poland indirectly, calculating that the sultan and the khan would reciprocate against Poland for damage done by the cossacks.[9] It may be that the cossacks approached the emperor first. According to one Habsburg source, Zaporozhians came to Rudolf in early 1593 and offered their services.[10] Probably these "Zaporozhians" were independent *szlachta* cossack adventurers,[11] and their offer was not accepted, but it stimulated Habsburg curiosity. The emperor asked permission of both the tsar and the Polish chancellor to use the cossacks,[12] and then determined that the cossacks were *de facto* autonomous agents: "Esse se homines liberos et milites voluntarios, qui cum hostibus Christiani nominis perpetuo concertent."[13]

When in December 1593 yet another "Zaporozhian" envoy, Stanislav Khlopitsky, a cossacking gentryman, arrived in Prague, the emperor responded. In February 1594 the emperor sent an envoy to the sich, Erich Lassota von Steblau, an experienced soldier and diplomat.[14]

Lassota's journey was arduous, and he kept a detailed diary. It took his party two months to reach Lvov. Late in April the Zaporozhians, hearing of Lassota's approach, sent guides to meet Lassota and his companions but they did not arrive at the sich until June 8, when they were received with an artillery salute. Lassota was impressed to learn that Zaporozhian hetman Mikoshinsky, with thirteen hundred cossacks and fifty boats, was away in a sea attack on the Tatars near Ochakov.

Lassota's two-week negotiations at the sich were tempestuous.

He brought the emperor's request that the cossacks invade Walla-chia to head off the Tatars' march to Hungary and prevent them from joining Turkish armies there. Lassota encountered numerous obstacles: First, Khlopitsky was neither their hetman nor represent-ative and had greatly overstated their strength. Second, while the cossacks were willing to work for the emperor, they wanted to choose their own campaigns. And third, the rank-and-file cossacks did not trust their officers. Lassota at first met only with officers. Then the rank and file learned of the secret negotiations and forced them into a full rada. As the rank and file entered the arena, they escalated cossack demands. Lassota was intimidated and frightened; in the end, without having reached any definite agreement, he gave the cossacks eight thousand gold ducats from the emperor, in a ceremony before the entire brotherhood, and then allowed the cossacks to dictate the terms of their service. These terms were: wages in advance, and at a higher rate than the officers had first proposed; the emperor to obtain Polish permission for them to cross Poland; detachments of the Muscovite army to aid them; and Lassota's companion, Jacob Henckel, to remain at the sich as a hostage! They now offered to supply six thousand "long-time, select cossacks," not including peasant recruits, they claimed. They gener-ously offered, while waiting for their payment, to undertake some sea expeditions to Kilia or Perekop, these being their favorite and most profitable looting targets at any time, and hardly even a challenge now that the Tatar army was away en route to Hungary.

Lassota seemed to think that there was a real possibility of cooperation with the Muscovites through the cossacks, which sug-gests that he was somewhat gullible. But who in his place could have sorted out the cossacks' truths from their bravura? Since we have no record of how the Zaporozhian proposals were received at the Habsburg or Muscovite courts, or of what happened to poor Henckel, we cannot evaluate Lassota's credibility. Still, his written appraisal of the cossacks' strengths gives us a view of how they appeared to a foreign power, a view which coincides with what we know of them from independent evidence. Lassota wrote that (1) they were brave and enterprising, had had military training since their youth, and knew the enemy well; (2) they were far cheaper to hire than mercenaries of any other nationality, and they had consid-erable artillery and experience in using it, thus obviating the neces-sity for hiring separate cannoneers; (3) they had already had dealings with the Great Prince of Muscovy, which was a valuable diplomatic connection; (4) their location was ideal for a rendezvous with the

Muscovite army; (5) it was important to keep the cossacks unavailable to Zamojski who also wanted to use them; (6) had negotiations broken off, the cossacks would have demanded payment for the two previous expeditions they claimed to have undertaken for the Emperor; and (7) "as concerns internal relations in Poland, as it was evident that revolution was threatened in the very near future, I considered it a matter of extraordinary importance to secure with an oath this mob, which not only had the greatest influence in the Ukraine but whom all Poland was watching."[15]

Whether or not the cossacks actually considered themselves to be serving the emperor and Christianity in their further raids into the principalities, the confidence and shrewdness of their diplomacy and their military self-salesmanship suggest that they did not cheat themselves. They were skeptical all along of promises of wages, though considering how often they had been cheated they were hardly skeptical enough. They may have had hopes of using negotiations with the emperor to win privileges in Poland. But however shabbily their employers behaved, the cossacks as employees were equally undependable. They tried to argue Lassota and the emperor into paying them for their privacy ventures into the Crimea or Turkish Bessarabia. When they were hired they could not be counted on to go where they said they would, and they were inclined to desert if the odds looked bad. They could be counted on to pillage any land they passed through, sparing no friends and

18. Rada at the sich. From Podhorodecki, *Sicz Zaporoska,* Warsaw, 1978.

acknowledging no allies. The cossacks were never disciplined mercenaries. They always considered themselves, in the last analysis, self-employed, and any wages they recived a kind of tribute.

Lassota left Zaporozhe on July 2, taking with him gifts from the cossack host for the emperor, including two janissary flags and a Tatar prisoner. Lassota's diary reports their arrival at the Habsburg court in September, and the emperor's decision to accept the cossack offer. We have no further direct evidence of these arrangements. It is possible to evaluate what might have been the Habsburg influence on future cossack military action, but only in connection with a second set of international negotiations, those of the cossacks with the Vatican.

There had been numerous previous contacts between the cossacks and the Vatican. In 1583 a cossack group had proposed to the pope an anti-Turkish crusade starring themselves.[16] Now a decade later a Dalmatian priest, Alexander Komulovich,[17] won over Pope Clement VIII to a similarly ambitious plan involving the cossacks. Komulovich had in mind a three–pronged military alliance against Turkey: Zamojski would lead the Polish army; the Cardinal Legate Sforza would march with his armies from Albania to Constantinople; and Cardinal Andrew Batory, another nephew of the late Polish King Stefan Batory, would lead a combined Translyvanian, Moldavian, and Wallachian army to be joined by cossack and Muscovite armies, pushing back the Turks until they joined the others at Constantinople.[18]

Although Komulovich's fantasies and Clement VIII's gullibility were partly to blame for the failure of this project, so were the cossacks' treachery and wilfulness. Komulovich went in early 1594 to the Principalities where he thought he persuaded Sigismund Batory, Mikhail and Aron to join his league.[19] In March he crossed into the Ukraine seeking cossack leaders; finding none, he saw the old Prince Ostrozhsky, whose name had been given him in Rome. Ostrozhsky seemed to sense the priest's gullibility and used it. A longtime enemy of Zamojski, Ostrozhsky was delighted to participate in a plot to subvert the chancellor's carefully nurtured peace. Besides, he saw profit for himself in acting as agent for the cossacks. He received Komulovich effusively, treated him to professions of the greatest anti-Turkish zeal, and got Zaporozhian hetman Mikoshinsky to agree to the vague proposals of the nuncio.[20] But when Komulovich wrote to Moldavia warning its Gospodar to welcome the cossacks, Aron backed down on everything he had promised. Belatedly beginning to understand the problems he was dealing with, Komulovich remarked that ". . . one does not know of whom he [Aron] was more afraid, the Turks or the cossacks."[21]

Luckily for Komulovich, the Turks and Tatars attacked Podolia and Pokutia on their route to Hungary, and Zamojski was forced to leave his neutralist policy and join the hostilities against the Turks. But despite this newly advantageous position, Komulovich was again trapped by his naivete. He fell into the hands of a Polish–Ruthenian noble adventurer with delusions almost as grandiose as his own, Nikolai (Mykola) Yazlovetsky.[22] The latter offered the services of the Zaporozhians to invade the Crimea or attack the Tatars on their return route from Hungary. Komulovich accepted the proposal and gave Yazlovetsky 10,000 florins as a first payment.[23] He was able to collect an army of both Zaporozhian and irregular cossacks, including groups led by Nalivaiko and Loboda. The cossacks' interpretations of the plan, however, differed significantly from Yazlovetsky's, it seemed—they were more interested in collecting booty than in fighting Tatars.[24] They were hardly to be blamed for taking this attitude, considering that Yazlovetsky had not shared with them the ten thousand florins he had received, but had hired them on the promise of future payment.[25] So, as Yazlovetsky led his army west to the Dniester, the cossacks began dropping off wherever they reached a likely town or village for pillaging. When he arrived at Belgorod, Yazlovetsky reportedly had only eighty men left with him.[26]

Yazlovetsky was ruined, materially and psychologically, by the experience of the desertion, but his cossack "allies" had gained strength from the episode. Deserting, Nalivaiko led his men into the Ukraine for the first time, to Bratslav, where they had broad popular support; Loboda and his followers appeared near Bar, also in Bratslav province. This was now autumn of 1594, and it was the beginning of a new phase in the adventures of the cossacks.

For almost a year afterward the cossacks moved rapidly in and out of the Ukraine, conducting land and sea raids against Turkish, Tatar and Balkan territory, and at other times stirring up trouble in the western Ukrainian provinces. Their feats grew in size and daring, and their accounts, perhaps, in exaggeration. Nalivaiko claimed to have raided over five hundred villages and captured four thousand Turks and Tatars on an expedition of September 1594.[27] In October Nalivaiko and Loboda joined forces for the first time (more of the significance of this alliance in the next chapter), and conducted the biggest raid yet, this time claiming to fight for the emperor.[28] They reportedly led twelve thousand men, seized a great deal of artillery from Jassy and controlled Jassy for a time before returning to Bratslav.[29] In February 1595 Nalivaiko and his cossacks fought in alliance with the anti-Turkish Danubian troops, simultaneously attacking three Turkish strongholds in the principalities—Tiagin (known today as Bender), Akkerman, and Kilia. The Turks were forced to provision the beseiged towns with galleys, but were unable to break the sieges[30] until the cossack–Danubian army disintegrated from internal conflicts.[31]

Early 1595 was the high point of the anti-Turkish successes. The Danubian princes had succeeded in liberating much of their territory; the Turks no longer exclusively controlled the Black Sea; Turkish control over Adrianople was threatened; the Danubian princes reneged on their financial obligations to their Turkish creditors and threatened to deprive Turkey of essential grain imports. Alarmed, Sinan Pasha resolved to crush the Balkan rebellions, and threw a great portion of his armed forces into that task.[32] Diplomatically, this required changes in the Sultan's policy towards Poland.

Until early 1594 the sultan had consistently attempted to avoid antagonizing Poland and to permit Zamojski to adhere to his neutrality policy. Indeed, Zamojski's stubborn rejections of the Habsburgs' and the Pope's crusading schemes gave the Sultan cause for gratitude. Nevertheless, for a large-scale campaign into Hungary the sultan had to ask for permission for Tatar troops to cross Poland on their way to join Turkish armies; and Zamojski had to refuse, having already promised the emperor not to permit such a crossing, and being well aware of the damage the Tatars were certain to inflict.[33] Zamojski was between Scylla and Charybdis, as Lev Sapieha described the problem: either desert Christian brothers in the Balkans and risk having to fight the infidels alone later, or aid the Christian league and commit himself to fighting them now, unprepared.[34] The Tatars not only entered Poland in July 1594 but raided the estates of powerful magnates in Volynia, Rus, and Pokutia, and Zamojski's already weak domestic political position was further weakened.[35] Futhermore, the anti-Polish Batory's hegemony in the Balkans was a serious threat, and Zamojski decided to act. Yet Zamojski's total armed forces at this moment, including the private retinues of the Lublin and Cracow governors, numbered only about seven thousand.[36] Naturally he had to turn to the cossacks for help, a bitter pill given his strong desire to weaken them and bring them under Polish control, but of course the traditional Polish solution. Throughout the winter of 1594–95 cossack sentries had gathered intelligence on Tatar movements and reported to Zamojski, making him aware—as they no doubt intended—of their value. As they had undoubtedly hoped, Zamojski wrote to Loboda for help: "Now is the fortuitous moment to earn the forgiveness and favor of the King," the chancellor begged.[37] But the cossacks had the advantage now and played hard to get. They demanded payment in advance; Zamojski could or would not oblige; and the cossacks refused to serve.[38]

At his most desperate Zamojski was often at his best. In a stunning display of surprise moves, Zamojski managed to recoup the situation by rapid diplomatic and military action. Turning his forces southwards into Moldavia, he occupied the country and installed his own puppet, Jeremiah Mogila, at the end of August 1595.[39] Having taken everyone by surprise, he thus gained time. He then accomplished the delicate diplomatic task of avoiding war with Turkey while retaining control over Moldavia, through a combination of flattery, bribery and duplicity, in separate dealings with the khan, Sinan Pasha, and Ahmad, head of the Tatar sandjak of Tiagin.[40]

This diplomacy did not free Zamojski of the cossack menace, however. In his agreement with the Turks, he had to promise to prevent further cossack attacks on Turkish lands.[41] It was not much to Zamojski's liking, then, that the cossacks immediately belied his word with two further looting expeditions into the principalities.[42]

In a further example of the divisions among cossacks, it appears that Loboda and the Zaporozhians complied, or represented themselves as obedient. Nalivaiko and his irregulars, however, persisted in their attacks. In a typical example of Nalivaiko's self-serving cant, he claimed to be serving both the Habsburgs and Poland!

> Having nothing to do in the [Polish] Kingdom, and being unaccustomed to idleness, having received a letter from the Christian Emperor, we set out for the Imperial lands; where, not for money but out of our love for knightly service, we served for some time, understanding that Mamutel along with the Transylvanian Voevoda were planning some action against Your Royal Highness [of Poland], and that . . . King [sic] Maximilian had sent the Voevoda to Wallachia against His Excellency the Chancellor, and I, being a subject of Your Royal Highness, could no longer endure; not accepting in this country either gift or money, and not succumbing to greed, I could not remain here, but knowing for certain that the Hetman [Zamojski] was going to Wallachia with his men immediately, being always obligated to my country I hurriedly left these regions for the service of my country.[43]

Actually, Nalivaiko and his men were driven out by the imperial forces after two months in Hungary.[44] Returning to Bratslav, they remained in the Ukraine for over a year where they continued to defy Zaporozhian as well as Polish discipline.[45]

The cossacks were emerging as an international mercenary force of significance; more and more they were seeking at least the fiction of having an employer to cover their looting expeditions. An identity as a permanent extra-national mercenary brotherhood promised them a stable identity and autonomy in Poland. As the Ukraine became more settled, they had to have a more defined status than they had previously acquired, and of all recognized catagories of the early modern era, "soldier" was the one they could most comfortably occupy. Had they continued in that direction, Ukrainian history would have been very different. They were blocked, however, by an inadequate market for their services. A more stable situation around the Black Sea and the Danube might have allowed them to become a permanent adjunct to some great power. But the unreliability of their employers combined with their own penchant for autonomous banditry kept them identifying the Zaporozhe as their headquarters and the Ukraine as their home land.

15. Urban Revolt

T HE "SPAWNING GROUND OF THE REBELLION," in the view of the crown officials, was the province of Bratslav, the westernmost part of the Ukraine, with the most coveted lands.[1] Bratslav towndwellers played a particularly large role in the Nalivaiko rebellion, so it is important to pay special attention to their situation. The government had not only made large land grants in Bratslav, but also granted generous privileges to towndwellers who settled there.[2] At first there was no apparent conflict between the magnates' and the towns' ambitions; the vulnerable location of Bratslav, on the favorite Tatar route to the north, made the magnates willing to tolerate autonomous towns if their residents would shoulder responsibilities for defense.

An example of this implicit bargain between lord and townspeople can be seen in developments in Chancellor Zamojski's own estate, Szarogrod, received from the king in 1579.[3] In 1583 the king granted Szarogrod burghers Magdeburg-like privileges, the right to conduct three markets a year, permission to trade with Wallachia, Turkey, and the Tatars as well as the rest of Poland, and exemption from many duties. In addition all merchants of whatever nationality who traded with Wallachia and Turkey were obliged, if they wished to trade with any Polish lands, to stop for at least two days to display their wares in Szarogrod—ensuring that it would become thus a major international market.[4] With such a potential for prosperity to defend, the Szarogrod burghers threw themselves enthusiastically into constructing a fort and providing for the defense of their town.

The growing prosperity of Bratslav, however, made town autonomy increasingly obnoxious to the magnates. The tendencies towards the whittling away of municipal privileges were most advanced in Bratslav, just as, and for the same reasons that, the enserfment of the peasantry proceeded more rapidly in the western than in the eastern Ukraine. Furthermore, all these changes occurred particularly rapidly in Bratslav, a single generation there witnessing the achievement and loss of privileges.

These factors partly explain why in the cossack rebellion of 1594–96, particularly in Bratslav, numerous towndwellers showed themselves prepared to join in armed defense of the cossacks against aristocratic privilege. The embryo of a town–cossack alliance developed during this rebellion and became a major Ukrainian phenomenon by the mid-seventeenth century.

In the 1590s the alliance was limited to opposition to a common enemy, not yet filled out by positive commitments—such as defense of Orthodoxy, or sense of national identity. Still more limiting, the enemy was not completely or always commonly identified. The alternatives were not yet clearly drawn and neither townspeople nor cossacks felt the need to destroy aristocratic power—both believed they could carve out autonomous places for themselves within it. Neither group, therefore, had revolutionary aims. Both groups anticipated making separate peaces, squeezing what concessions they could out of the Poles. Thus the town–cossack alliance was tenuous as well as tentative. It played a significant part in early cossack victories while its disintegration played a central part in the cossack defeat.[5]

The uprising in Bratslav, which reached its greatest size in the autumn of 1595, was seeded and cultivated by numerous cossack visits in 1594 between forays to the Danube. They did not come here to stir up rebellion, although their long-standing hostility to Sheriff Jakub Strus made them behave provocatively; primarily they came to rest themselves and their horses, to get fresh horses, to seek "cossack bread." They were not a disciplined guerrilla army following the time-honored rules of winning over rural populations— never steal, never use without compensation, help the peasants. They were high-handed, confiscated property, and disregarded local interests. That the local population supported the cossack forces, and transformed cossack hegemony into social rebellion, was due less to the tactics of the cossacks than the grievances of the Bratslavians. While the cossacks "used" the Ukrainian population, stirring them up into rebellion in support of the cossacks' own demands for privilege, the peasant and town populations also "used" the cossacks as leadership for their own purposes.

At the end of 1593 there were reports of peasant disturbances in Bratslav, although the Kosinsky rebellion had not generally affected that province.[6] In March 1594 there were complaints about insubordination among the Bratslav townspeople toward their sheriff, Strus.[7] Then in the second half of 1594, the cossacks made three separate excursions into Bratslav.

First some of the cossacks led by Nalivaiko, returning from summer raids into Moldavia, fled into Bratslav. These, like Nalivaiko, were largely irregular, non-Zaporozhian cossacks; and Bratslav was one of their favorite territories.[8] They went directly to the town of Bratslav, chased out the Strus administration, and installed their own. Then they began systematically to exact quartering, supplies, and horses from the local nobles. They accomplished this with the help (or treachery, in the aristocratic view) of the Bratslav townspeople—artisans, merchants, petty servitors.[9]

In this attack, Nalivaiko and the Bratslavians had separate but coinciding motivations. The townspeople evidently had an existing animosity against Sheriff Strus and his rule. Nalivaiko had a personal grudge against another important Bratslav lord, Kalinovsky (who later succeeded Strus as Bratslav sheriff). The latter had killed Nalivaiko's father, or so the cossack leader believed; and the motive, again in Nalivaiko's story, was to usurp land. This land, now in Kalinovsky's possession, Nalivaiko claimed as his own; and collecting a following of irregular cossacks and peasants, including some of Kalinovsky's own tenants, he robbed the Kalinovsky estate.[10]

Nalivaiko relieved this first siege of the Bratslav nobility by setting off again to Wallachia in August 1594. When Gospodar Aron chased the cossacks out and took away their horses, they fled again to Bratslav. Again Nalivaiko challenged the existing administration, demanding horses, supplies, and quartering of the nobles assembled for assizes. The nobles fearfully dispersed. The Bratslav town council then accepted Nalivaiko as their *de facto* ruler, granting him a large measure of autonomy and authority, and he settled himself in again, taking what he needed primarily from the surrounding estates.[11]

The events in Bratslav were once again interrupted in early October when Loboda and Nalivaiko returned to Wallachia for revenge against Aron. Their absence, for less than two weeks, gave the forces of order some time to regroup. Rumors that the cossacks had suffered heavy losses in Wallachia helped the nobility regain some of their nerve and they decided to reconvene the Bratslav assizes. They ordered the Bratslav town corporation not to give any supplies or quarter to the cossacks and threatened to punish not only the cossacks but any who remained loyal to them. As the nobles neared Bratslav and camped for the night, Nalivaiko's cossacks, back from Wallachia, attacked, taking them by surprise, killed many and robbed them—removing all their money, clothes, horses, and documents.[12] In the spring of 1595, when the cossacks left again and Zolkiewski re-established crown authority in Bratslav, the residents were found with the property taken that night and were forced to return it.[13]

The town never recovered, however, its book of records which the cossacks had stolen.[14] The cossacks always looked for documents wherever they attacked, out of both rational and superstitious motives. At times they were seeking evidence that they had been cheated, even under Polish law, by finding land titles, rent records, or the like. At other times their obsession with and hatred for documents reflected a naive and illiterate view that the documents themselves were the source of aristocratic power and privilege, a naiveté typical of pre-industrial rebels. Still, the continual cossack theft of documents symbolized their stubborn and short-sighted conviction that they could get the liberty and justice they sought within the existing Polish constitutional and legal framework.

The night attack on the Bratslav nobility was a turning point in the rebellion because it re-established cossack and popular control by an act of open war; and also because, as never previously, it was supported by the town burgomaster and the rest of the Bratslav magistracy.[15] With the help of the cossacks they freed themselves from aristocratic rule. The town of Bratslav became autonomous and self-governing under cossack protection. Disinclined to accept much administrative responsibility themselves, these irregular cossacks were more than willing to allow the burghers independence in return for their respect for cossack privileges of free movement, exemption from taxation or service burdens, and "cossack bread."

Simultaneously Loboda and his Zaporozhian cossacks, returning with Nalivaiko from Wallachia, had gone to the town of Bar, also in Bratslav province. Here the Zaporozhians installed themselves with an organization duplicating that at the sich. They held a rada; set up a sentry system, permitting no one to enter or leave the city without their permission; issued a series of orders requisitioning the necessary supplies and sent out detachments to collect what they needed. When they took the fortress at Bar they demanded of the sheriff a full inventory of all his stores.[16]

The distinction between the Bar and Bratslav organizations at this point well illustrates differences between Zaporozhian and independent cossacks. The former had more highly developed administrative skills and self-confidence, and an ability to transform military discipline and organization into at least rudimentary civil authority. Had the cossack "armies" of this rebellion all been Zaporozhians, experienced in self-government and accustomed to centralized leadership, the cossack power in the Ukraine might have been somewhat more long-lasting and their defense against royal and aristocratic counter-insurgency more effective. But the cossack armies were heterogenous, including not only Nalivaiko's irregulars, having no practice in or loyalty to any discipline other than the immediate tyranny of an individual leader, but also peasant rebels who had not even campaigned with a group of cossacks previously. Nor did the different cossack groups remain separate. Here as later Nalivaiko's men joined the Zaporozhians, wanted or not;[17] and the process of fusion was troubled and imperfect. This difference in administrative style was but one of many ways in which the cossacks' tendency to accumulate followers was simultaneously a strength and a weakness, increasing their numerical power but often decreasing their organizational coherence. Cossack heterogeneity meant that they could evolve no consistent policy towards the Bratslav townspeople, could not steadily exploit the animosity between town and nobility. The cossack–burgher municipal governments were unstable and brief.

The municipal rebellions were further destabilized by the reappearance of peasant uprisings at this time, late 1594. Crowds of hangers-on began to collect; as always they included some disaffected and outlawed nobles, too, but the majority was peasant.[18] Illustrating the fusion of cossacks with peasants, Zolkiewski wrote that there was "no peace due to the insubordination and rebellion of these accursed peasants."[19] "God save me from another Kosinsky," he added on March 4.[20]

Still, the Bratslav unrest was notable for the participation of townspeople. In a royal Universal the Chancellor complained that the townspeople had defied numerous royal orders and even death sentences in continuing to resist the lawful authority of sheriff Strus: He ordered the nobles to bring the culprits to justice[21]—in his helplessness Zamojski gallantly empowered the nobility to do exactly what they would have done anyway if they had been able.

The Bratslavian nobles and officials were terrified. The army was far away, the crown offered only empty threats. Many fled to Lvov. "I am almost alone here, except for a few servants," wrote Jakub Pretvich, sheriff of Terebovl. "If God will not help us and the King provide for us and Your Grace care for us then they will pillage everything we own." This he wrote to Zolkiewski on November 25, 1594; two hours after writing the letter he added a postscript saying that news had come that the cossacks had arrived at Zinkovo, two miles away, and he hurriedly packed up his family and fled himself.[22]

Ostrozhsky, in Volynia, was also nervous. He remained on his estates, relying on his intelligence system to give him adequate warning of an impending attack. He not only had informants among the cossacks and a special messenger in Mezhibozh, but also received letters from Loboda himself keeping him abreast of events![23] At this point Ostrozhsky and Loboda were both attempting to remain on good terms with each other: the former hoped to divert the cossacks' attacks away from himself, fearful of a repetition of Kosinsky and not trusting the crown to offer real assistance; the latter guaranteeing Ostrozhsky the safety of his estates, wanting to preserve Ostrozhsky's neutrality in case of need. Nevertheless, in late December of 1594, Ostrozhsky wrote to Lithuanian Commander-in-Chief Radziwill that the cossacks were gaining dangerously in strength, numbering now 10,000, he estimated; and that new outbreaks were likely.[24] By the beginning of February 1595, Ostrozhsky raised his estimate to 12,000. The two-thousand-man army that the king was raising would be much too small, he predicted.[25]

When Nalivaiko returned to Moldavia in the spring of 1595, Zolkiewski sent a small armed force which was able to retake the town of Bratslav and return it to the jurisdiction of Strus. Much as the Bratslavian townspeople enjoyed their independence, they had organized no defense, nor had the cossacks helped them to do so. In May Nalivaiko came back to Bratslav and took it again away from Strus.[26] He and his men stayed nearby for three weeks. Their strength was so alarming that Lithuanian Chancellor Sapieha believed that several thousand cossacks were advancing on Cracow.[27] But at the end of the summer of 1595 the Polish army subdued the town of Bratslav and exacted a lasting surrender from its people.[28] Nalivaiko's army had been able to hold off—more accurately, to frighten off—royal forces; but the cossacks had not been able to create any lasting civilian power.

The defeat of the "bourgeois republic of Bratslav" is hardly surprising in the context of sixteenth-century Ukraine. The surprise was that it existed for any time at all. It did not, as we know from earlier discussion of the economic development of the Ukrainian towns, reflect the strength of a large merchant class. It arose out of a combination of temporary circumstances peculiar to the Ukraine. The impetus to this outburst of town autonomy came from the tension between the frontier's loose social categories and the imposition of Poland's rigid ones; and between a growing and needed urban population and a social system that allowed it no privileges at all. The possibility for that autonomy was created by the temporary military hegemony of a cossack force and a desperate peasantry, forces whose creation owed little to the townspeople.

Nevertheless, without the support from the Bratslavian (and later Kievan) townspeople, the cossack rebellion would have taken on a different appearance. It would have been driven more quickly than it was into the "wild steppe," and therefore would have had less time to attract reinforcements from among the peasantry. It would always have had its centers in small villages; it would have probably been unable to take fortresses, and, therefore, would have had no artillery. In all these ways the rebellions might have been weaker without the support of town dwellers. The significance of the cossack strength in the towns was greatest as a portent of the future. As the cossacks became an Orthodox and a nationalist force—a transformation to be examined in the next chapter—their greatest strength came from their urban support.

On the other hand, when the cossack army was face to face with a large royal army, and the risks involved in loyalty to the cossacks were much higher than previously, the townspeople almost all deserted the cossacks and left them unexpectedly isolated. Fair-weather allies can be dangerous when they are too much relied on. For the townspeople, defection was the only rational course. They had no positive interest in a cossack victory, for the cossacks had no commitment to serving the interest of the townspeople. The latter had supported the cossacks in only one of their implicit goals: to destroy aristocratic power in the Ukraine. When the cossacks were no longer likely to achieve that goal, they were useless as allies.

16. A Holy War?

ONE PART OF the Nalivaiko rebellion is distinct because it bears some of the marks of a religious struggle. From spring 1595 until the end of 1596 cossacks led by Nalivaiko carried out a series of attacks in Volynia in which Prince Konstantin-Vasili Ostrozhsky played a powerful but shadowy role. The Poles later charged that he instigated cossack attacks on Catholic and Uniate leaders,[1] in effect using the cossacks as personal servitors in his campaign against the Catholic–Orthodox Union. Evaluating these charges requires disentangling the Volynian events from what was now a mass uprising. By April 1595 large parts of Kiev and Polesia were ruled by Zaporozhians; by autumn of that year no part of the Ukraine was untouched and the rebellion had spread into Belorussia. The cossack rebellion had been enclosed in a popular uprising.

Although there is room for doubt about the religious convictions of the cossacks, in these Volynian episodes the insurgency of the cossacks and Ukrainian lower classes took on a partially religious identification, through particular association with Orthodox magnate K.-V. Ostrozhsky. Although Ostrozhsky had always been closely connected to cossacks, in this period he appeared primarily as a perpetrator, not as victim. Personal grievance continued to explain many of the cossack-led attacks, but their anti-Uniate consistency is so striking that coincidence does not seem a convincing explanation. The collaboration between Ostrozhsky and the cossacks, and the combination of cossack aims with religious grievances, moved the Zaporozhians a significant distance towards an identification and self-identification as defenders of Orthodoxy in the Ukraine.

Several specific factors preceding the 1595 attacks made this identification possible. First there was the peculiar role of the old Prince Ostrozhsky. An enemy of the Zaporozhians under Kosinsky, as a leading Ukrainian magnate he was threatened by the cossacks' ability to disrupt the service position of peasants and burghers. On the other hand, Nalivaiko had been in Ostrozhsky's retinue and the latter was skilled at using cossacks, even if merely by negotiating deals which directed their activities away from his own territories. Ostrozhsky's experience with Kosinsky undoubtedly strengthened his conviction that he needed an individual, flexible cossack strategy, for he had seen that he could count on military aid from neither the Crown nor the rest of the nobility.

A second factor conditioning the 1595 attacks was religious tension. The cossacks, and the peasants who joined them were almost exclusively Orthodox. The town-dwellers and nobles were divided between Catholicism and Orthodoxy; the process of Polonization and Catholicization, which moved rapidly after the 1569 Union of Lublin, had not yet captured all of the Ukrainian ruling class. Ostrozhsky was one of the minority of magnates who had remained Orthodox. These differences, however, were not usually marked by overt hostility prior to the campaign for the religious Union. Peasants, to be sure, recognized in Catholicism the religion of the oppressor, an alien religion, and peasants may have been the most intolerant stratum of Ukrainian society at that time. Ostrozhsky's own tolerance prior to the Union—he married the daughter of the Catholic Polish magnate Count Tarnowski, and supported a Dominican monastery at Ostrog[2]—was not atypical of urban and upper-class attitudes.

The plan for the Orthodox–Catholic Union, however, disrupted this religious peace. The Orthodox hierarchy was threatened by this attack on its privileges and wealth. The Orthodox lower clergy was in a different situation. Not well supported, many had had to put themselves under the patronage of local landlords in order to survive.[3] Since many of these latter were Catholic, and increasingly interested in converting their peasants, many of the lower rural clergy were forced to convert themselves. Simultaneously, many Ruthenian nobles had been converting to Catholicism as a means to increase their power and influence in the Rzecz Pospolita.[4] The conversions produced a vicious circle: the more the nobles converted, the more Orthodoxy became particularly a religion of peasants; and the more it became a religion of peasants, the more the nobles despised it and felt ashamed to be associated with it.

In the face of this increasing debilitation, a union seemed to many supporters of Orthodoxy a possible source of help to the church. Union would mean a significant inflow of money, which could be controlled and spent on constructive educational projects; it would mean a granting of full political and social equality to all the Orthodox and their clergy and thus, it was hoped, remove some of the incentive for conversion to Roman Catholicism. The original plan for the Union would have allowed the Orthodox Church to keep the Eastern Rite and the marriage of the clergy. The idea of union also had an important diplomatic dimension, in resisting Muscovite influence over the Orthodox, for in 1589 the Moscow patriarchate had claimed jurisdiction over Lithuania and the Ukraine.[5]

Ostrozhsky had at first been not only a supporter but an instigator of the Union plan. Representatives of both sides—for examples, the Jesuit priest Peter Skarga and the Jesuit-hater Kurbsky—saw Ostrozhsky as the key man for their side. And despite Kurbsky's eloquent pleas to Ostrozhsky not to enter into disputations with the "cunning Latins,"[6] in 1585 Ostrozhsky had written to Pope Gregory XIII requesting Union. Ostrozhsky's 1593 list of conditions became the basis of the final agreement.[7]

In 1593 the Union seemed destined to go through without significant opposition.[8] Ostrozhsky's change of mind contributed significantly to the reversal of its political chances. Beginning in 1595 Ostrozhsky appeared as the chief spokesman for an anti-Union opposition based on the Orthodox brotherhoods of Lvov, Vilna and Kiev in particular and among the Ruthenian lesser gentry more generally.[9] Ostrozhsky's motive for this change was in part a re-evaluation of his own political power position: he feared that Polish magnates planned to use the Union to bring them fuller control of Belorussia and the Ukraine and that his autonomy would be better served by clinging to a separate church, of which he could continue to be the *de facto* head.[10] Ostrozhsky and the brotherhoods fought hard against the Union. The prince attempted to bribe Metropolitan Rogoza with a gift of twenty villages to denounce the Union, and to intervene against the pro-Union Voevoda Mogila in Moldavia. He denounced vehemently the "turncoat" Orthodox clergy who supported the Union, and tried to intimidate them.[11]

Oddly, in the end both Ostrozhsky and the Union failed. Ostrozhsky failed to check the flow of Ukrainian nobles into the Catholic Church, and by 1630 his successor as Kiev governor, Dominik Zaslavsky, was able to order all Ukrainian priests to submit to the Uniate Metropolitan.[12] But in the long run the Union also cost Catholic Poland an enormous price: peasant Orthodoxy and anti-Polish feeling had been consolidated, and in the seventeenth century the cossacks came to symbolize and then to lead this resistance to achieve Ukrainian secession.

The germs of this secessionist movement were planted in the 1590s. Before the Nalivaiko rebellion, cossacks had attacked Catholics and Orthodox (and Moslems) alike. The Ostrozhsky–Nalivaiko team behaved differently. In the spring of 1595 the cossacks concentrated several attacks near Lutsk in Volynia. The frightened bishop, nobles and merchants tried to pacify them with gifts (up to several thousand zlotys), but with no results. The cossacks took the gifts and collected "tribute" of their own choosing from the churches and the nobles. In autumn 1595 they terrorized Lutsk for three days and burnt many villages.[13] Although they took some ammunition and gunpowder, the military objectives of these attacks were minimal: they took no artillery, nor did they try to hold Lutsk as a base.

Indeed, the only rational pattern in the attacks was in the identity of their victims. One was Nalivaiko's personal enemy, Kalinovsky;[14] several others were pro-Union enemies of Ostrozhsky. The first ambush of a Uniate leader could be explained as chance; the succeeding attacks could not.

Victim number one was Kiril Terletsky, Bishop of Lutsk. Ostrozhsky considered him a traitor: once thought of as a loyal Orthodox, Terletsky had been given a *carte blanche* by the council of anti-Union bishops to represent them, had broken faith and become a supporter of the Union.[15] He was to become a Catholic the following year.[16] Terletsky was also one of the most notoriously corrupt of the clergy; a veritable gangster, he had been tried for murder, rape, and brigandage.[17] At this time Terletsky was on his way to Rome for negotiations on the Union.[18] His servants were bringing letters, deeds, other important documents and valuables from his residence in Cracow to the Lutsk cathedral for safe-keeping when the cossacks fell upon them, beat and robbed them.[19]

Uniate forces and even the King himself immediately suspected Ostrozhsky's hand.[20] The attack occurred just after the latter's manifesto to the Ukrainian people denouncing Terletsky. Furthermore, Terletsky and his travelling companion, Ipaty Potei, Bishop of Vladimir, had accused Ostrozhsky of sending cossacks to harass them while they were en route to Cracow previously.[21] Nevertheless, the cossacks *might* have come upon Terletsky's men by chance, discovered who they were and what they were carrying, and robbed them spontaneously.[22]

If the first attack was accidental, the ensuing ones could not have been. They relied extensively on Nalivaiko's older brother

Damian, who was Ostrozhsky's private priest and confessor at Ostrog, as a participant and a receiver for stolen goods, in preplanned ambushes.[23] In January 1596, with Terletsky in Rome, the cossacks, led by the Nalivaiko brothers, pillaged his and his family's holdings. Going then to Pinsk, the cossacks raided the home of a burgher who was guarding some of Terletsky's episcopal treasures and "two parchment documents to which he attributed great importance." In Pinsk, no doubt, the word spread about what they were planning, for when they went to the estates of Jarosh Terletsky, the bishop's brother, they were joined by two former servitors and current enemies of Terletsky, Florian Gedroit and Pavel Kmit. Having added many Pinsk dwellers, both commoners and nobles, to their number, they attacked many nearby villages, stealing documents, money, clothing, gold and silver; they killed and wounded many of Jarosh Terletsky's servants. Damian Nalivaiko retired to Ostrog while Severin Nalivaiko and Gedroit went to Stepan, another of Ostrozhsky's estates, with the booty. There they divided it and sent part to Damian, part to the steward of Stepan (in return for quartering them?), and another part to Ostrog to be melted down for manufacturing.[24]

19. Fortress at Ostrog. From Hrushevsky, *Pro Stari Chasy na Ukraini*, 1907.

The cossacks then singled out another victim—Alexander Semashko, sheriff of Lutsk, a Roman Catholic since 1586.[25] A series of attacks, perhaps more accurately described as a campaign, was made on Semashko. He charged that the attacks were instigated and led by Andrei Gansky, a noble who was also a servitor of Ostrozhsky. Severin Nalivaiko did not participate in them, but Damian did, bringing with him about one hundred men. Another piece of evidence for Ostrozhsky's influence was the participation of Loboda, despite his tense relations with Nalivaiko. Although Loboda was not present here, several of Loboda's cossack companies were, commanded by Ostafy Slutsky. In addition there was a group of two hundred led by Okhrim Gumenitsky, a burgher from Mezhirich, who also identified himself as a captain under Loboda.[26] Attacking several of Semashko's estates, they stole the best livestock and much of the other moveable property.[27] At one estate, Korostiatin, they killed many when they apparently met resistance; Slutsky was killed and several other cossacks captured. At another estate, Tuchin, two noble cossacks, Prince Voronetsky and Gulevich, both Ostrozhsky's servitors, the former also a priest, cut off the ears of eleven peasants. Damian brought all the booty to Ostrog, including seven travelling horses, seventeen stallions, and seven horses-of-all-work which he claimed for himself personally.[28]

Both Semashko and Terletsky attempted to bring legal action against Ostrozhsky. The bishop sent two of his agents with a bailiff to Ostrog in November 1596 (when Nalivaiko had already been defeated and captured by the Poles), demanding the arrest of Gedroit, then at Ostrog, and the return of his property. Zhdano Borovitsky, the sheriff of Ostrog, threw Terletsky's messengers into jail. On the next day a "commission of inquiry" came to interview the Stepan steward who had quartered Nalivaiko and Gedroit, and an Ostrog commoner who had fetched Terletsky's silver from Stepan to Ostrog. Borovitsky also arrested this entire commission.[29] Attempting to use the law against those protected by Ostrozhsky was not safe. Not only did Terletsky fail to obtain any satisfaction from Ostrozhsky, but by 1598 the latter had managed, by a variety of means, to deprive the bishop of his Ostrog estate and of the villages of Buderazh, Busha, Borshchevka, and Pivcha.[30]

Semashko also sent a bailiff to Ostrog who recognized there three of Semashko's horses; he was repelled by Borovitsky.[31] Later the bailiff went to Mezhirich castle where, again, he saw livestock and horses belonging to Semashko. At this castle two hundred townspeople and peasants, the bailiff wrote, "who called themselves cossacks," undoubtedly the people who had fought under Gumenitsky, chased him out.[32] In December 1596 Semashko attempted to have Ostrozhsky subpoenaed. The unfortunate bailiff was too frightened even to deliver the summons![33] (It seems odd that Semashko should have been so naive as to think he could use Ostrozhsky's courts and Ostrozhsky's provincial administration against Ostrozhsky. Perhaps he had a strategy of forcing the crown to interfere, but Ostrozhsky outmaneuvered him.)

When Ostrozhsky could not legally protect the cossacks, the population often would. The peasants not only had a strong suspicion of written documents, but also of those who administered them. Thus they were hostile to the bailiff seeking evidence against Ostrozhsky. Even more striking is the story of those who were captured at Korostiatin. Three were commoners, three nobles; all were sentenced to death—the nobles with the written permission of the king, which was required before capital punishment could be administered to a noble. As the prisoners were being led to their

20. Kiev seminary students. From an engraving of the 1690s, reprinted in *Istoria Ukrainskoi Kultury*, Winnipeg, 1964

execution past the Holy Trinity Church in Lutsk, built by Ostrozhsky in 1582,[34] the seminarians attacked and were able to free one of the convicts.[35] Divinity students might be expected to be sympathetic to cossacks on social grounds, since the seminaries drew many students from the middle and lower classes, but this episode suggests that in addition the cossacks were beginning to be seen as defenders of the faith against the Polish enemies.

This cossack reputation as religious partisans was not (yet) deserved.[36] The evidence of Ostrozhsky's role does not necessarily signify that the cossacks shared his religious convictions. Ostrozhsky and the cossacks were using each other. When the cossacks operated independently they never included any religious demands in the numerous sets of conditions and grievances they presented to the crown or to various magnates. There were no priests or church at the sich at this time. The papal nuncio in Poland, Malaspina, followed the cossack rebellion closely but did not consider it at all connected with the Union.[37] Neither did Zamojski.[38] The Catholic Bishop Vereshchinsky remained on the best terms with the cossacks throughout this period.[39] Surely the rank-and-file cossacks and their followers shared some anti-Catholicism, but this was an attitude, not a policy, and a rather complex attitude, composed as much of social and economic as of religious grievances; and this lower-class anti-Catholicism thus contained many views and grievances hardly shared by Ostrozhsky.

Yet Ostrozhsky had injected some lasting religious and national consciousness into cossackdom. So had the Orthodox brotherhoods and the Orthodox peasant and urban populations, by their support of the cossacks and their attribution of motives to the cossacks. Throughout the cossacks' history, cossack "traditions" were developed and changed by what others attributed to them as well as by the cossacks' own initiative. The associations of cossacks and anti-Union forces in the minds of their mutual enemies further strengthened those connections. For example, the Uniate Bishop Potei, immediately after the Brest Union, called the Vilna Orthodox Brotherhood a "Nalivaiko horde."[40] Indeed, the word *Nalivaikovtsy* soon came to mean Orthodox die-hards in Polish usage.[41]

In the context of the 1595–96 rebellion, the religious issue quickly died down. The uprisings grew so rapidly in size and extent, and the socioeconomic issues grew so overwhelming, that the Union grievances paled by comparison. Furthermore, Catholics, Uniates and Orthodox were divided, all groups found on both sides of the conflict. The association of the rebels with Orthodoxy was a

Polish legend which grew in retrospect, as the events were retold and re-examined. It was not until the seventeenth-century cossack rebellions that the cossacks' reputation, combined with new pressures and options to make defense of Orthodoxy a genuine and integral part of the cossack program.

17. Peasant Rebellion

I

N NOVEMBER 1595 Nalivaiko and his cossacks burst into Belorussia and sparked a major peasant uprising. As in the Ukraine, the cossacks did little to court the peasants; yet the latter joined the cossacks immediately as if in response to an arranged signal. The cossacks did not aspire to become liberators of the Belorussian peasants; the peasants appointed them to that role.[1] This chapter will use the Belorussian events of 1594–96 to illuminate several aspects of cossack–peasant relations, and to contrast the style and content of a primarily peasant uprising with the Bratslav situation, where the cossacks also had substantial urban support.

Throughout the fifteenth and sixteenth centuries there had been frequent peasant uprisings in Belorussia.[2] Ukrainian cossacks had invaded in 1588 and 1590, both times amassing peasant support.[3] Nalivaiko claimed that Belorussia was one of the traditional places where the cossacks were entitled to seek "bread."[4] Yet the Belorussians did not produce their own cossacks. This was partly because their terrain lacked the dry, flat plains of the Ukraine which facilitated horse travel; and also because there was no dangerous frontier stimulating para-military organization. Furthermore, by the sixteenth century Belorussian peasants were more firmly restricted by servile land relations than Ukrainian peasants. At the same time the Belorussian peasants' burdens were heavy and rapidly increasing,[5] making the people angry and desperate.

Thus from the first appearance of the cossacks, in late 1594, Belorussian peasants grativated towards them. The uprising spread faster and wider here than previously in the Ukraine, perhaps because the exploitation of the peasantry was more severe, perhaps because the news travelled faster in this more populated territory.

Returning from their autumn 1594 campaign into Moldavia, in December the Zaporozhians came to Ovruch, near the border between Kievan Polesia and Belorussia. Here they quickly collected a "rabble" of eight thousand.[6] By the spring of 1595 there were at least three separate cossack armies in Belorussia, each with their separate followings numbered in the thousands. The rulers feared not only the numbers but the intentions of the insurgents. Lithuanian Chancellor Sapieha wrote, in January 1596, "the peasants, our subjects, are overrunning, plundering, stealing and fighting, and they rule us, and our hands are tied; not only are we not strong enough to retaliate but we cannot even defend ourselves."[7] Sapieha's sense of the size of the problem was shared by the other magnates. "And in every inn they are drinking to the health of Nalivaiko," wrote N. K. Radziwill, grand marshal of Lithuania and later governor of Vilna.[8] Increasingly, too, they were also aware that the peasant movement was gaining its own momentum, not always relying on cossacks to propel them into action. The uprising had spread into Mazowia, where there were no cossacks. Small bands of rebels and bandits roamed, with leaders who called themselves "hetmans," robbing and terrorizing, usually but not always limiting their targets to noble estates. Everywhere peasants were calling themselves cossacks. Fugitive soldiers, too, were swelling the cossack bands, for they were tired, mistreated, and, as perennially in Polish armies, unpaid. Sapieha compared the rebellion to the German peasant wars.[9]

Although the cossacks had surely "stirred up" the peasants, the latter had also had an effect on the cossack uprising. The Zaporozhian rada held at Ovruch in December 1594 was irregular and disorderly due to the pressure from these non-Zaporozhian hangers-on.[10] The relation between the peasant "followers" and the cossacks was complex and ambiguous. The "followers" were a threatening pressure upon cossack leadership. The peasants were untrained and undisciplined. In attacks they supplied useful strength, but in retreat they slowed cossack mobility, sometimes bringing families with them. Once away from their homes they needed to be provisioned, thus increasing the amount of "bread" or "tribute" the cossacks needed to collect and distribute. And the peasant-cossacks had of course different goals. The cossack demands for their "traditional liberties" left room for negotiation and compromise on points such as the register, the autonomy of the sich, and military payment, while the peasants had only simple and uncompromisable demands: land and freedom. (This conflict will be discussed further below, in the story of the defeat of the rebellion.)

The accumulation of these peasant supporters split the cossack

leadership and hastened its defeat. In the fall of 1594 the Zaporozhians under Loboda and the irregular cossacks under Nalivaiko had fought jointly, in Bratslav. Nalivaiko had then gone on
one of his campaigns into Moldavia, but when he returned in
December of 1594 it again appeared that a unified cossack army
might form. Both groups had swollen enormously during 1594, and
a sign of their potential power can be seen in the fact that the
Lithuanian nobels feared nothing so much as their conjoining.[11] At
Ovruch, the Zaporozhians held a rada.[12] At this meeting there were
heated debates and frequent interventions, often violent, from the
"rabble" who surrounded the cossacks and looked to them for
leadership and protection. When the rada broke up, Loboda and one
group of cossacks remained while Shaul, taking all the artillery,
headed for Mozyr in Belorussia.[13] He was aiming to join another
renegade Zaporozhian, Fedor Polous.[14]

Loboda, nobleman and official hetman, was overthrown because of the rabble's influence; Shaul had been more willing and
able to cater to their demands. Loboda responded to his overthrow
by denouncing Nalivaiko to the authorities, specifically Lithuanian
Commander-in-Chief Radziwill, attempting to distinguish himself
as a dutiful registered cossack. "And of that licentious man Nalivaiko," he said, "who has almost forgotten the fear of God and is
without respect for anything in the world . . . we know nothing and
wish to know nothing . . . for we are not against the authority of His
Royal Grace or the orders of Your Grace." Justifying his previous
raids on the Danube, Loboda argued that he had gone there only "to
serve the Crown."[15] Evidence that Loboda was not entirely isolated
in this posture, but retained the loyalty of a group of registered
cossacks, lies in the fact that he was not killed when deposed, as had
been customary among Zaporozhians. Loboda returned to Zaporozhe and functioned separately at the head of a group of Zaporozhians for almost a year. He was drawn into yet another attempt
at cossack unity a year later, when Nalivaiko was fleeing from a
crown army; but ultimately he was lynched by the "rabble" he
refused to accept.

Meanwhile Shaul, Polous, and Nalivaiko, leading separate
groups, were all in Belorussia. Polous and Shaul reached Mozyr
sometime in the spring of 1595 and dug in there. Polous' cossacks
took "bread" from the local nobility but remained for a time on
royal lands, perhaps hoping thus to avoid forcing the Lithuanian
magnates into immediate action to defend their property. Indeed,
Polous in a letter to Radziwill took pains to point out that he had

not touched Radziwill property, and addressed him only as a magnate, ignoring his official position as vice-chancellor and Lithuanian commander-in-chief. And, in fact, Radziwill threatened but took no military steps against them.[16] That autumn, however, Nalivaiko adopted more provocative tactics. With an army estimated at one thousand, he headed for Slutsk, the territory of Vilna marshal Khodkevich, head of what was probably the second most powerful Lithuanian family. En route he raided many small villages belonging to Khodkevich.[17] Shaul meanwhile ravaged not only Mozyr but also Bykhov, Propoisk and Ostry, finally returning to Kiev. N. K. Radziwill wrote to his brother the Lithuanian hetman that Shaul could be the equal of Nalivaiko and that they were definitely equal as robbers.[18]

A significant re-orientation had occurred: a segment of Zaporozhians, pressured by the mass, desperate, violent support they received, had become indistinguishable from the "godless" Nalivaiko men. The uprising now took on some of the traditional lineaments of a *jacquerie:* robbery and murder, burning houses, stealing or destroying documents, kidnapping or "liberating" serfs, vandalizing nobles' property. The roving cossack–peasant bands rarely stayed in any one place long, except in seasons when travel was difficult. The desperation of their followers is reflected in the willingness of so many to leave their homes.

The uprising was extremely violent, and its violence often appears, particularly to the observer familiar with modern revolutions, aimless, even gratuitous. Peasants were murdered, women raped and murdered, the victims often mutilated. Property was stolen only to be discarded because it could not be carried; immoveable property was destroyed. This kind of violence has been characteristic of some peasant uprisings, and is related to a lack of clear political and social goals rather than simply the excesses of class hatred. Violence in the service of clearly defined political or social aims may be equally severe but is often more disciplined, limited and focused. As the cossacks became more driven by the needs of peasant masses, their already limited strategic aims—autonomy, self-government, etc.—were still further submerged. As a result the violence became, as it were, insatiable and indiscriminate, on both sides, as the next chapter shows; it continued until one side was exhausted or decimated.

However, even at its most massive, peasant-dominated moment, the cossack-led rebellion still retained other characteristics which distinguished it from a peasant uprising. Several historians have suggested taxonomies of popular uprisings and social banditry, and distinguished between urban and rural revolts.[19] The cossack rebellions of this period were complex because they retained elements of both social banditry and urban revolt.

The cossacks were, of course, archtypical social bandits. In times of mass passivity, peasants, townspeople and even the gentry entertained themselves with true and tall tales of cossack exploits. For those with grievances, as Hobsbawm has suggested, the bandit represents "a surrogate for the failure of the mass to lift itself out of its own poverty, helplessness and meekness."[20] That reputation enabled the cossacks to provide leadership for peasant rebellion. But it may also, conversely, have eliminated the incentive for peasant self-organization that would have led to more effectively strategized and lasting rebellions. It may even have obstructed some organized peasant action. Social bandits tend towards a tight, often secretive, para-military form of organization, with strong leadership and strong sanctions for violation of "traditions" or of fraternal loyalty. As a result their organizations tend to be excluding and impenetrable to outsiders; hence their patterns of success at avoiding infiltration and betrayal. The cossacks in warfare retained many of these organizational patterns developed at the sich and in their smaller piratical and mercenary adventures. When confronted with masses of followers, or with territory to hold, they had organizational habits with which they tried to exercise control, but they did not open up new, democratic forms of participation. Radziwill described how the cossacks seized "documents from messengers on the roads . . . which having read they re-sealed with their own seals [!] and gave back to the messengers . . ."[21]—to assert a governmental authority. In Bratslav, with urban support, the cossacks temporarily substituted a revolutionary government for Crown-gentry authority; in Belorussia they hinted at the same. But these "governments" represented no one but cossacks. The peasant followers accepted them as separate, alien governments. At moments of maximum disorganization, peasant masses might call themselves cossacks and join the radas, as at Ovruch. However, they did not challenge nor alter cossack organizational forms, style, or leadership.

Because of the particular social, religious and economic situation of the Lithuanian lands, the cossacks in rebellion usually had some potential urban support as well. In Bratslav, where it materialized most, the Nalivaiko rebellion became as a result more powerful, a real revolutionary threat. In Belorussia it did not materialize, because of differing behavior among townspeople and cossacks; as a result the uprising in Belorussia was less a rebellion and more an extended *jacquerie*. The difference created by the actions of townspeople can be better understood through a brief description of the cossacks' experience in two Belorussian towns, Slutsk and Mogilev.

When Nalivaiko went to Slutsk in autumn of 1595 he demanded recognition and tribute from the town corporation. The town refused and he took the castle by force, stealing artillery and a great deal of valuable moveable property from the town.[22] (By comparison in Bratslav, Nalivaiko had approached the town first through overthrowing the administration of a hated sheriff; perhaps in Slutsk there was no similar grievance against its ruler, Khodkevich.) Using Slutsk as headquarters, Nalivaiko attempted to create a cossack administration, much as in Bratslav, in order to organize and legitimize collection of tribute from the nobles. He distributed proclamations claiming to be acting on orders from Zamojski![23] (Perhaps this was a crude attempt at exploiting distrust between Poles and Lithuanians.) But the Slutsk townspeople continued to be noncooperative. In late November a group of about five hundred cossacks was lured to the nearby town of Kopyla, possibly with the collaboration of the townspeople, into an ambush by a private army of Khodkevich. Most of the cossacks were killed.[24]

Despite this loss, Nalivaiko's ranks swelled quickly again, to an estimated 2,000 by November 30.[25] In addition Nalivaiko had an estimated 12-14 cannon, 80 matchlock guns, 700 rifles, a great deal of Lithuanian money, much booty and many horses stolen from Slutsk.[26] The cossack snowball had not been stopped and the Belorussian nobility was frightened; hence they responded rather efficiently to Radziwill's call for a gentry militia to suppress the culprits.[27] Within two weeks Radziwill's deputy, Buivid, left with six hundred cavalry to head off Nalivaiko at Mogilev, on the Dnieper, where he was believed to have gone.[28]

Nalivaiko had indeed gone to Mogilev. In a letter written a few months later, Nalivaiko emphasized that he had gone there because it was a *royal* town where he could expect fair treatment, as opposed to persecution by the magnates—"hoping to eat our bread in peace."[29] The cossacks were again attempting to exploit the Commonwealth's chief weakness: lack of gentry loyalty to the central government.

Ironically, en route to Mogilev, the cossacks were dealt a blow by *their* chief weakness, at least in Belorussia—poor relations with townspeople. At Kopyla again, a group of Nalivaiko's cossacks was again ambushed, murdered in their sleep, this time by the townspeople themselves.[30] And arriving at Mogilev, they received no support from the townspeople. So the cossacks resorted to force: a few bursts from their artillery were enough to terrorize the burghers into surrendering, despite their strong fortifications. Possibly because they were angered by the lack of cooperation, the cossacks then went on a two-week spree of extreme destructiveness and cruelty, revenging themselves without apparent gain.[31]

The cossacks were blamed for more than they actually did at Mogilev, however. The chronicles of one noble clergyman recorded that they burned five hundred houses and four hundred stores, killed many nobles, townspeople and peasants, including women and children, and destroyed two churches, finally burning down virtually the entire town. But this was the same chronicler who claimed that the Lithuanians had an army of eighteen thousand, a grossly inflated figure.[32] For once we have alternative accounts which leave no doubt that he was exaggerating, probably maliciously. In February 1596, after the Lithuanian army had retaken Mogilev, Sapieha wrote that it was becoming "difficult to conceal, considering that all who are arriving from there, and especially the Mogilevians themselves, are giving it out, that not the cossacks but our people burned Mogilev."[33] This should not suggest that the cossacks were blameless. More reliable sources indicate that they did rob and burn extensively.[34] But the town was razed by the cossacks' enemies. The Lithuanian army threatened the townspeople with death should they cooperate with the cossacks, and then ordered them to set fires to force the cossacks out.[35]

Thus in Belorussia it was the noble-burgher alliance that was effective, not the cossack-peasant-burgher alliance. The fact that the counter-insurgents did not spare the townsfolk in their military response may have changed the possibility of future such alliances, but at this time the cossacks had almost completely failed to mobilize urban support. There may well have been objective reasons for this, in material differences between the Belorussian and the Bratslavian towns' situations. The Belorussian burghers were in the late sixteenth century still expanding their privileges and autonomy.[36] In their regions, aristocratic power was still checked by grand-ducal power, while in Polish-administered Ukraine, the nobility had overwhelmed most of its urban opposition.[37] In both parts of the Commonwealth town autonomy was an object of class struggle between burghers and the landowning classes, but in Lithuania the latter were still on the defensive. Hence the Lithuanian army, composed of nobles and their retinues, may not have been entirely reluctant to see Mogilev burn. At the same time, the Belorussian burghers, optimistic about their future, may have been understandably disinterested in supporting rebels.

The consequences of the failure of urban support for the cossacks in Belorussia were heavy. Belorussia was the turning point, after which the cossacks were thrown permanently on the defensive. Had they been able to stay for a while in Belorussia, to consolidate their gains and organize their new adherents, they might have been able to conduct a longer offensive; and their inability to hole up for any length of time there was largely due to their betrayal by townspeople. In Bratslav, by contrast, the support of the burghers had established the cossacks as a genuine rebel force, providing them with artillery, with headquarters that commanded administrative and communications centers, with time to organize the collection of supplies, and with quarters so that they did not have to return to the sich and disperse. Of course the burghers had given nothing away, and the cossacks had given them a chance at municipal self-government. The Belorussian burghers did not, perhaps, perceive the cossacks as offering anything; or perhaps self-government did not interest them, as they were doing well without it. Whatever the explanation, it was the cossacks' loss. Only in alliance with burghers did the cossacks demonstrate the capacity to administer territory other than their sich. With peasant allies only, they could not hold territory.

It is also important to recognize that, from the peasants' point of view, the cossacks were terrible allies. We have already seen that an elite portion of the Zaporozhians chose to preserve their privileges rather than risk them by aligning with the "rabble."

In the victorious campaign of a crown army against the cossacks that soon followed, virtually all the cossack leadership betrayed their followers. The finale of the cossacks' invasion of Belorussia already indicated the potential for that betrayal. From Mogilev, a town held only by military force, Nalivaiko chose to continue roving piracy in Belorussia, rather than defending his headquarters or standing and fighting back after the town was razed. Offering no leadership to the mass of peasants that had collected, Nalivaiko allowed the group to fight over the distribution of booty and to disperse into many different raiding groups.[38] Nalivaiko then quickly left Belorussia, travelling swiftly with a much smaller group of immediate followers, leaving many of his erstwhile peasant supporters deserted. On the way back into Volynia, Nalivaiko wrote a lengthy, self-pitying and self-justifying letter to King Sigismund.[39] It was a treacherous and a naive document, demonstrating both disinterest towards the fate of the army of runaway serfs that the cossacks had attracted, and innocence of the ways in which those peasants could have built the cossacks' own power.

> . . .wanting, because of the weariness of our horses, to rest in our usual cossack territory on the Dnieper until the occasion for service to the Rzecz Pospolita presented itself, we set off to Lithuanian territory, into which we had hardly set foot, so to speak [sic], when the Lithuanian lords . . . without any provocation from us, except our seeking a little bread . . . attacked us in Slutsk . . . From there, greatly disturbed, having used the town only for our rest, . . . we set out directly for your Royal Highness' town Mogilev, hoping to eat our bread there in peace. But while on the road, the army, taking in peasants from all the villages . . . became such a great force . . . that the burghers appealed to the lords not to allow us to enter there, for people from all the Mogilevian villages and from other districts as well were gathered in rebellion, numbering 10-20 thousands. . .

This long letter contained many of the typical cossack gambits: their attempt to depict themselves as victims, to exploit crown-magnate distrust, their self-righteousness and perhaps genuine feeling of entitlement. Also notable however is Nalivaiko's distancing himself from the peasants. Attached to the letter was a set of "Conditions" offered to the king, the fulfillment of which would persuade the cossacks to cease their insubordination.[40] The primary demand was for land, a piece between the Bug and the Dniester, along the River Szenosed, almost at the Tatar–Turkish travel route between Tiagin and Ochakov, twenty miles below Bratslav, "where since the creation of the world no one has lived, and on which route his majesty would wish to build towns and castles and populate it with cossacks. . . ." In return for this land grant to a new group of cossacks, who would thereby become "regulars," Nalivaiko offered that:

> All of the insubordinate cossacks not in the official register he, Nalivaiko, would "suppress." Those who were nobles would be sent to the king for punishment. He would cut off the ears and noses of those who were serfs and not permit them in the Army.[!]

Neither bandits nor outlaws would be permitted among the new cossack group to be assembled for settling the new land: any outlaws apprehended would be immediately handed over to the Ukrainian royal officials. . . .

The letter received no reply; it may never have reached the king. But no matter. The logic of it was predictable—it was as much an extension of governmental as of cossack thought about the "cossack problem." The most subversive of the cossack rebel leaders was willing to "sell out" for the price of a place on the inside. Nalivaiko even offered to give up the time-honored cossack title "hetman" and to call himself "lieutenant." So individualist was his intention that he did not even attempt to bargain about the number of cossacks he could take with him to join his new recognized official group. "Sell out" is of course an inappropriate and ahistorical term to describe Nalivaiko's attempt. He had not asked to be, and did not conceive of himself as, a mass leader or even a social bandit. He had not demanded an end to serfdom. Far from it: he wanted an army commission and a chance to become, perhaps, a serfowner himself.

18. A Royal Victory?

In 1596 the cossacks were decisively defeated by a crown army. The Polish victory was not easy, and required a long and costly chase out onto the "wild steppe." The story of the six-month series of battles, negotiations, betrayals, mutinies, ambushes, and atrocities has the characteristics of a fine war narrative, small-scale but exotic. We will however touch only upon the highlights of that story here (enough perhaps to satisfy the lovers of military history) and we will focus on those events which communicate not only the tactics that were finally successful against the cossacks, but also some of the reasons for their defeat. The 1596 chase will help us evaluate the social significance of the cossacks in the sixteenth century, for we will see that their military strengths and weakneses reflected rather closely their strengths and weaknesses as social leaders. Their war aims in this battle were indistinguishable from their whole *raison d'etre*.

In the short run, the cossacks' 1596 defeat seemed to make little difference. Having signed a surrender in June of that year, in September cossack groups were again raiding in the Ukraine, and the new crown-appointed Zaporozhian hetman was leading campaigns against the Tatars in defiance of the crown's prohibition.[1] Nevertheless, in the long run the 1596 battle was portentous. The cossacks saw their enemies, crown and nobility, Polish and Lithuanian, unite, making it clearer than before how difficult the cossack struggle for autonomy in the changing Polish Kingdom was to become. Further, the cossacks saw a crown army follow them even onto the "wild steppe," previously their seemingly inviolable space. The frontier, which had been a condition of the cossacks' existence, was shrinking.

191

The Gathering of the Counter-insurgents

The Poles finally organized themselves to restore order in the Ukraine in January 1596. Zamojski would have preferred to act earlier. He had been under constant pressure from the Ukrainian and Lithuanian magnates to send military assistance. Furthermore he had personal reasons for concern: beginning in 1576 he had been steadily expanding his own land holdings in the Ukraine.[2] He had actually raised an army against the cossacks in Bratslav in 1594, but "a greater danger [war with Turkey] appeared and we had to divert it. Remember that I reminded the Diet many times about this rebelliousness . . . I myself wishing to take action . . ."[3]

Finally Crown General Stanislaw Zolkiewski was assigned the job of suppressing the cossacks. It was to be the first campaign that he commanded alone, and the first time a Polish army was to fight cossacks. In the end, the anti-cossack campaign helped build Zolkiewski's career and make him a national hero; it also taught him much that he was to employ in his later invasion of Muscovy. But in 1595 he had just returned, exhausted, from the Balkans, with only one thousand men, many of them wounded, and no fresh horses.

For these reasons the crown first made another attempt at a peaceful settlement, again, as with Kosinsky, appointing a royal commission to go to the Ukraine. Its charge was to punish both cossacks and those who abetted them.[4] In an impressive display of masochistic obtuseness, some of the magnates who had served on the Kosinsky commission appeared here as commissars again;[5] or was it because they were most well acquainted with the magnitude of the cossack menace and therefore most dreaded open warfare?

The commission achieved nothing.[6] Resigning himself to the inevitable, the king agreed to provide two thousand crown soldiers, half of them cavalry, and arms. There was no money to be spared, neither in the crown nor the Lithuanian treasury, so it was necessary to collect a special military tax, first used in 1591. Simultaneously Zolkiewski's thousand men were ordered forward, and Kremenets in Volynia was selected as the assembly point.[7]

On January 27 the king called upon the Volynian nobility to join as a militia with the royal army, "not as a duty," he argued weakly, "but out of love for country and for your own security."[8] (Such was the authority of the crown!) Zolkiewski personally canvassed the Ukraine to get the magnates to join the effort, but with little success. He got promises but no action from Stanislav Gulski, Janush Zaslavsky, and Bratslav governor Janush Zbarazhsky; Kamenets magnate Jan Potocki did not even reply to his requests. Later, as the cossack menace grew, the magnates fell into line. In April Potocki and Lithuanian general Khodkevich—the Commonwealth's greatest military figures—joined the Zolkiewski army with their retinues; their presence labelled the cossack "insubordination" a significant military challenge and brought out other private armed forces. Ostrozhsky Senior, however, continued to subvert Zolkiewski's efforts with his "neutrality:" he remained peacefully on his estate at Konstantinov while the cossacks continued to avoid disturbing him or his interests.[9] They knew well the narrowness of the magnates' interpretation of their self-interest, and were undoubtedly skeptical about the prospects for the creation of any effective army in the Ukraine at all.

Many factors worked in favor of the cossacks: the magnates' hostility to the presence of a crown army in the Ukraine; their refusal to put up any money for it; their individual hopes that they could each, like Ostrozhsky, deal separately with the cossacks and divert cossack belligerence towards another landowner. In the end these factors were not so strong as the fear the cossacks evoked. Cossack success united the opposition. But the cossacks did not perceive this, as they did not understand how successful they were; because they had no clear collective political goals, they had no collective criteria for measuring success. They could measure only booty, and the length of time they spent unchecked. They did not know why their enemies were so frightened.

The Lithuanians acted with somewhat more alacrity than the Poles. Ironically, the destructiveness of Nalivaiko's and Shaul's raids in Belorussia may have been more frightening than the greater *political* threat of the cossack-supported insurgency in Bratslav. In driving the cossacks out of Lithuania, Radziwill had already assembled an army of several thousand, including hired Tatars, mercenaries who were a regular part of the Lithuanian army.[10] By mid-February 1596 about three thousand had "volunteered" to join the crown army,[11] and money had been taken from a royal slush fund to pay for more mercenaries. Furthermore, the government resolved to ask the Muscovites to chase the cossacks should they try to flee to the east; and to ask the Diet to decree, as rewards for all those who would join in subduing the cossacks, amnesty for all past crimes, and exemption from certain large taxes.[12]

Zolkiewski set out from Kremenets in icy February. His plan

was to take the cossacks by surprise before they could flee to the steppe or the sich. He also hoped to forestall unification of the separate cossack forces and to defeat the cossack groups one by one. He knew the strengths of the cossacks as fighters. The further into the Ukraine, the better they knew the terrain and the worse Zolkiewski's forces did. The cossacks had better horses; could travel very light and therefore much faster, because they could get food and supplies from the population and from hidden stores; they could often rely on local populations for information, secrecy and quartering. They had the possibility of escape into Muscovy, or Crimea, or the land of the Don cossacks. Understanding all this, it is not surprising that Zolkiewski hoped for a quick recovery.

When the first gambit failed, however, he had no choice but to chase them, which he did for four months and two hundred miles. The chase exacted a heavy toll from his own army and at times the cossacks eluded him completely. Just as they were on the very edge of Muscovy and about to slip out of his grasp he managed to surround them and then to starve and thirst them into submission. That the cossacks did not stay beaten, Zolkiewski might have added, was the fault of the politicians, not the generals.

The Cossacks Seek Refuge

After being driven out of Mogilev in Belorussia, and seeing the town burned, the cossacks had to flee. At first they attempted to stay in Belorussia, and had camped on a nearby field, making their usual tabor. The Lithuanians surrounded them but, lacking artillery, could not break the cossack defense.[13] Both sides suffered from the severe weather conditions, the magnates' army probably more so since they were less hardened. When the cossacks held fast, desertions among the nobles' retinues mounted; some simply fled the cold, while others were attracted by the prospects of looting in the smoking ruins of Mogilev.[14] Thus one night the cossacks were able to break camp and flee, unnoticed, to the south.[15] Some of the Belorussian peasants accompanied Nalivaiko all the way to Ostrog in Ukrainian Volynia, on Ostrozhsky's lands. Here Nalivaiko hoped again to be able to stay.

Zolkiewski, however, surprised the cossacks. Instead of waiting for better weather, the end of mud season, and a larger army, he left Kremenets in late February 1596, hoping to ambush the cossacks at

Ostrog. The cossack intelligence network gave warning and Nali-vaiko left, heading southwards towards Bratslav, where the cossacks usually found their strongest popular support.[16] Nalivaiko was confident not only of his strength but of Zolkiewski's weakness. He did not hurry, thinking that the general would wait. This miscalculation led to the first in a series of setbacks to the cossacks. They learned too late that they had both underestimated their enemy and overestimated their popular support.

Because Nalivaiko took his time, he and his followers were almost ambushed in camp by a Zolkiewski advance group. The cossacks were slower than usual because they were carrying artillery.[17] Furthermore, the additional peasants, fugitives, deserters and poor townspeople who joined them as they headed south [18] slowed their speed. The lack of discipline among this mob immediately caused a defeat: At Martirichi, a village between Konstantinov and Ostropol where they had stopped off to attack and loot a noble's estate, they found a keg of brandy and drank themselves into a stupor; some of Zolkiewski's advance detachments came upon them half asleep and burned the whole village, killing several hundred cossacks and peasants.[19]

The heaviest blow to the cossacks, however, was their desertion by the Bratslav townspeople upon whom they had counted. At the village of Charnov some cossack rearguards remaining behind after the cossack main force had departed were turned over by the residents to the Poles, most of them to be killed.[20] At Pikov the townspeople refused to let the cossacks in, and Nalivaiko did not feel strong enough to attack them. Instead he sent ahead a messenger to Bratslav with a letter to its residents, recalling the past friendship of Bratslavians and cossacks. The town was extremely well fortified, and Nalivaiko hoped to hole up there at least to give himself and his men a chance to rest. But the Bratslavians either did not answer or replied negatively, and two miles from Bratslav, Nalivaiko and his men were forced to head southeast into the "wild steppe" beyond the Sob river.[21]

The Bratslav burghers were not rewarded for their betrayal of the cossacks. When Zolkiewski arrived in Bratslav he had the mayor publicly executed for his cooperation with the cossacks in 1594.[22] Had the Bratslavians helped the cossacks in 1596, they probably would have fared no worse and might have done better, putting themselves into a bargaining position. But the cossacks had not rewarded them for their past help, either. Nalivaiko's forces were robbing and vandalizing through Volynia and Bratslav. Once more the cossacks were weakened by their own failure to appreciate the value of allies.

Running eastwards towards Kiev, the cossacks again approached the townspeople with high hopes for support. The Kievan towns—Kanev, Belotserkov, Cherkassy, Korsun, and Kiev itself—were often second homes for Zaporozhians, many of whom had houses, farms and families there.[23] But even in Kiev the cossacks' success was mixed. Some burghers did aid them, in Belotserkov and Korsun; but as the Zolkiewski army's punitive brutality grew, the cossacks encountered betrayal from Kievan townsfolk as well. Even when the cossacks tried to treat their allies well, their decreasing military strength left them with less to offer their allies. From the point of view of the burghers, the risk of association with a losing side was high. Thus it was not entirely a function of cossack short-sightedness or selfishness that they lost supporters. Nevertheless, the flabbiness of the towns reflected the limits of what they had to gain from a cossack victory.

As in Belorussia, the disappearance of town facilities to use as headquarters cut off a main cossack option and forced them to look to the wilderness for refuge. Without forts, the cossacks' defense would have to be constructed out of speed and their ability to survive in the uninhabited steppe. But in this latter task, their large non-cossack following was now a detriment; and the cossacks were unable to identify and exploit the possible advantages that a large peasant mass might have brought them. As mercenaries, the cossacks were unfamiliar with the use and education of untrained "enlisted men;" furthermore they were unfamiliar with military techniques of using large armies, and the cossack leaders had such contempt for their peasant following that they hardly communicated with them. Ironically, those unhappy peasants, whose help the cossacks never asked for and whose interests they never intended to defend, caused the cossacks' defeat.

Nalivaiko headed for the wild Uman steppe, the "horses eating grass and the cossacks eating the horses." He was forced to put his cannon into the river and bury the ammunition for later recovery in order to speed his flight.[24] These losses would have been less significant for a small and speedy cossack force of a few hundred which could lose itself in the steppe or at the sich. With at least a thousand, probably several thousand, in tow, however, not all of them mounted, shedding the heavy artillery did not produce much more speed; and a crowd of that size could not disappear, despite lead time. Zolkiewski did not follow at first; he had neither provisions nor wagons on which to transport them, and many of his horses were sick and lame. Waiting at the edge of the steppe, he built his army, as new detachments arrived, to number fifteen hundred: the regular army, including the Tatar divisions, about three hundred Hungarian cavalry, and several hundred men of the personal retinues of various Ukrainian nobles.[25]

When Thieves Fall Out

Impressed with Zolkiewski's growing strength, Nalivaiko tried to slough off his own weaknesses. These weaknesses happened to be people, the "rabble" followers. He may not have perceived his own actions as treacherous, but his followers did. In mid-March Nalivaiko sent a cossack to Jakob Strus, Bratslav magnate and once the target of his strongest attacks, asking him to serve as a go-between to Zolkiewski. Nalivaiko offered to give up his guns and disperse his forces in return for a pardon for himself.[26] Strus, swallowing what must have been a great desire for revenge, did as requested, and Zolkiewski responded favorably, saying he wanted neither Nalivaiko's nor the cossacks' blood, and even promised to intercede with the king for Nalivaiko. But the peasants and cossack irregulars discovered these secret negotiations and nearly murdered Nalivaiko. Many deserted him at this point, understanding that they could expect no protection from their leader. But others, with nowhere to go, had no choice but to stay and try to control Nalivaiko. Helpless before his own army, Nalivaiko rejected Zolkiewski's feeler.[27]

Seeking another solution, Nalivaiko turned now to Loboda and the Zaporozhians for help, despite their previous disavowal of him. The Zaporozhians had themselves left the sich and gone into Kiev, as they often did during the winter; here they too "gained" many irregular followers, produced by the massive peasant insubordination throughout the Ukraine. It was no doubt the influence of these new cossackized peasants that led a Zaporozhian rada to agree to "accept" Nalivaiko, although the latter was now a beggar—his artillery scuttled, his horses exhausted.[28]

Such was the pressure from below that this union was effected despite Zolkiewski's steady efforts to keep the two groups separated. The general had written Loboda that he considered Nalivaiko to be the only culprit, promised that the Zaporozhians could serve the king as before, and offered to intercede personally for Loboda. Furthermore, Loboda had shown no previous loyalty to the cossack "cause;" he almost certainly knew of Nalivaiko's similar attempts at a private "deal" with Zolkiewski; and he had previously been eager to work with Polish authorities. Loboda was now, however, no longer free to make his own decisions. Zolkiewski's envoy was intercepted by the cossack rank and file before he reached Laboda or the officers; the envoy turned out to be a former cossack, which did not increase his popularity. They threatened to kill him, and Loboda managed to save his life only by joining in the outcry against him and attempting to calm the crowd.[29] Zolkiewski made another, similar, offer to cossack leader Sasko Fedorovich, promising amnesty in return for betraying his followers; probably unanswered, the letter was found on Sasko's body when he was killed in April.[30]

The cossack masses had to be vigilant about intercepting and rejecting such offers because they knew that their interests could only be furthered by total victory. Zolkiewski would never offer them freedom from serfdom. This fact divided the rank-and-file cossacks from their officers. Between these two groups—peasant and noble, registered and unregistered—the tension now began to intensify markedly, dividing and weakening the cossacks when they most needed their strength. This division was Zolkiewski's chief advantage.

It was an advantage, however, only if the Polish leadership could recognize and exploit it. At first they could not. Perhaps they were not fully aware of the potential for division. The cossack leaders were now together, in virtual control of Kiev, with as many as eight thousand men under them.[31] The countryside was in complete disorder, if by that is meant disregard for legal authority. The majority of the peasants recognized the authority of the cossack hetman and elders. From Belotserkov Zolkiewski wrote: "All Ukraine is cossackized, full of traitors and spies."[32] Again Zolkiewski tried to act quickly, but his haste made a major tactical error.

Himself waiting for more troops, Zolkiewski sent Prince Kirik Ruzhinsky with five hundred horsemen and some of the infantry ahead to the Kievan town of Pavolotsk. Ruzhinsky had his own opinions about dealing with the cossacks, and he instituted a terror, an indiscriminate execution of peasants. Even Zolkiewski was dismayed at Ruzhinsky's cruelty,[33] not to mention its inefficacy, for the terror only drove more peasants into the cossack bands.

Ruzhinsky's attacks were a direct challenge to the cossacks' authority, since their reputation depended on their ability to defend their comrades, and they had to act immediately against him even though they were not yet well organized as a single force. They were also offended because of who Ruzhinsky was: a former cossack, son of a cossack hetman, he had received two Kievan villages for his service; since then he had gained notoriety even in the disorderly Kiev province for his ruthlessness and violence, even against other landlords, in his drive for land. He kept a private retinue of some five hundred of his own cossacks and a goodly stock of artillery.[34] The Zaporozhians thought of him as a turncoat, an upstart, and a dishonorable man.

No sooner had he heard news of the terror than Loboda sent Sasko after Ruzhinsky. But Sasko let his vanguard fall into Ruzhinsky's hands; the cossacks were slaughtered and Sasko quickly retreated.[35] The cossacks immediately mounted a second attack, more elaborate than the first. Shaul wrote deceptive letters to both Zolkiewski and Ruzhinsky, offering a peaceful mission from the Zaporozhians.[36] Meanwhile Shaul asked Nalivaiko to join him in an attack.[37] Ruzhinsky retreated to Belotserkov, to be closer to his property.[38]

"Despising his enemy," as Heidenstein wrote, Ruzhinsky could not really believe they would attack him there.[39] He went directly into the town with his soldiers and began looting. The Belotserkov residents, not particularly pleased with the Ruzhinsky regime in their town, opened another gate to the town and let Nalivaiko and his men in.[40] These destroyed the Polish camp in the town and massacred the sleeping soldiers; continued out the other side of the town and attacked the remainder of Ruzhinsky's army, now caught between Nalivaiko and Shaul. Ruzhinsky and the survivors managed to get back into the castle, where they waited for Zolkiewski.[41]

The cossacks fled east, towards Tripolye, another center of cossack strength, with Zolkiewski close behind. Many of the cossacks were now on foot, however, and much slower than usual, so they had to make a stand. They stopped at the little village of Ostry Kamen and made their tabor. Zolkiewski had fewer men but much better arms and more cavalry, and he knew that if he could crush this group it would be much easier to take care of the rest back in Kiev. Furthermore, cossack prisoners and deserters convinced him that the cossacks were frightened—in fact they were undoubtedly terrified, at what was for many of them a first glimpse of the military power of a great state. On the other hand Zolkiewski, wiser than Ruzhinsky, also knew that it would be difficult to defeat desperate people and wanted to leave them hope. He planned to attack, strike them a decisive blow, frighten them into running and wear them down psychologically so that they would surrender.[42]

But Zolkiewski was overruled by his vengeful officers and their private armies, as he had been overruled in effect by Ruzhinsky's unauthorized action. Ultimately Zolkiewski did not have control over his conglomerate army, composed of sections of regulars, mercenaries, and the private servitors of the nobles. The latter insisted on storming the tabor. They attacked the next morning, April 3, and fought all day long, but the cossack defense held. The Polish casualties, and surprise at their total failure, abruptly demoralized them. They quit after this one attempt and retreated to Belotserkov, leaving Kiev to the cossacks.[43]

Cossack casualties were also great. Sasko was killed, Loboda and Nalivaiko both wounded, and Shaul's hand was ripped off by a cannonball. But the Polish humiliation was significant and a strong show of force by the cossacks now might have frightened them into hesitating.

Unfortunately the urban support that had enabled the cossacks to defeat Ruzhinsky, and had been responsible for so many of their previous victories, was still unreliable; as was the cossack unity forged in Kiev.[44] Nalivaiko believed that the Kievan towns would stick with the cossacks.[45] Not only had the Belotserkov burghers helped trap the Poles, but Nalivaiko was now well-treated in Korsun, where he had holed up, his army continuing to swell. Hoping for a continuation of this support, the cossacks rushed to Kiev town, crossed the river and dug in on the left bank. The Polish army arrived just afterwards only to find that there were no boats in which to cross the Dnieper. The Kievans, however, betrayed their cossack friends and agreed to raise their boats for the Poles and to build more. Like the Bratslavians before them, they had picked the likely winner.[46]

Producing the boats took time, however, and meanwhile Zolkiewski again used guile to stall and deceive. Negotiations began, initiated by floating logs across the river with messages. Zolkiewski began the rumor that a large part of his army was being sent to Pereaslav under Potocki, and even sent Potocki in that direction, but instructed him to double back and return to Kiev. At the same time he sent two soldiers to pose as deserters to the cossacks and to announce that another huge army was expected any day from Lithuania. To make the story credible, Zolkiewski then demanded that the deserters be returned, which the cossacks refused to do. One of these unfortunate soldiers died in the last battle, and the other the cossacks later hung and quartered.[47]

The result of this trickery was that the cossacks quit the shore and went rapidly to Pereaslav, where the (by now) large majority of the cossacks who were not professional Zaporozhians had left their wives and children. Despite Zolkiewski's wishes, parts of his army had continued indiscriminate terrorism against the peasantry, thus forcing the peasants in the cossack camp into greater determination, as surrender came to seem likely to include not only enserfment but massacre. This intense pressure again split the cossacks. At a long, chaotic, and violent rada in Pereaslav, the Zaporozhian elite advocated compromise with the Poles, while the majority refused. Of the majority, some wanted to stay and make a stand in Pereaslav; but it was a difficult town to defend, and furthermore there were now ten thousand horses and eight to ten thousand people to feed. The other option, going out onto the steppe, meant dragging heavy artillery and ammunition plus all the women and children. But the steppe also meant the possibility that the Poles would not follow—a slim chance, but really their only chance. They headed east and stopped at Lubny, a castle of Prince Vishnevetsky on the Sula River, only twelve to fifteen miles from Putivl, a Muscovite fort.[48]

Lubny was a new, seven-year-old castle, preceded by a very long bridge over a shallow and marshy river, the Sula. The cossacks apparently planned to destroy the bridge after crossing, thus making the castle accessible only from the steppe. They were still depending on their two traditional strengths—superior mobility, and ability to exist without carrying provisions—when in fact they had lost both. The women and children, plus the heavy artillery, made them very slow. They had such a large concentration of people that it was difficult to find enough food; nor did they dare sacrifice their horses, without which they were helpless in the open steppe. Ignoring, or refusing to face, these facts, the cossacks miscalculated.

They arrived at Lubny exhausted and began the debate all over again—to stay and make a stand or flee to Muscovy or the Don cossacks. In fact their lead on Zolkiewski was so short that he made their decision for them: he sent ahead a small, fast detachment to cross the Sula several miles below Lubny and come upon the cossacks from the east. After it was in position, Zolkiewski's vanguard advanced to the Lubny bridge; the cossacks set fire to it, only to find themselves attacked from behind simultaneously.[49]

Still the cossacks had the better position, on a height, with strong earth ramparts and trenches. Zolkiewski could not storm the encampment until his long-range artillery came from Kiev, so he besiegcd them. It was very hot and the water shortage soon became even more acute than the food shortage, especially since all the salt supplies had been stolen by the Poles. The cossacks fought back with guerrilla harassment tactics: small bands of cossacks would steal out at night to get food; they attacked the edges of the Polish camp; lured the Poles out of their camp and ambushed them; stole Polish supplies; freed Polish horses. The Poles, as the cossacks well knew, were hungry and thirsty too. Their morale suffered particularly as cossacks captured Polish sentries, executed them, and waved their heads on staffs so the Polish camp could see them.

Zolkiewski had by now learned the value of internal dissension in the enemy camp, and through a correspondence with Loboda again stimulated Nalivaiko's and his followers' fear of betrayal.[50] Just as Zolkiewski began an artillery attack, Loboda was lynched and murdered by an angry cossack mob. This provoked a counter-rebellion on the part of Loboda's followers, so that the cossack camp was already in a state of disintegration when Zolkiewski's cannon began firing. After two days of siege a fight broke out among the cossacks, so violent that the Poles could hear the shouting; and a mob emerged to hand Nalivaiko over to the Poles and ask for Zolkiewski's conditions.[51] Their leaders had frequently tried to buy personal amnesty by surrendering the peasant-cossacks; now the rank and file was trying to reverse the deal by surrendering Nalivaiko. Only in their absolute desperation had they thought of their own interests as separate from those of their hetmans; but this distinction came too late, and without sufficient planning, to help them. They had nothing to offer the Poles.

Revenge

Zolkiewski's conditions were so unrealistic, in terms of the constitution of the cossack forces at this point, that one wonders if the commander was not, like the cossack hetmans, under severe pressure from his own men. The Polish army demanded that the cossacks: (1) disperse and never again assemble without royal permission; (2) surrender their leaders, flags and tokens of foreign powers (important symbols of the cossacks' autonomy to engage themselves as mercenaries and thus obtain independent income); (3) return stolen property and booty to thc Polish army; (4) return all peasant fugitives to their lords.[52] The cossacks found the last condition unacceptable, of course. It would have meant unconditional surrender for most of them. Hence the cossack envoys rejected it and threatened to renew fighting. The commander-in-chief responded by crying to his eager officers, *"Bronciez."* ("Go ahead.") The Poles attacked, not even giving the cossack messengers time to return to their camp and tell the results of their mission. There followed not a battle but a riot and a massacre as the soldiers rushed into the cossack camp, motivated both by anger and by their awareness of the booty there.[53] Only about fifteen hundred out of the eight thousand cossacks escaped to the sich. The rest were murdered or kidnapped by the serf-hungry lords. "And they were so merciless that for a mile or more corpse lay upon corpse," reported a Polish chronicler.[54]

The Poles' violent rampage, begun by uncontrolled and greedy soldiers, soon became a policy decision. Nalivaiko was imprisoned for a year, probably tortured during this period; then he was beheaded, quartered, and put on public display.[55] Shaul and Shostak were executed simultaneously, also in a manner designed to terrorize.[56] Other parts of the "revenge" were more materially profitable. The rank and file of Zolkiewski's army had looted at Lubny, and got very little; the Ukrainian magnates waited until after the victory and began a legal looting of the cossacks' wealth. From September 1596 to the end of 1597 the property of all cossacks—not only land but commercial enterprises as well—was legally confiscated and redistributed to the magnates. The lands of Trekhtemirov and Barishpol, granted to the Zaporozhians but a few years earlier,[57] were given to Zolkiewski.[58] The crown awarded Loboda's estate to a Kievan noble in return for the latter's services to the royal cause.[59] Other nobles quarrelled over their claims to cossack property. For example, Shaul, too, left valuable lands, which were originally bestowed upon Erazmo Komorovsky;[60] but by July 1600 Prince Roman Ruzhinsky claimed part of this windfall.[61] The same Komorovsky fought with another noble, Alexander Ostroukh, for the estate of Sasko Fedorovich.[62] Numerous houses in Kiev, valuable commercial properties in several towns, and innumerable agricultural estates were given out to magnates and even to those lesser gentry lucky enough to have fought on the winning side.[63]

Conclusion

Having seen the cossacks in action, and experienced their relation to the Ukranian population, Zolkiewski returned to Poland skeptical about his own accomplishment. He pointed out to the government that many cossacks had escaped to the sich; that the conditions of the Ukraine would produce new cossacks consistently; and that this type of insurgency could not be prevented by single "decisive" battles but only by constant vigilance.[1] His warnings had little impact. The treasury was low, as usual, and king and senators shared a preference for making problems disappear by not thinking about them. Furthermore, Zamojski found it politically expedient to present the campaign as a great victory. He organized numerous triumphal ceremonies,[2] and informed the papal legate that he had defeated the Habsburgs—since the Austrian flags carried by the cossacks had fallen to him![3]

Yet the emptiness of the victory was evident even before the celebrations and punishments were over. The Diet renewed the constitution of 1590 which had proved absolutely unworkable several times. The Diet also increased the fines levied on runaway serfs by 700 percent, an equally unavailing gesture.[4] The crown ordered that groups should be dispersed whenever five or six men gathered; that "idlers," that is, all commoners not in the service of the crown or the lords, should be arrested; that those who did "mischief" should be executed without formality; that those without defined occupations and residences, or who were unable to give a satisfactory account of themselves, should be apprehended.[5] This edict merely licensed the magnates to do what they tried to do for themselves anyway, and there were no royal agents who could enforce these provisions in the interest of national security rather than the enlargement of their personal retinue.

Meanwhile the cossacks' defiance continued almost without

205

pause. The new crown-appointed hetman, Kristof Nechkovsky, was not resisted by the Zaporozhians only because resistance was unnecessary. Nechkovsky immediately became indistinguishable from earlier irregular hetmans. Already in July 1596 he announced a Zaporozhian campaign against the Tatars in defiance of the crown prohibition.[6] Soon the cossacks' "old friend" Jacob Pretvich, sheriff of Terebovl and soon to be governor of Podolia, himself instigated an attack on the Turks.[7] By September the crown already admitted that:

> . . .from the recently destroyed army of rebellious cossacks some rebels are still pressing upon Our castles, towns and villages, and upon the villages of Our nobles, and without rendering service they are again collecting in large mobs and spreading threats. . .[8]

Within four years the cossacks had won amnesty and were again operating above ground and with great autonomy in the Ukraine. Furthermore they got back their communal lands and the individual rights to own property and bequeath it.[9] The reason for this about-face in government policy should be familiar by now: cossacks were needed as recruits for an imminent war with Sweden.

In the half century between these early uprisings and the secession of the Ukraine from Poland, many of the themes of the 1590s were repeated even more strongly.[10] The military dependence of the Commonwealth upon the cossacks in time of foreign war grew until it was absolute, as wars, with Turkey in particular, escalated and the central Polish state weakened. The crown continued attempts to create a stable cossack register, separating loyal from disloyal, controlled from uncontrolled, cossacks. But the registers were undermined—and ultimately virtually destroyed—by the foreign wars and the need for troops. At the same time the splits among the cossacks, exacerbated by the process of registration, deepened. Official cossacks increased their privileges, as the efforts of magnates to force others into serfdom became steadily more tenacious. These divisions, embryonic class divisions, underlay the ultimate destiny of the Ukraine, for they led the gentry cossack leader Bohdan Khmelnitsky to rely more on foreign alliances than on mass insurgency in his final war against Poland.[11]

The politicization of the cossacks also increased and, as in the 1590s, proceeded primarily in religious terms. The reaction to the Union drew the cossacks ever more firmly into association with the

Orthodox Church, and in the 1620s cossack groups took on military defense of the Orthodox brotherhoods as one of their purposes; to this end they used the government's military dependence on them as leverage, refusing service in time of war until guarantees of Orthodox autonomy were made. The death of Sigismund in 1632 signalled a renewed Ukrainian campaign for religious rights in which the Ukrainian senators presented a united front, with the cossacks and the Ukrainian population, for Orthodox rights. Impending war with Muscovy forced the new King Wladyslaw to concede on the religious issue. Cossack committment to Orthodoxy by no means proceeded steadily, however. Well into the seventeenth century observers took seriously the possibility of cossack alliances with Moslem powers. Certainly individual cossack leaders occasionally conducted negotiations with Turkey for joint action against Poland or Muscovy, and that these consistently failed may have had more to do with Turkish than with cossack reluctance.[12]

However, the cossacks' increasing identification with the Orthodox cause greatly increased their ability to transcend class divisions, both within the cossack groups and between cossacks and other Ukrainians. The rise of the Orthodox brotherhoods greatly strengthened the town–cossack alliance, which was transitory and fragmented in the 1590s. The peasant–cossack alliance was also intensified by Orthodox religious commitment, and by the growth of cossack strength itself.

Peasant support became steadily more crucial to cossack strategy. In the 1620s the cossacks could threaten the Poles with armies in excess of one hundred thousand; and the cossacks' autonomous control over the steppe Ukraine in time of mobilization became more widespread and more solid in the first half of the seventeenth century.[13] But the peasant–cossack alliance continued unstable because of the frequent "sell-out" agreements in which cossack hetmans agreed to accept privileged status for a relatively small group of cossacks in exchange for peace and the return of the "rabble" to bound labor.[14]

The cossack defeats were hastened not only by this difference in privilege, but also by the continuing cossack unclarity about war aims which we met in the 1590s. Cossack leadership, until after 1650, remained focused on winning concessions for cossacks from the Polish government, not on conquering any permanent area of independence—geographical, social or political—for Ukrainians. Neither the religious cause nor the cossacks' own desire for autonomy was sufficient to support a Ukrainian independence movement strong enough to resist Muscovite expansionism after the original Khmelnitsky rebellion.

These instances of continuity between the 1590s and 1650s should not imply that there was nothing new in the Ukraine. Muscovite power was a large new factor, felt from the first years of the seventeenth century when tsar pretenders in the Ukraine stimulated cossack intervention into Muscovy. Another important new factor was that the Zaporozhian sich became more often the headquarters of unregistered, defiant cossacks, the registered staying in royal forts. Furthermore, as magnate economic power became more established in the Ukraine, the losers in peasant–cossack revolts began to flee to Muscovy, to the region of the upper Donets basin (near modern Kharkov) in large numbers, thus establishing an internal base for Ukrainian annexation by Muscovy.

Nevertheless, the fundamental trajectory of cossack–Ukrainian–Polish relations was already established by the 1590s. Not only the internal but even the large external factors—the military threats to Poland, the economic drive for Ukrainian agricultural lands and produce—had arisen over a period of decades during the sixteenth, even the fifteenth, centuries. And the cossack response, too, arose from patterns of organization, self-image and leadership well-established by the beginning of the seventeenth century.

The cossacks, a relatively small group in world-historical terms, were at the center of some of the largest changes in early-modern history: Turkey's decline, Poland's eventual complete destruction, and Muscovy's annexation of its most important colonial territory—indeed, the territory which enabled it to become a great world power—the Ukraine. The cossacks were also participants in the process by which eastern Europe was confirmed in a status of subordination to a capitalist industrial western Europe. The contrast between the great changes and the small cossack groups should not, however, contribute to a view of the cossacks as pawns, actors reading from a script written by others even outside the Ukraine.

The cossacks were both objects and subjects of Ukrainian and even European history. It seems useful now to return to that two-sided view of the cossacks in summarizing their significance and achievements in the sixteenth century.

The preceding narrative of the 1590s uprisings provides much evidence of the reactive role of the cossacks: As mercenaries, they were reacting to pressures from many great state powers. As Ukrainian settlers, they were reacting without conscious plan to an offensive by others, particularly Polish-Lithuanian magnates, to colonize the steppe. As a military brotherhood, their shifting degree of autonomy was conditioned by international diplomatic and military struggles between Poland, Muscovy, the Holy Roman Empire, Turkey, and their client states. The cossacks had no articulate political nor national goals, and even their religious identity was a response to a movement outside their organization, an identity attributed to them by the non-cossack Orthodox. They did not consider themselves leaders of "Ukrainians," nor did they display any consistent sense of responsibility to any social group.

Furthermore, to the extent that the cossacks were initiators of events, they do not easily fit the usual conception of history makers because their motives were so personal. Their uprisings, as their banditry, were motivated primarily by search for personal profit, privilege or aggrandizement; or by defense of privileges they had held. It would, however, be a simplistic and inaccurate view of politics to assume that having personal, selfish motives predominant is somehow in contradistinction with being a political actor. As we pointed out above, people rarely feel economic forces or political desires or even nationalist passions in the abstract; rather these are formed in connection with personal passions, towards kin and friends, towards personal security and gain. Rebels learn about justice in defending their own rights against personally damaging attacks. To view the cossacks correctly thus requires revising some conventional concepts of leadership. To say that they were the leaders of Ukrainians does not mean that they knew what was good for the people and then convinced the people of that. Rather, the Cossacks' greatest leadership achievements came when they were taught by others what was needed, and put into positions of leadership almost involuntarily.

It was the cossacks' fighting ability that made them desirable as leaders. Indeed, it was their banditry, even their most greedy and brutal piracy, that made them candidates for political/national leadership. However "low" their motives and however brutal their form of "self-government," what was crucial to the Ukraine's further history, and most definitely not determined by outside forces, was the cossacks' success at defending autonomous space. The existence of the Zaporozhian sich, and later other centers of "free" cossack activity, was an essential condition for the development of opposition to Polish domination. Nothing could have predicted, no script prescribed, the cossacks' ability to hold this space.

Ironically for Poland, the cossacks' very success at defying state control strengthened the cossacks militarily and made them more desirable as a striking force for the Polish army. The Polish need for them then further strengthened the cossacks, their self-confidence spiralling upwards.

Through ability to maintain their autonomous space, military prowess and assertiveness in demanding liberties, the cossacks frequently created dual-power situations, to use the classic terms of history of revolutions. In other words, the cossacks, consciously or not, periodically created alternative power centers to that of the central government. In both the Kosinsky and Nalivaiko rebellions there were moments in which many nonbelligerent Ukrainians looked to the cossacks as much as to Cracow for the maintenance of order. It was the cossacks' military force, not moral nor political pretensions, which gave them that power. The comparative study of revolutions shows the vital importance of the creation of a credible alternative to the success of movements that try to challenge "legitimate" governments. Without that credibility, without the ability to convince others that there is a good chance of winning, no amount of discontent is adequate to create an effective insurgency. Of course, the weakness of the legitimate government contributed significantly to the credibility of the cossacks' challenge. But the challenges would not have been made were it not for the "selfish," individual motives of the cossack bandits.

In such a context, even the cossacks' victims became their supporters. The kind of support that was operative was not moral approval, friendly feelings or political comradeship, but respect. There is a subtle but substantial difference between respect and fear. The respect would not have been forthcoming had the cossacks' looting and mercenary activity been totally indiscriminate. There would have been no reason to support the cossacks had the cossacks not protected their friends and punished their enemies. Above all the cossacks made rebellion a reasonable risk, because their control of the Zaporozhe provided a possible escape should there be a temporary government military victory.

Through the considerable influence they gained in the Ukraine, the cossacks were directly responsible for some of the major transformations of that region. They not only contributed to the weakening of the Polish central government, but they were one of the largest single factors in exposing that weakness internationally. They contributed more than any other social group to changing the very meaning of the word Ukraine—from a general descriptive term, *ukraina*, borderland, to a proper noun, denoting a unique area. They then helped give substance to the embryonic national identity of the people who lived there. By the early seventeenth century cossacking was perhaps the leading connotation in the popular understanding of what went on in the Ukraine. The cossacks did not alone create the Ukrainian nationality, but they contributed greatly to identifying the Ukraine as a unique and potentially independent region.

This transformation of the Ukraine into a nation was also conditioned by the cossack form of organization. The brotherhood model, albeit a military-mercenary rather than a political form, was a communal form that was open to expansion. It might be described as a network of connections and loyalties in between kinship and nation. In the movement towards national consciousness, the cossacks provided a crucial step in expanding beyond their core of full-time "professional" bandits and frontiersmen to include peasants with families, part-time fighters who also worked the land to earn a living. Thus there appeared cossack women and children, and whole communities which reproduced themselves, making cossackness hereditary, one of the requirements of nationality. The snowballing of the cossack groups in times of rebellion, and their spreading reputation even in peacetime, provided a point of identity for people who were neither kin nor neighbors. Clearly other conditions were necessary for this identity to become "national," such as religion and language. The cossack brotherhood offered symbolic connective tissue, however, essential to the new national organism. Furthermore, the brotherhood developed a rough model of self-government that provided rudimentary training in leadership and mechanisms for collective decision-making.

The cossack influence pushed the Ukrainians towards a new group identity, but at the same time limited the political content of and strategy for the group's development. At an early stage, the cossack brotherhood stimulated a "national" identification, but ultimately the cossacks' continuing self-identification as a military group held back a drive for national autonomy. Mercenary activity, after all, hardly reinforces national patriotism. Ultimately, under Muscovite rule, it was the cossacks' identification as a military brotherhood that allowed them to be converted into a branch of the Imperial Russian army, losing all their autonomy and ability to lead a Ukrainian independence struggle. Even before this, it was their military organization, and subordination under a single hetman, that brought them into Muscovy in the first place. Furthermore, their military organization held back their development of a model for a state structure. Their radas emphasized extreme centralization of leadership, with little delegated authority; offered representation only to fighters, and rewarded military exploits over diplomatic or administrative achievements. They retained a narrow range of jurisdiction, leaving issues of the social relations of agriculture, for example, largely unquestioned. In general the cossacks' primary interest in fighting offered them little incentive to develop a political program and social ideology for their "people."

Indeed, not only was the cossacks' social and political program negligible, it lagged behind that of other groups in their society. Certainly the Polish nobility had a more developed sense of the kind of state and economy that would benefit its interests, and of the nature of threats to those interests. Even the peasantry identified its class interests as the prevention or abolition of serfdom, for example, in other words, a structural change. The cossacks continued to seek only individual exemptions and waivers of oppressive practices.

The cossacks' social program and self-understanding also lagged behind their own actions. To some extent, despite their machismo and bravado, this lag reflected an underestimation of themselves. They entirely failed to conceptualize their relation to the peasant masses who followed them, could not change their military strategy to accomodate and use these followers, and could not even appreciate the great strength that these mass armies might bring them. They could not benefit from their own supporters. They frequently failed to call upon even the passive loyalty of followers, to reward their supporters, to pay any regard to those outside the brotherhood. They often withdrew from confrontations they might have won. Even Bohdan Khmelnitsky fought several years before forming the intention of actually seceding from Polish rule.

The cossacks' limitations in political vision must be seen as reflecting their corporate view of society. They conceived of themselves as one social group, or estate, fighting for a place in a society composed of several such estates in balance, not a nation composed of citizens. The fact that they were only "primitive" rebels, in Hobsbawm's terms, means not only that they lacked a modern individualist view of government and politics, but that they had an alternative view. Their very successes in creating and defending an autonomous area reinforced this backward-looking ideology. Surely they could not have anticipated an era in which nation states would come to dominate even southeastern Europe.

Yet while cossack activities at first accelerated the development of Ukrainian nationalism, their country was not one of those able to achieve independence. Their power to disrupt, even to destroy, one kingdom only left them absorbed by another. Had they been more purposive in a quest for independence, might it have been different? This is of course an ahistorical question—we have just argued some of the reasons they were incapable of leading such a quest or even forming such an aspiration. Suspending this historical skepticism for a moment, one would still have to answer in the negative. The powers with which the cossacks were contending were very strong. And above all they were trapped in an enormous irony stemming from the nature of their country: their great influence was in part owing to the economically rich potential of their land, and that richness, which would have made it easily viable as an independent nation, also made Moscow's hold on it tenacious. Particularly as Russia moved towards its own export agriculture and then industrialism, the Ukraine's fertility and mineral resources made it the very heart of the Russian economy.

One might ask a similar question about what might have happened if the cossacks had been more systematic in seeking to destroy serfdom. (And again, to consider the question we must think a bit ahistorically, forgetting for the moment the reasons that the cossacks did not try to do this.) Here the economic determinists would say, of course, that nothing could have been different. The pull of the market, combined with the fertility of the Ukraine, made intensified labor exploitation inevitable. I have already made numerous criticisms of this thesis—that the evidence for the pull of the foreign grain market on the Ukraine is not definitive, that intensified labor exploitation might have occurred in many ways, that actual serfdom in the Ukraine was tenuous and that many local, specific patterns of class, social and cultural relations affected its outcome. Had the cossacks been even slightly more conscious of their power as peasant leaders, it seems possible that events might have turned out differently. The cossacks were able to mobilize extremely large forces by sixteenth-century standards. Their social banditry took consonant symbolic forms, travelled the same frequency, so to speak, with the discontent of tens of thousands. Their communicative speed and range could call up giant choruses of support. Is it possible that a system of small freeholding could have installed itself in the Ukraine? Or would the expropriation of the magnates have led to their replacement by a cossack landowning elite?

No definitive answer to these questions arises from the evidence. It is in the nature of social movements that elements of unpredictability cannot be eliminated from them, or from historians' explanations of them. Yet, that such speculations appear at all attests to the power and potential power embodied in the cossack groups. We have tried in the preceding narrative and analysis to suggest the sources of that power, its drawing together of many discontents among the Ukrainian population. It is deceptively easy to think one has adequately defined the cossacks through categorizations such as mercenaries, rebels, social bandits, frontiersmen. Their actual activity, however, breaks through these categories, creating a spirit and moments of possibility in the Ukraine that were greater than the sum of these separate aspects. No contemporaries, not even the cossacks, appreciated specifically and precisely what these possibilities were. Yet the heroism attributed to the cossacks in the romantic and, later, the nationalist folklore about them suggests that, in unspecific imprecise forms, it was just these possibilities that the cossacks symbolized—possibilities for a free, prosperous and independent existence for the Ukrainians. Though unrealized, these aspirations were an operative force in Ukrainian history. The cossacks' ability to symbolize them was a central part of their historical significance. Their romanticized reputation, thus, is as much a part of their historical contribution as their actions.

Notes

Because the bibliography is subdivided, the first reference to any items in the notes will be marked as follows, in order to help readers find the full citation quickly: (Ch) means the item is listed among "Contemporary Chronicles and Letters; (D) means the item is listed among "Collections of Documents." References without marks can be found in the section on secondary works if a full citation is not given in the notes.

1. THE LAND

1. Frank Friedeberg Seeley, "Russia and the Slave Trade," p. 126.
2. Although this view is not unchallenged, particularly in Soviet historiography. My own description of nomadism is influenced by S. E. Tolybekov, "O Patriarkhalno-Feodalnykh Otnosheniakh u Kochevykh Narodov," p. 77.
3. Perry Anderson, *Passages from Antiquity to Feudalism*, pp. 219–25.
4. Pierre Chevalier, *Discourse of the Original, Countrey, Manners, Government and Religion of the Cossacks . . .* (Ch), p. 19.
5. Seeley, p. 127. On the importance of nomadism as an influence in east-Slavic society and culture, see Henryk Łowmianski, "The Russian Peasantry," p. 105.
6. William Hardy McNeill, *Europe's Steppe Frontier 1500–1800*, p. 4.

2. THE PEOPLE

1. Quoted in M. Chubaty, "The Ukrainian and Russian Conceptions of the History of Eastern Europe," 1: 11.
2. See my historiographical essay in this volume.
3. George W. Simpson, "The Names 'Rus,' 'Russia,' 'Ukraine,' and Their Historical Background," p. 14.
4. Nicholas L. Freischyn–Chirovsky, *Old Ukraine*, pp. 1–2; Simpson, "Names," pp. 15–16.

5. Estimates of Ukrainian population in the medieval and early-modern periods have been controversial (see Chapter 4, n. 12) and inaccurate. It was in the interests of many settlers to avoid the tax-collector, who was the census-taker. On the basis of 1545 and 1552 revenue records, historian Vladimirsky-Budanov estimated that 34,000 people lived in the Ukraine then. Even if twentieth-century historian Baranovich is correct that this must be an underestimate, there was still a sparse population in this area of 277,000 square miles (area is that of the contemporary Ukraine). See M. F. Vladimirsky-Budanov, "Naselenie Yugo-Zapadnoi Rossii ot Poloviny XIII do Poliviny XV Veka," Part 7, vol. 2 (1886), p. 33; and A. I. Baranovich, "Naselenie Predstepnoi Ukrainy v XVI v.," pp. 199–210.

6. W. E. D. Allen, *The Ukraine*, p. 66.

7. A. I. Baranovich, *Ukraina Nakanune Osvoboditelnoi Voiny Serediny XVII v.* pp. 21–26; A. Ya. Efimenko, *Ocherki Istorii Pravoberezhnoi Ukrainy*, pp. 15–22.

8. Freischyn-Chirovsky, pp. 158, 202.

9. Ibid., pp. 158, 174 ff., 198 ff., and 200 ff.; McNeill, p. 22; C. Max Kortepeter, *Ottoman Imperialism During the Reformation*, p. 17.

10. Baranovich, *Ukraina*, p. 67; A. O. Turtsevich, *Russkie Krestiane pod Vladychestvom Litvy i Polshi*, pp. 10–36; Mykhailo Hrushevsky, *Istoria Ukrainskavo Kozachestva* 1: 335–36; V. O. Holobutsky, *Zaporozhskoe Kazachestvo*, p. 96.

11. Baranovich, *Ukraina*, p. 67; Turtsevich, pp. 36–37.

12. Turtsevich, pp. 14–15.

13. M. K. Liubavsky, "Nachalnaya Istoria Malorusskovo Kazachestva," pp. 234–35.

14. Hrushevsky, loc. cit.

3. THE RULERS

1. Kortepeter, *Ottoman Imperialism*, Chapter 1.

2. C. M. Kortepeter, "Gazi Giray II, Khan of the Crimea, and Ottoman Policy in Eastern Europe and the Caucasus, 1588-94," pp. 140–43.

3. McNeill, pp. 16–22.

4. Bohdan Baranowski, *Chłop Polski w Walce z Tatarami*, pp. 9–12; Kortepeter, *Ottoman Imperialism*, pp. 32–33, 57.

5. Baranovich, *Ukraina*, pp. 124–25.

6. Robert William Seton-Watson, *A History of the Roumanians from Roman Times to the Completion of Unity*, p. 59; Oscar Halecki, *Borderlands of Western Civilization*, p. 159.

7. Perry Anderson, *Lineages of the Absolutist State*, p. 279.

8. This interpretation is indebted to three works by P. Skwarczynski: "The Problem of Feudalism in Poland up to the Beginning of the 16th Century;" "Poland and Lithuania;" and "The Constitution of Poland before the Partitions."

9. Le Comte Michel Tyszkiewicz, ed., *Documents Historiques sur l'Ukraine et ses Relations Avec le Pologne, la Russie et la Suede (1569-1769)* (D), ##3–4.

10. J. Siemieński, "Constitutional Conditions in the Fifteenth and Sixteenth Centuries," 1: 432.

11. A. Zanaczkowski, "Cadres Structurels de la Noblesse," *Annales ESC* (Jan.-Feb. 1968), pp. 88–102.

12. The internal structure of the *szlachta* raises the question of feudalism in Poland. In general there have been two extreme and rather simple opinions on this question. Those using the older paradigm of feudalism, based particularly on the French experience, emphasized legal stratification within the landowning class, the fief system of land tenure, as the essence of the system. In other words, feudalism required hierarchical chains of dependence and loyalty within a landowning ruling class which were recognized by legal ranks. This requirement did not pertain in the Rzecz Pospolita. Absolute land tenure dominated there, and between 1561 and 1588 the Diet transformed remaining conditional landholdings into allodial tenure. The undivided authority of landowners over their estates tended to create virtually independent principalities. At the other extreme has been a definition of feudalism as a universal precapitalist stage of economic development, a peasant society with a landowning class extracting an unearned surplus. Rodney H. Hilton defined feudalism as "a system of economic and social relationships based on the legalized and institutionalized claim of a ruling group to a substantial part of the surplus of peasant production," in his "Peasant Society, Peasant Movements and Feudalism in Medieval Europe," p. 71. Soviet Marxists particularly use this definition, but so do some non-Marxists. See, for example, Rushton Coulbourn, ed., *Feudalism in History*. A useful interpretation of definitions of feudalism can be found in Łowmianski, "Russian Peasantry," pp. 102–9.

In the past decades, the question of feudalism in Poland has been addressed with much greater complexity by Polish historians, notably Witold Kula in his *Economic Theory of the Feudal System*. Kula has argued a fuller definition that is not exclusively juridical but also not tautologous, as those emphasizing simply a "precapitalist form" tend to be. He has added to the definition specifications including the presence of extra-economic coercion; the lack of influence of a goods or labor market; a low level of productive forces. Above all he has tried to see the system from the perspective of its laborers, "a corporate system in which the basic unit of production is a large landed estate surrounded by the small plots of peasants who are dependent on the former both economically and juridically, and who have to furnish various services to the lord and submit to his authority".

Compelling as is Kula's argument, the scope of this study and above all the evidence available do not permit its critical examination with respect to the Ukraine. But my arguments here do not rest on such definitions or abstractions. I have attempted to specify the relevant social, legal, and economic relationships without judgment on the propriety of the term "feudalism." In any case, the events surrounding the cossacks in the sixteenth century show that, however one names it, the Ukrainian situation was unstable and rapidly metamorphizing.

4. THE SIXTEENTH-CENTURY CRISIS

1. I will not offer here an analysis of the origins of the cossacks, which has been done elsewhere. See reference notes to Chapter 5.

2. Immanuel Wallerstein, *The Modern World-System;* Marian Małowist, "Problem Genezy Podziału Gospodarczego Europe w XV-XVII w."; idem, "The Economic and Social Development of the Baltic Countries from the Fifteenth to the Seventeenth Centuries," pp. 177–89; idem, "Poland, Russia and Western Trade in the Fifteenth and Sixteenth Centuries," pp. 26–39; idem, "La commerce de la Baltique et le problème des luttes sociales eh Pologne aux XVe et XVIe siècles," pp. 125–46. It is also the interpretation offered by Leonid Żytkowicz in his "Okres Gospodarki Folwarczno-Pańszczyznianej (XVI-XVII w.)," in Stefan Inglot, ed., *Historia Chłopów Polskich* (Częstochowa: 1970), 1: 247–308, 393–397; and in idem, "The Peasant's Farm and the Landlord's Farm in Poland from the Sixteenth to the Middle of the Eighteenth Century," pp. 135–54. The same interpretation is used by Karl von Loewe, "Commerce and Agriculture in Lithuania, 1400-1600," pp. 23–35; Jerome Blum, "The Rise of Serfdom in Eastern Europe," pp. 807–36; Mykhailo Hrushevsky, *Istoria Ukrainy-Rusy;* Aleksander Jabłonowski, "Handel Ukrainy w XV Wieku," *Athenum*, 2 (1895); Stanisław Hoszowski, "The Polish Baltic Trade in the Fifteenth–Eighteenth Centuries," pp. 117–54, esp. pp. 121–22; Henry Kamen, *The Iron Century;* Frances Dvornik, *The Slavs in European History and Civilization* pp. 340–41; Andrzej Wyczański, "Tentative Estimate of Polish Rye Trade in the Sixteenth Century," pp. 119–31.

3. This is argued, notably, by Wallerstein, Małowist, von Loewe, Hoszowski, and Kamen.

4. This is argued, notably, by Wallerstein.

5. For elucidations of this phrase, see Rod Aya, "The Present as 'Jumbo History,' " *Race and Class*, 17 (Autumn 1975), pp. 179–88; Keith Thomas, "Jumbo History," *New York Review of Books* (April 17, 1975), pp. 26–28.

6. This definition is taken from Raymond Williams, *Keywords: A Vocabulary of Culture and Society* (N.Y.: 1976), pp. 87–91.

7. See my historiographical essay in this volume.

8. This "general crisis" is variously dated: for example, McNeill calls it 1570 to 1650; Hobsbawm and Trevor-Roper consider it coincident with the seventeenth century, in their essays collected in Trevor Aston's *Crisis in Europe;* Aston himself dates it 1560 to 1660.

9. McNeill, p. 58; Małowist, "Commerce," p. 129.

10. The phrase "second serfdom" was first used by Friedrich Engels in

his "The Peasant War in Germany." The second serfdom may, however, have been in continuity with an interrupted process of enserfment which had been in train in eastern Europe since the first western migrations there. See R. E. F. Smith, *The Enserfment of the Russian Peasantry*, particularly introd. by R. H. Hilton and Smith, pp. 9–19.

11. See particularly previous citations to Wallerstein, Małowist, Kamen, Blum, Hrushevsky, Żytkowicz; and Anderson, *Passages* and *Lineages*.

12. Skwarczynski, "Poland and Lithuania," p. 380. Until recently most historians agreed that the Ukrainian lands were almost empty of settled population from the thirteenth through the sixteenth centuries; see Baranovich, *Ukraina*, pp. 17–19; Élie Borschak, *La Légende Historique de l'Ukraine*, p. 11. This was an exaggeration perpetuated, in part, by the official Polish chroniclers to support the image of the Poles as civilizers of the Slavs; see Baranovich, "Naselenie," p. 198. However, the low population estimates were also accepted by leading Ukrainian and Great Russian historians; see, respectively, Hrushevsky, *Istoria Ukrainy-Rusy*, 7: 41–47, and V. O. Kluchevsky, *Kurs Russkoi Istorii* 3: 111. They were first challenged by the Ukrainian M. F. Vladimirsky-Budanov in his "Naselenie Yugo-Zapadnoi Rossii ot Poloviny XIII do Poloviny XV Veka." The challenge was reinforced by more evidence published in the 1950s by Baranovich in both the above-mentioned works.

13. Skwarczynski, "Poland and Lithuania," p. 377; Baranovich, "Naselenie," p. 209.

14. Baranovich, *Ukraina*, pp. 52–53; Efimenko, *Ocherki Istorii Pravoberezhnoi Ukrainy*, pp. 29–31; I. I. Lappo, *Velikoe Kniazhestvo Litovskoe* 1: 255–56; Iu. M. Grossman, "Razvitie Folvarochnovo Proizvodstva v Russkom i Belzkom Voevodstvakh vo Vtoroi Polovine XVI—Pervoi Polovine XVII v.," in *Ezhegodnik po Agrarnoi Istorii Vostochnoi Evropy 1965 g.* (Moscow: 1970), pp. 71–79.

15. V. B. Antonovych, *O Proiskhozhdenii Shliakhetskikh Rodov v Yugo-Zapadnoi Rossii*, pp. 4–8; Antonovych, introd. to *Soderzhanie Aktov o Kozakakh 1500–1648*, Part 3, vol. 10 of *Arkhiv Yugo-Zapadnoi Rossii*, p. liv; George Vernadsky, *Russia at the Dawn of the Modern Age*, p. 199; Małowist, "Commerce," pp. 141–43.

16. Skwarczynski, "Poland and Lithuania," p. 378.

17. Ibid., p. 380.

18. Baranovich, *Ukraina*, pp. 67–71.

19. Antoni Mączak, "The Social Distribution of Landed Property in Poland from the Sixteenth to the Eighteenth Century," p. 461.

20. A. I. Baranovich, *Zaliudnennia Volynskovo Voevodstva v Pershii Polovini XVII St.*, pp. 23–25.

21. Indeed, a century before our period, in 1459, an earlier Ostrozhsky had tried to make the office of *voevoda* hereditary, with the title of prince, but he had not then had the power to force the Diet to accept his proposal. Ostrozhsky, "Monumentum pro comitiis generalibus Regni, 1467," in *Starodawne Prawa Polskiego Pomniki* (Cracow: 1878), vol. 5.

22. Skwarczynski, "Problem of Feudalism," pp. 292–310; Siemieński, 1: 416–40.

23. An early twentieth-century Russian interpretation of this agrarian reform argued that it was directed against the nobility. This logic focused primarily on the fact that the land survey gave the Grand Duke some authority over nobles' lands; see V. I. Picheta, *Agrarnaya Reforma Sigizmunda-Avgusta v Litovsko-Russkom Gosudarstve*, pp. 285 ff. However, studies since then agree in the main that it is more correctly seen as part of the seigneurial reaction, benefiting the development of aristocratic demesnes. See D. L. Pokhylevich, *Krestiane Belorussii i Litvy v XVI-XVII vv.*; idem, "O Reaktsionnom Kharaktere Agrarnoi Reformy Sigizmunda-Avgusta v Litovskom Gosudarstve," *Uchenie Zapiski Yaroslavskovo Pedinstitute*, 7 (Yaroslavl: 1945), pp. 1–42; and Jerzy Ochmański, "La Grande Réforme Agraire en Lituanie et en Ruthénie Blanche au XVIe Siècle," pp. 329–30.

24. Baranovich, *Ukraina*, pp. 32–33.

25. Małowist, "Commerce," p. 139.

26. von Loewe, pp. 27 ff.; Baranovich, *Ukraina*, pp. 72–75.

27. A. O. Turtsevich, *Russkie Krestiane pod Vladychestvom Litvy i Polshi*, passim; Peter I. Lyashchenko, *History of the National Economy of Russia*, p. 260.

28. Turtsevich, passim; Baranovich, *Ukraina*, p. 72.

29. Bohdan Baranowski, *Powstania Chłopskie na Ziemiach Dawnej Rzeczypospolitej*, pp. 23–25; Turtsevich, ibid., passim.

30. Małowist, "Commerce," p. 134.

31. Turtsevich, passim; Baranovich, *Ukraina*, p. 72.

32. This pattern was characteristic of all Poland–Lithuania; see Andrzej Kamiński, "Neo-Serfdom in Poland–Lithuania," pp. 262–63, for references on this point.

33. Skwarczynski, "Poland and Lithuania," p. 379; F. C. Spooner, "The Economy of Europe 1559–1609," in *New Cambridge Modern History*, ed. R. B. Wernham (Cambridge: University Press, 1968), 322–23; Wallerstein, passim.

34. Turtsevich, passim; Baranovich, *Ukraina*, p. 72.

35. Baranovich, *Ukraina*, p. 71.

36. The standard plot was called *sluzhba* in Lithuania, *dvorishch* in Volynia and Polesia, *osedlyi dym* in the southwestern Ukraine. Turtsevich, pp. 12–13.

37. Ibid., pp. 20–22; *Akty Vilenskoi Arkh. Kommissia (D)*, passim.

38. Małowist, "Commerce" pp. 141–43.

39. Skwarczynski, "Poland and Lithuania," p. 380.

40. Turtsevich, pp. 59–63; Pokhylevich, *Krestiane*, pp. 96–98; Aleksander Tarnawski, *Działalność Gospodarcza Jana Zamoyskiego*, p. 361; S. Śreniowski, *Zbiegostwo Chłopów w Dawnej Polsce jako Zagadnienie Ustroju Społecznego*, chap. 6; Inglot, 25–27, 401–6.

41. Tarnawski, *Działalność*, p. 361.

42. Ibid.; Pokhylevich, *Krestiane*, pp. 96–98; Turtsevich, p. 63.

43. Małowist, "Commerce," p. 132.

44. These figures are for the early seventeenth century and are taken from Skwarczynski, "Poland and Lithuania," p. 377. For population comparison between east and west Europe, also see Smith, p. 4.

45. Here the evidence is less clear, for there are good records only from older, well-ordered estates, rarely in the Ukraine.

46. Freischyn-Chirovsky, p. 169. Wyczański, "Tentative Estimate," p. 120, gives a slightly different figure for rye (36% in 1560–70) but does not compare it to other grains.

47. Kamiński, pp. 256–57.

48. Żytkowicz, "Peasant's Farm," p. 144.

49. Baranovich, *Ukraina*, p. 56; Nikolai Sementovsky, *Starina Malorossiiskaya, Zaporozhskaya i Donskaya*, p. 58. A dispute within Ukrainian historiography about whether these urban rights are better called Magdeburg privileges, or described as a *sui generis* Ukrainian form, is mainly ideological in nature, concerning how much influence is attributed to western cultural and institutional forms. F. P. Shevchenko, a somewhat anti-Stalinist Soviet Ukrainian historian, called them Magdeburg privileges, in his *Politychni ta Ekonomichni Zviazky Ukrainy z Rossieiu v Seredyni XVIII St.*, pp. 29, 270; the opposite is maintained by A. I. Pashuk, *Sud i Sudochystvo na Livoberezhnii Ukraini v XVII-XVIII St.*, pp. 75–76, and V. D. Otamanovsky, "Razvitie Gorodskovo Stroya na Ukraine v XIV-XVIII vv. i Magdeburgskoe Pravo," pp. 122–35.

50. Baranovich, *Ukraina*, pp. 56–60; *Arkhiv Yugo-Zapadnoi Rossii (D)*, pt. 8, vol. 5, ##82; 90, 96.

51. Dvornik, p. 339.

52. Anderson, *Passages*, p. 254; Freischyn-Chirovsky, pp. 148–49; Baranovich, *Ukraina*, p. 100; M. Hrushevsky, *Barskoe Starostvo*, pp. 262–63.

53. Baranovich, ibid., pp. 104; Hrushevsky, ibid., pp. 261–63. Aristocratic control over the towns grew unevenly, however. During these years some towns were still *gaining* privileges. See Hrushevsky, ibid., pp. 261–63, and Baranovich, ibid., pp. 56–60. Religion sometimes mediated town-gentry relations. For example, in the western Ukraine, in towns that were mainly Polish and Catholic such as Lvov and Kamenets-Podolsk, burghers tended to be hostile to the surrounding Orthodox peasants and looked towards the Polish nobility as their protectors. Where town populations were predominantly Ruthenian and Orthodox, the opposite was the case: here Armenians and Jews tended to look more favorably upon aristocratic control to protect them from the united front of the Orthodox. Another factor complicating town–gentry relations was the difference between outright ownership and political control. Some magnates began to buy large parts of towns. For example, in Vladimir in 1629, 349 households belonged to the municipality, 52 to the bishop, and 44 to Prince Janush Vishnevetsky. In Kremenets in that year, out of a total of 1,224 households, 436 belonged to the

municipality, 169 to Jews, and 507 to the noble sheriff. See Baranovich, *Ukraina*, pp. 100-109. Outright ownership was a shortcut to political power, but it created situations in which the legal rights and duties of townspeople were different within single towns. Still, an overall tendency that placed towns on the defensive was unmistakable.

54. Hoszowski, "Polish Baltic Trade," pp. 121–22; Kamiński, p. 261 n.; Kamen, p. 221.

55. Kamen, pp. 58, 67, 212–14, 218; Marian Małowist, "The Problem of the Inequality of Economic Development in Europe in the Later Middle Ages," p. 27. The fact that the Ukraine was of course also one of those countries without easy access to the northern seas will be discussed later.

56. Hoszowski, "Polish Baltic Trade," p. 123; von Loewe, p. 31; Wyczański, "Tentative Estimate," passim.

57. Małowist, "Economic and Sovial Development."

58. S. Hoszowski, "The Revolution of Prices in Poland in the 16th and 17th Centuries," pp. 8, 11–12.

59. Kamiński, p. 259.

60. Ibid., pp. 256, 256n.; Anderson, *Passages*, pp. 258–59.

61. Hoszowski, "Revolution," pp. 8, 11–12. The reason for Lvov's higher rate of price rise was that it began its foreign-market role later than, for example, Danzig, which had shown higher rates of price increase in the sixteenth century, according to this interpreter.

62. von Loewe, p. 32.

63. Wallerstein, pp. 300 ff. and passim; also Kamen, p. 227. There is not, however, enough evidence yet compiled about the Ukraine to make a certain judgment about its position in this regard.

64. This phenomenon is neglected by Kamiński, a serious omission in his otherwise thorough critique of recent Polish historiography on neo-serfdom.

65. These religious factors will be discussed more fully later in this chapter.

66. Małowist, "Commerce," p. 131; Blum, p. 820; Małowist, "Poland, Russia and Western Trade," pp. 27–29; Kamen, p. 221; von Loewe, p. 27; Pokhylevich, "Dvizhenie Feodalnoi Zemelnoi Renty v Velikom Kniazhestve Litovskom v XV-XVI vv.," *Istorichiskie Zapiski*, 31 (1950), pp. 210–11. For this reason some Polish historians have credited the first stages of this transformation to domestic trade demands; for example, see Żytkowicz, "Peasant's Farm," p. 137; and for an earlier version of the argument, Pokhylevich, "Dvizhenie," pp. 208–9.

67. Żytkowicz, ibid., pp. 138, 138 n.

68. Anderson, *Passages*, p. 259; Małowist, "Commerce," p. 129.

69. Małowist, "Commerce," p. 130.

70. Ibid., passim.

71. Anderson, *Passages*, pp. 260–61; Małowist, "Poland, Russia and Western Trade," p. 31.

72. I am indebted to Anderson, *Lineages*, p. 269, for this observation.

73. Robert Brenner, "Agrarian Class Structure and Economic Development in Pre-Industrial Europe," p. 51; Smith, p. 4.

74. Malowist, "Commerce," pp. 141–43.

75. These three theoretical objections to the foreign-market explanation of early-modern European economic development have also appeared in controversies among Marxists. I am particularly indebted to Brenner's critique of Wallerstein.

76. Kliuchevsky, 3: 102; Maria Bogucka, "Towns in Poland and the Reformation," pp. 55–74.

77. M. Yuzefovich, "Predislovie," pp. xii and xv ff.

78. F. Nowak, "Sigismund III," in *Cambridge History of Poland*, ed. W. F. Reddaway, 1: 459; Baranovich, *Ukraina*, p. 111.

79. Baranovich, ibid., pp. 112–17; Yuzefovich, pp. xii and xv ff.

80. Not because he was against union, but because he clung to visions of a more complete union including the patriarchates of Constantinople and Muscovy and the Moldavian Orthodox Church; see Skwarczynski, "Poland and Lithuania, p. 389.

81. *Akty Yugo–Zapadnoi Rossii (D)*, 1: 280–89.

82. Baranovich, *Ukraina*, p. 118; Oscar Halecki, *From Florence to Brest (1439–1596)*, pp. 344–62.

83. Maurycy Horn, "Żydowski Ruch Osadniczy w Miastach Rusi Czerwonej do 1648 R., pp. 3–24.

84. Bernard Dov Weinryb, *The Jews of Poland*, p. 116.

85. N. P. Bykov, *Kniazia Ostrozhskie i Volyn*, p. 23; Weinryb, p. 129.

86. These percentages were probably exaggerations, since more Christian than Jewish settlers were likely to have been able to evade the tax collectors.

87. This is a high estimate. The best authority estimates only 150,000 Jews in the entire Commonwealth at the advent of Batory in 1576. See Salo Wittmayer Baron, *A Social and Religious History of the Jews, vol. 21, Poland–Lithuania 1500–1650*, 2nd ed. (New York: 1976), p. 207. However, the period 1576–1648 was one of enormous increase in the Jewish population of the Commonwealth, which rose from 2 percent of the total population in 1576 to 4.5 percent in 1648, when it reached 450,000. This was, of course, the period of greatest Jewish immigration from central Europe; inversely, the rapid increase in Jewish population supplied further evidence for the increasing commercialization of the Commonwealth economy.

88. Bykov, p. 24; Baranovich, *Ukraina*, p. 106.

89. Bykov, pp. 24–25; Freischyn-Chirovsky, p. 151; McNeill, p. 86.

90. Baron, pp. 140 ff.; Israel Cohen, *History of the Jews in Vilna*, p. 25.

91. Baron, pp. 106 ff. Note that this was also true in the West, notably in Spain, Germany and Italy, where artisans led pogroms in the late Middle Ages.

92. Cohen, pp. 22, 48–49; S. M. Dubnow, *History of the Jews in Russia and Poland*, 1:94. These restrictions were also found in France, Sicily and the Papal States in the same century.

93. Other "foreigners"—such as Greeks, Serbs, Armenians, Germans, Dutchmen, and even some Englishmen—also did this work. See McNeill, pp. 104, 130. However, we do not have evidence on Jews in these trades in the Ukraine specifically. Furthermore, Małowist has pointed out that the Baltic grain trade was controlled by the nobles, who kept urban merchants as their agents. Małowist, "Poland, Russia, and the Western Trade," pp. 30–31.

94. Israel Friedlaender, *The Jews of Russia and Poland* p. 74; Baron, pp. 122 ff.

95. *Pamiatniki* (1898) (D), ##9–11, gives three typical contracts from the year 1595.

96. Cohen, p. 21; Dubnow, 1:93.

97. Friedlaender, pp. 66–67.

98. Ibid., p. 64.

99. Dubnow, 1:95–96; Cohen, pp. 20–25.

100. In 1612, on the campaign to Moscow, there was even a special Jewish section among the Zaporozhians.

101. V. O. Holobutsky, *Zaporozhskoe Kazachestvo*, p. 226.

102. Friedlaender, p. 80.

5. FRONTIERSMEN: THE OPPORTUNITIES OF THE STEPPE

1. The best etymological accounts are given by Philip Longworth, *The Cossacks*, p. 344 n.; Gunther Stökl, *Die Entstehung des Kosakentums*, pp. 39–41; and O. Pritsak, "Etymolohia ta zmist nazvy Kosak," pp. 76–78.

2. For example, see Nikon Chronicle, *Polnoe Sobranie Russkikh Letopisei*, pp. 12:61 ff.; Dmytro Doroshenko, *History of the Ukraine*, p. 141; Stökl, pp. 53 ff.

3. Imperatorskoe Russkoe Istoricheskoe Obshchestvo, *Sbornik* 41:194–96; Liubavsky, p. 226.

4. See examples in Ivan M. Kamanin, "K Voprosu o Kozachestve do Bogdana Khmelnitskovo," pp. 60–61.

5. For example, in 1489 the Muscovite Prince complained to the Lithuanian Grand Duke that *cherkassy* had attacked Muscovite merchants on the Dnieper; in 1492 the Khan complained that *cherkassy* had looted a Tatar ship; in ibid.

6. E. J. Hobsbawm, *Primitive Rebels: Studies in Archaic Forms of Social Movement in the 19th and 20th Centuries*, and idem, *Bandits*.

7. Antoine Blok, "The Peasant and the Brigand: Social Banditry Reconsidered," and reply of Hobsbawm, in *Comparative Studies in Society and History*, 14 (Sept. 1972), pp. 494–502.

8. Quoted in D. I. Evarnitsky, *Istoria Zaporozhskikh Kozakov* (St. Petersburg; 1892), 1:1.

9. The best summary of Muscovite cossack patterns is Longworth's.

On the Ukrainian cossacks, see V. B. Antonovych, introd. to *Soderzhanie Aktov o Kozakakh 1500–1648 (D)*, pp. ii–xxv; Kamanin, "Voprosu o Kozachestve," pp. 67–69; N. I. Kostomarov, *Istoricheskie Monografii i Izsledovania*, 1:60–72; O. M. Apanovych, "Natsionalno-vyzvolni Viiny v Epochu Feodalizmu," pp. 29–38; I. D. Boiko, "Do Pytannia pro Derzhavnist Ukrainskoho Narodu v Period Feodalizmu," pp. 27–38.

10. E.g., V. B. Antonovych, *Besidy pro Chasy Kozatsky na Ukrainy.*

11. Kamanin, "Voprosu o Kozachestve,"

12. This distinction is well illuminated by the debate between I. L. Rudnytsky in his review of Longworth's book, "Study of Cossack History," *Slavic Review*, 31 (Dec. 1972), pp. 870–75, and Longworth in his response in *Slavic Review*, 33 (June 1974), pp. 411–16.

13. See L. J. D. Collins, "The Military Organization and Tactics of the Crimean Tatars during the Sixteenth and Seventeenth Centuries," pp. 258–9.

14. Blok, p. 499.

15. M. K. Liubavsky, "Nachalnaya Istoria Malorusskovo Kazachestva," pp. 224–27; Kamanin, "Voprosu o Kozachestve," pp. 59–63; Doroshenko, p. 142; *Soderzhamie Aktov*, pp. xxvi–xxvii.

16. Hobsbawm, *Bandits*, p. 19.

17. For contemporary understandings of this phenomenon, see *Listy Stanisława Żółkiewskiego, 1584–1623* (Ch) #60, p. 89; and W. Tomkiewicz, "O Składzie Społecznym i Etnicznym Kozaczyzny Ukrainnej na Przełomie XVI i XVII Wieku," pp. 248–60.

18. Hobsbawm, *Bandits*, p. 73.

19. Longworth, p. 345 n.

20. Apanovych, p. 37; Boiko, p. 30; Efimenko, *Ocherki Istorii Pravoberezhnoi Ukrainy*, p. 37; D. I. Evarnitsky, *Zaporozhe v Ostatkakh Stariny i Predaniakh Naroda* 1:199; F. P. Shevchenko, *Politychni ta Ekonomichni Zviazky Ukrainy z Rossieiu v Seredyni XVIII St.*, pp. 275 ff.

21. The nationalistic interpretations date from the nineteenth century, beginning with Kostomarov, and later in that century historians influenced by Ukrainian radical populism attempted to merge national and class interpretations. There is a dispute within Soviet historiography today, with the dominant position being that the cossacks were exclusively of the lower classes; see Holobutsky, *Zaporozhskoe Kozachestvo*, pp. 95–96; and K. Huslystyi and O. Apanovych, *Zaporozka Sich ta ii Progresyvna Rola v Istorii Ukrainskovo Narodu* (Kiev: 1954). See historiographical essay.

22. Imperatorskoe Russkoe Istoricheskoe Obshchestvo, *Sbornik* (D), 41:194–96; Dmitro Ivanovich Bagalei (Bahaliy), "Ocherki iz Istorii Kolonizatsii Stepnoi Okrainy Moskovskavo Gosudarstva," p. 75.

23. *Prawa Konstytucye y Przywileie; Krolestwá Polskiego, y Wielkiego Xięstwá Litewskiego* (D), 2:1345–46.

24. Evarnitsky, *Istoria*, 1:187.

25. Quoted in Tomkiewicz, p. 251.

26. Ibid.

27. *Listy Żółkiewskiego* (Ch), loc. cit.

28. Bagalei, chap. 3, passim.

29. *Żródła Dźiejowe: Pod Względem Geograficzno-statystycznym* (D), 22:423; Tomkiewicz, p. 253–54.

30. *Pisma Stanisława Żółkiewskiego* (Ch), pp. 317, 320, 332, for example.

31. *Arkhiv Yugo-Zapadnoi Rossii*, pt. 7, vol. 1, 308; *Zródła Dźiejowe* (D), 5:132; Hrushevsky, "Materialy do Istorii Kozatskykh Rukhiv 1590-kh rr.," (D), p. 5.

32. *Arkhiv Yugo-Zapadnoi Rossii*, pt. 7, vol. 2, #17, pp. 366–70.

33. Ludwik Boratyński, "Kozacy i Watykan," pp. 23–24; Tomkiewicz, pp. 248–51.

34. Quoted in Hrushevsky, *Istoria Ukrainskavo Kozachestva*, 1:347–48.

35. Efimenko, *Ocherki*, p. 38.

36. E.g., Lassota von Steblau, *Putevia Zapiski* (Ch), p. 39.

37. *Zherela do Istorii Ukrainy-Rusy* (D), 8, ##48, 90, 109, 114; Boratyński, p. 24.

38. Tomkiewicz, p. 255.

39. *Zherela*, 8, #31.

40. Tomkiewicz, p. 259; *Żródła Dźiejowe*, 20:151–64.

41. Krasinski (Ch), pp. 83–84.

42. Tomkiewicz, p. 259; *Żródła Dźiejowe*, 20:151–64.

43. The question of the ethnicity of the Ukrainian cossacks is controversial, bringing into play opposing national tendencies to make nationalist-political points. Thus Ukrainian historians outside the Soviet Union tend to emphasize the Ruthenian, sometimes called "Ukrainian", ethnic composition of the cossacks; for example, Lubomyr Wynar, "Birth of Democracy on the Dnieper River: Zaporozhian Kozakdom in the XVIIth Century," p. 46. Polish historians tend to emphasize the multinational character of the cossacks, for example, Tomkiewicz, pp. 248–60; or Zbigniew Wójcik, *Dzikie Pola w Ogniu*, p. 14.

44. Tomkiewicz, pp. 257–58.

6. WARRIORS: MILITARY ORGANIZATION AND TECHNIQUE

1. Except where otherwise noted, the descriptions of Tatar military technique are taken from Collins, "Military Organization."

2. Chevalier, *Discourse* (Ch), p. 16.

3. Guillaume le Vasseur Beauplan, "A Description of Ukraine . . . ," (Ch), 1:531–32; Chevalier (Ch), pp. 16–17. On the tabor, see also Wojskowy Instytut Historyczny, *Zarys Dziejów Wojskowości Polskiej do Roku 1864* (D), 2:72–73.

4. Chevalier, pp. 20–21; Beauplan, *Description de l'Ukranie* (Paris: 1861), pp. 105–9; Krasinski, pp. 20–21.

5. Chevalier, p. 21.
6. Krasinski, pp. 21–22.
7. Beauplan (Paris), p. 110.
8. Beauplan (Paris), pp. 105–12; Chevalier, pp. 19–23; Krasinski, pp. 21–24.
9. Mary Ann Clawson, "Early Modern Fraternalism and the Patriarchal Family," *Feminist Studies*, 6, #2 (Summer 1980), pp. 368–91.
10. Krasinski, Beauplan, Chevalier, passim.
11. Krasinski, p. 81.
12. Krasinski, passim.
13. Hrushevsky, "Materialy do Istorii Kozatskykh Rukhiv 1590-kh rr.," (D), pp. 4–6, and ##13–16; Kamanin, "Voprosu," pp. 84–95; Kamanin, "Materialy po Istorii Kozatskovo Zemlevladenia, 1494–1668," (D), ##3, #9, and p. 8; *Arkhiv Yugo-Zapadnoi Rossii*, pt. 7, vol. 1, pp. 86, 185 ff., 610; Vasil Domanitsky, "Kozachchina na Perelomi XVI-XVII Stoletii (1591–1603)," pp. 160–69.
14. Kamanin, "Materialy," #2.
15. Lassota (Ch), pp. 32–36.

7. THE REGISTER: DISCIPLINING THE UNRULY CHILD

1. *Sbornik Letopisei, Otnosiashchikhsia k Istorii Yuzhnoi i Zapadnoi Rusi* (D), p. 3; Kamanin, "K Voprosu," p. 8; Krasinski, p. 14.
2. Kamanin, loc. cit.
3. *Listy Żołkiewskiego*, introd. by J. T. Lubomirski, p. 20. At least one of the ransomed cossacks was a noble, so the king's action may have been a case of protecting his aristocracy.
4. *Akty . . . Yuzhnoi i Zapadnoi Rossii*, 1, #105.
5. Ibid., 2, p. 394; *Źródła Dziejowe*, 22, p. 418; *Arkhiv Yugo-Zapadnoi Rossii*, pt. 7, vol. 1, ##14–19, 84.
6. *Arkhiv Yugo-Zapadnoi Rossii*, pt. 3, vol. 1, pp. 4–6.
7. *Zherela*, 8, #34; Panteleimon Alexandrovich Kulish, *Materialy dlia Istorii Vozsoedinenia Rusi*, p. 58.
8. Hrushevsky, *Istoria Ukrainskavo Kozachestva*, 1:349–50, gives many examples.
9. *Sprawy Wojenne Króla Stefana Batorego*, vol. 11 of *Acta Historica Res Gestas Poloniae Illustrantia* (D), p. 61, #XLI.
10. *Akty . . . Yuzhnoi i Zapadnoi Rossii*, 2, #149, pp. 175–76.
11. Hrushevsky, *Istoria Ukrainskavo Kozachestva*, 1:197, 208; Hrushevsky, *Istoria Ukrainy-Rusy*, 7:144.
12. Antonovych, introd. to *Soderzhanie Aktov o Kozakakh*, p. xxviii; A. V. Storozhenko, *Stefan Batorii i Dneprovskie Kozaki, Izsledovania, Pamiatniki, Dokumenty i Zametki*, pp. 34–53; Edouard Kuntze, "Les Rapports de la Pologne avec le Saint-Siege a l'Epoque d'Etienne Bátory," p. 186.

13. Kulish, *Materialy*, #1.
14. Ibid., #6; Storozhenko, *Stefan Batorii*, p. 77–78.
15. Evarnitsky, *Istoria*, 1:2.
16. Hrushevsky, *Istoria Ukrainskavo Kozachestva*, 1:197–99; Kulish, *Materialy*, ##1–3.
17. *Arkhiv Yugo-Zapadnoi Rossii*, pt. 3, vol. 1, #6, p. 14.
18. Chevalier, *Discourse*, p. 3.
19. Kulish, loc. cit.
20. E.g., Kulish, Antonovych, Hrushevsky, Storozhenko, Holobutsky.
21. Hrushevsky, *Istoria Ukrainskavo Kozachestva*, 1:198; Storozhenko, *Stefan Batorii*, p. 74.
22. *Źródła Dziejowe*, 22:418; Konstanty Marian Górski, *Historya Piechoty Polskiej*, pp. 35–36.
23. Storozhenko, *Stefan Batorii*, p. 83.
24. Ibid., p. 261.
25. Antonovych, intro. to *Soderzhanie Aktov o Kozakakh*, p. xxxv.
26. Ibid., p. xxxvi; Storozhenko, *Stefan Batorii*, p. 119; Hrushevsky, *Istoria Ukrainskavo Kozachestva*, 1:338–41.
27. McNeill, pp. 76 ff.
28. This point is also made by Wynar, "Birth of Democracy," pt. 2, p. 147.
29. Hrushevsky, "Materialy," pp. 4–6.
30. Velychenko, "The Origins of the Ukrainian Revolution of 1648," p. 20; Wynar, "Birth of Democracy," pt. 2, p. 147.
31. See the critique of this error by Lubomyr R. Wynar, "Birth of Democracy," pt. 2, p. 154.

8. COSSACKS AGAINST INFIDELS: PIRACY AND POLISH POLITICS

1. Charles Sienkiewicz, introd. to Zamojski, *La Deffaicte des Tartares et Turcs faicte par le Seigneur Jean Zamoisky* (Ch), pp. vi–vii.
2. Kortepeter, *Ottoman Imperialism*, pp. 5–6.
3. Dorothy M. Vaughan, *Europe and the Turk: A Pattern of Alliances 1350–1700*, p. 176.
4. McNeill, pp. 47–51.
5. Imperatorskoe Russkoe Istoricheskoe Obshchestvo, *Sbornik*, 41, #5, pp. 23, 194–95; Evarnitsky, *Istoria*, 2:9–10.
6. Jan Zamojski, *La Deffaicte*, pp. 1–3; Kulish, *Materialy*, I–V; Storozhenko, *Stefan Batorii*, pp. 34, 81, 94, 100, 112, 159; Kortepeter, *Ottoman Imperialism*, passim.
7. In the early 1570s a Podolian noble, Swierczowski or Svirhovsky, led a cossack army to aid Moldavian ruler Ivon (Ivonia) III, who was in rebellion against the Turks: they were defeated in 1574. Then, under Ivan Podkova, who claimed to be Ivon's brother but was probably a cossack leader,

cossacks went again to Moldavia and overthrew the Turkish-appointed governor in 1577; they in turn were defeated by a Transylvanian army in 1578, and the Poles beheaded Podkova at the insistence of the Sultan. An alleged brother of Podkova led the cossacks back yet again in the same year. Borschak, pp. 59–60; Storozhenko, *Stefan Batorii*, pp. 46–47, 59–68; Antonovych, *Soderzhanie Aktov*, p. xxxviii; S. M. Solovev, *Istoria Rossii s Drevneishikh Vremen* 7:368–69; Kortepeter, *Ottoman Imperialism*, pp. 32–33.

8. The powerful Zborowski family had a long-standing feud with Zamojski, giving Samuil no doubt a double motivation for his cossack adventures. When at the Zaporozhian sich he claimed to have a letter from the khan promising him the governorship of Moldavia in return for bringing cossack aid against Persia. Kulish, *Istoria Vozsoedinenia Rusi* 1:112–30.

9. It appears that he incurred the wrath of Prince Mikhail Vishnevetsky who was at this time trying to get the Zaporozhians to join his campaign into Muscovy. Storozhenko, op. cit., pp. 92–93.

10. Kortepeter, pp. 151–54; *Cambridge History of Poland*, 1:455.

11. Zamojski, *La Deffaicte*, pp. 18–20; dated Oct. 27, year of Mohammed 900.

12. Kortepeter, *Ottoman Imperialism*, p. 129.

13. Storozhenko, op. cit., p. 260.

14. *Zherela*, 8, #38.

15. Sinan Bassa [sic], "Letter to Queen Elizabeth of June 12, 1590," in Hakluyt, *The Principal Navigations, Voiages, Traffiques and Discoveries of the English Nation* . . . (Ch), 5, 2, Part 2, p. 295.

16. Kulish, *Istoria*, 2:5–7; Kortepeter, "Gazi Giray II," pp. 151–54; *Cambridge History of Poland*, 1:455; Kostomarov, "Yuzhnaya Rus v Kontsye XVI Veka," in *Istoricheskie Monografii i Izsledovaniya*, 3:241–42; Sinan Bassa, loc. cit.

17. This emissary, Ukhansky, had a difficult time: he broke his leg en route, and arrived late and in great pain with only 600 zlotys, hardly enough to bribe a senior Turkish general. He was apparently under the delusion that the infidels he was dealing with would be stupid and easily deceived; the Beylerbey broke off negotiations, possibly uncovering some ruse or feeling insulted at the size of the bribe he was offered. The Beylerbey may then have taken more extreme action, for it was later reported that Ukhansky had died on December 1, 1589. Kulish, *Istoria*, 2:11–14; Kostomarov, ibid., pp. 242–45.

18. Sinan Bassa, loc. cit.

19. Quoted in Kulish, *Istoria*, 2:14–15; see also Kostomarov, *Istoricheskie Monografii*, p. 245.

20. Kulish, *Istoria*, 2:15–19; Kostomarov, ibid., p. 246.

21. Sinan Bassa, loc. cit.

22. Rajnold Hejdensztejn, *Dzieje Polski, od Śmierci Zygmunta Augusta do Roku 1594* (Ch), 2:294; Kulish, *Istoria*, 2:21; Kostomarov, pp. 243–46; Kortepeter, p. 154.

23. *Arkhiv Yugo-Zapadnoi Rossii*, pt. 3, vol. 1, #11. The editor of this volume of the *Arkhiv* apparently thought that "Kremenchug on the Dniester" was an error and changed it to read "on the Dnieper," possibly unaware that a Kremenchug existed in Bessarabia. The historian Storozhenko has pointed out that, in 1590, the Bessarabian location was the more likely because both Poles and Turks were primarily concerned with cossack raids into the Danubian principalities. See Storozhenko, *Stefan Batorii*, p. 260; and *Kievskaya Starina*, #64, Sec. 2 (1899), p. 18.

24. See Part V, Chapter 14.

25. Storozhenko, *Stefan Batorii*, p. 260; Hejdensztejn, II, 300; Joachim Bielski, *Dalszy Ciąg Kroniki Polskiej* (Ch), p. 152; F. D. Nikolaichik, "Pervye Kozatskia Dvizhenia v Rechi Pospolitoi," 3:428.

26. *Prawa Konstytucye v Przywileie; Krolestwá Polskiego, y Wielkiego Xięstwá Litewskiego ...*, pp. 1329–32; *Inventarz Nowy Praw, Statutow, Konstytucyi Koronnych, y W. X. Litew* (D), pp. 257–58.

27. *Prawa*, loc. cit.

9. PERSONAL GRIEVANCES, SOCIAL BANDITRY

1. In 1586 Kosinsky had been employed as a sentry at Tavan, an outpost below the Dnieper rapids. *Listy Żółkiewskiego*, p.34.

2. Ibid., p. 27.

3. Beyond these facts, Kosinsky's background is uncertain. One contemporary chronicler, Bielski, by no means noted for his accuracy, reported that he came from Podlesia (p. 188), where the population was then predominantly Ruthenian. Kosinsky wrote in Polish, but so did other sixteenth-century men known to be Ruthenian. His spelling of his first name, Kristof, suggests that he was Catholic, or at least educated in a Latin school. Yet one historian argued that he must have been a Lutheran, and the traditional Ukrainian chroniclers of his heroism insisted, of course, that he was a devout Orthodox. See Kulish, *Istoria*, 2:26.

4. *Źródła Dziejowe*, 22:120.

5. At this time Janush Ostrozhsky, as sheriff of both Belotserkov and Boguslav, was subordinate to his father Konstantin-Vasili who was governor of Kiev; Janush himself was also governor of Volynia, however.

6. *Źródła Dziejowe*, 20:38.

7. Frontier lands were often awarded on the condition that they be populated, and on occasion the Diet ruled that lands given out but thereafter unsettled should revert to the crown for redistribution. The Rokitna lands were included in a list of areas classified by the 1590 Diet as empty and available for distribution. Rulikowski, entry on Rokitna, in *Słownik Geograficzny Królestwa Polskiego i Innych Krajow Słowiańskich*, 9:704.

8. At some time between 1590 and 1599 a Vishnevetsky owned the Rokitna lands again; and in 1599 they were held by Janush Ostrozhsky.

Archiwum Domu Radziwiłłow. Listy Ks. M. K. Radziwiłła Sierotki, Jana Zamoyskiego, Lwa Sapiehy (Ch), 8:147; Kulish, *Istoria*, 2:446–47. As Ostrozhsky told the story, everything was quite legal. Kosinsky sold his land to Vishnevetsky, and then Ostrozhsky found it "necessary" to buy it from Vishnevetsky: "entering into a neighborhood of discord, for my own peace [I] had to buy these villages in perpetuity from Prince Vishnevetsky, whom I paid as much as he demanded." Kulish, loc. cit.

9. *Arkhiv Yugo-Zapadnoi Rossii*, pt. 3, vol. 1, #12.

10. One or both of the magnates might have argued that the grant to Kosinsky was invalid because the Rokitna estate was traditionally part of the Belotserkov royal lands and ought to remain with the sheriff's other holdings. Ostrozhsky had raised such an objection when Prince Zbarazhsky, himself a powerful magnate, bought some lands near his Volodarka estate. See *Żródła Dziejowe*, 12:392. At other times such land-grabbing had occurred without the magnates feeling the need for a justification.

11. Domanitsky, "Kozachchina," p. 162.

12. Storozhenko, *Stefan Batorii*, p. 310.

13. *Listy Żółkiewskiego*, #13. In dating this letter I have followed Hrushevsky; the editor of the *Listy* dates it 1592.

14. *Arkhiv Yugo-Zapadnoi Rossii*, pt. 3, vol. 1, #14.

15. Ibid, p. 12.

16. *Zherela*, 8, #48.

17. Ibid.; *Arkhiv Yugo-Zapadnoi Rossii*, pt. 3, vol. 1, #14.

18. *Zherela*, 8, ##43 and 48.

19. *Arkhiv Yugo-Zapadnoi Rossii*, pt. 8, vol. 5, #58. The commissioners included Jakub Pretvich.

20. Ibid.

21. Ibid., #56.

10. THE NATURE OF COSSACK INSURGENCY

1. On the Ukrainian outbreaks, see *Zherela*, 8, ##41–54; *Arkhiv Yugo-Zapadnoi Rossii*, pt. 3, vol. 1, ##15–21; Hejdensztejn, 2:317; Bielski, pp. 178, 188. In Muscovy, the Putivl governor reported in 1591 that the "cherkassy" had attacked many places, threatened the royal sentries and villages, and made passage through Putivl dangerous; see Solovev, 7:640. Elsewhere, Muscovite documents contain very accurate reports of the Kosinsky affair itself, suggesting the size and significance contemporaries attributed to it; see ibid., 9:1454. A Belorussian chronicle reported unrest in Chernigov, Gomel, Liubech, Streshin, Rechitsa, Rogachov, and Krichov; see "Borkulabovskaya Khronika 1563-1608," in Kulish, *Materialy*, p. 62.

2. Diets of Vilna, Poznan, Kalish, Kamenets, Novgorod, and Cracow; see *Zherela*, 8, ##41, 45–47, 51–52.

3. Surprisingly, since taking and ransoming of prisoners was a favorite trick of the Turks and Tartars, especially Crimeans, from whom the Cossacks learned so many of their combat techniques.

4. Ibid, ##41, 43, 51; *Arkhiv Yugo-Zapadnoi Rossii,* pt. 3, vol. 1, #17.

5. Declaration of szlachta of Vladimir, 29 Jan. 1593, in *Arkhiv Yugo-Zapadnoi Rossii,* pt. 3, vol. 1, p. 183; see also, e.g., *Zherela,* 8, ##45–46.

6. *Arkhiv Yugo-Zapadnoi Rossii,* pt. 3, vol. 1, #13.

7. *Zherela,* 3, #48.

8. *Bielski,* p. 188; *Zherela,* loc cit.

9. *Listy Żółkiewskiego,* #12.

10. *Zherela,* loc. cit., incorrectly dates it 1591. We do not have the text of the decree itself, but only a description of it in the Diet's project for a new "constitution" for the cossacks.

11. *Prawa,* pp. 1329–32.

12. *Zherela,* 8, ##43, 48.

13. Domanitsky, "Kozachchina," p. 11.

14. *Źródła Dziejowe,* 20:58; Efimenko, *Ocherki,* pp. 4–5, 17–19, 29–37; M. V. Dovnar-Zapolsky, "Ukrainskia Starostva v Pervoi Polovine XVI v., p. 40; Hrushevsky, *Istoria Ukrainy-Rusy,* 6:1 and 5:202–3.

15. Hrushevsky, loc. cit.; Baranovich, *Ukraina,* p. 37.

16. Efimenko, p. 44.

17. Bielski, p. 178. Kosinsky's adventures in Bratslav are not clearly ascertainable. Bielski says that the old man Ostrozhsky raised an army, did battle with Kosinsky in the late summer of 1592, and was defeated by the cossacks. The story is reasonable, but unverifiable in other sources. Ostrozhsky probably surmised, from rumors and from the cossacks' path, that Koskinsky was heading for Ostropol. Assuming that Ostrozhsky went into Bratslav to strike an offensive blow against the cossacks, his defeat would be understandable. Especially in northern Bratslav, Kosinsky would have had broad popular support against Ostrozhsky.

18. Bielski, p. 188; Hejdensztejn, 2:317, although the latter mistakenly calls it "Tarnopol."

19. Domanitsky, "Kozachchina," p. 11, Evarnitsky, 2:90.

20. Kulish, *Istoria,* 2:34.

21. *Zherela,* 7, ##41–52.

22. "Borkulabovskaya Khronika," (Ch), pp. 57, 62.

23. *Arkhiv Yugo-Zapadnoi Rossii,* pt. 3, vol. 1, #15.

24. Ibid., 14.

11. THE NATURE OF ARISTOCRATIC DEFENSE

1. *Zherela,* 7, ##41–52.

2. *Dyaryusze i Akta Sejmowe 1591-92* (D), p. 100; see also Domanitsky, "Kozachchina," p. 162.

3. *Dyaryusze Sejmowe 1591-92,* p. 306; *Listy Żółkiewskiego,* #14.

4. *Dyaryusze Sejmowe 1591-92*, p. 101.

5. Ibid., pp. 111, 115, 227–278.

6. *Zherela*, 8, #48.

7. *Arkhiv Yugo-Zapadnoi Rossii*, pt. 3, vol. 1, #14. Ostrozhsky's insistence on this bureaucratic maneuver seems out of place with his independence and his traditional *modus operandi* as a sovereign ruler of his own lands. He may have been replying to a reprimand from the king. It is also possible that funds intended for the upkeep of fortifications had been put to other, unauthorized, uses. There is evidence that the Kievan fortresses were indeed in disrepair. See Kostomarov, citing an unpublished letter of Sigismund Augustus, p. 250.

8. Efimenko, p. 45.

9. Kulish, *Otpadenie Malorossii ot Polshi (1340-1654)* 1:61. Tarnopol was the birthplace of Janush Ostrozhsky's mother and as such a locale of potential support.

10. Hejdensztejn, 2:317; Domanitsky, p. 11.

11. 16 Jan. 1593, in *Arkhiv Yugo-Zapadnoi Rossii*, pt. 3, vol. 1, #17.

12. Kulish, *Otpadenie*, 1:61; Domanitsky, p. 13.

13. Hejdensztejn, loc. cit.

14. Kulish, *Istoria*, 2:34.

15. Hejdensztejn, loc. cit; Bielski, p. 188. Piatka was in Zhitomir, in the far eastern portion of Volynia, practically on the Kievan border, and it belonged to Janush Ostrozhsky.

16. Efimenko, p. 45; Domanitsky, "Kozachchina," p. 13; *Słownik Geograficzny*, 8:65.

17. Bielski, pp. 188–89.

18. Evarnitsky, 2:92.

19. Bielski, loc. cit.; Hejdensztejn, loc. cit.

20. Bielski, loc. cit.; Hejdensztejn, loc cit., *Listy Żółkiewskiego*, #16.

21. *Listy Żółkiewskiego*, loc. cit.

22. There is some confusion among the sources about the dates of the Piatka battle and the end of the siege of Ostropol. In the *Listy Żółkiewskiego* we read that Kosinsky surrendered on Feb. 1; Bielski wrote March 15, possibly because that is the date on which the capitulation was inscribed in the official records of Vladimir district; Kostomarov (p. 252) for some reason writes March 10.

23. One Polish officer reported that Kosinsky was first made to fall on his knees, beg forgiveness and kiss the feet of Ostrozhsky and his son three times. *Listy Żółkiewskiego*, loc. cit., and Bielski, p. 189. A charming but unlikely adornment to the story, it hardly suits the temperament or style of the Zaporozhian hetman. Ostrozhsky claimed that he "took pity on them and especially on the people of the Ukrainian districts . . . and, having put down his anger," made a peace. *Listy Żółkiewskiego*, loc. cit.

24. *Arkhiv Yugo-Zapadnoi Rossii*, pt. 3, vol. 1, #19; or *Listy Żółkiewskiego*, #15.

25. E.g., the Ostrozhsky, Vishnevetsky, Sangushko, Zaslavsky,

Koretsky, Pronsky, Kovelsky, Kashirsky, Kosik and Kurtsevich families considered themselves descendants of Gedymin.

26. *Listy Żółkiewskiego*, loc. cit.

27. Efimenko, p. 46.

28. S. Orgelbrand, ed., *Encyklopedyja Powszechna*, 2d ed. (Warsaw: 1884). His was a family of relatively new wealth and power, having received their land from Sigismund I in return for military service.

29. Vishnevetsky probably had closer dealings with the Zaporozhians than any other magnate. His ancestor Dmitri, according to legend, was an early Zaporozhian hetman. Borschak, pp. 54–55.

30. Baranovich, *Zaliudnennia*, passim.

31. Domanitsky "Kozachchina," p. 13, Nikolaichik, p. 436; Efimenko, p. 45; Kulish, *Otpadenie*, 1:60–61.

32. For examples see Domanitsky, "Kozachchina," p. 163.

33. Beauplan, *Description de l'Ukranie*, pp. 22–23.

34. Antonovych, *O Proiskhozhdenii Shliakhetskikh Rodov v Yugo-Zapadnoi Rossii*, pp. 4–8.

35. *Zherela*, 8:121; Tomkiewicz, pp. 249–55.

36. Baranovich, *Zaliudnennia*, p. 144.

37. *Arkhiv Yugo-Zapadnoi Rossii*, pt. 3, vol. 1, #4.

38. Ibid., #20.

39. Ibid., #44.

40. Ibid., #43.

41. *Prawa*, pp. 1329–32.

12. THE AMBIGUITY OF DEFEAT

1. Domanitsky, "Kozachchina,", p. 18.

2. Hejdensztejn, 2:318; Bielski, p. 190.

3. *Prawa*, p. 1402; *Iventarz*, p. 258.

4. Hejdensztejn, 2:320, Domanitsky, "Kozachchina," p. 18#n. According to the *Listy Żółkiewskiego*, #16, the Tatars had been collecting an army for many months; undoubtedly they had timed their expedition to coincide with the Diet, when so much of the military leadership would be absent from the Ukraine.

5. *Listy Żółkiewskiego*, #17.

6. Even Zamojski's secretary believed that the cossacks had arranged the Tatar attacks as revenge upon Ostrozhsky; Hejdensztejn, 2:319.

7. Domanitsky, "Kozachchina," p. 19.

8. *Arkhiv Yugo-Zapadnoi Rossii*, pt. 3, vol. 1, #20.

9. Hejdensztejn, 2:318; Bielski, p. 190, Evarnitsky, 1:95.

10. *Listy Żółkiewskiego*, #17.

11. Hejdensztejn, loc. cit.; Bielski, loc. cit.

12. Bielski, loc. cit.

13. Listy Żółkiewskiego, loc. cit.

14. Storozhenko, *Stefan Batorii*, pp. 307–9, and 313.
15. *Arkhiv Yugo-Zapadnoi Rossii*, pt. 3, vol. 1, #21.
16. *Listy Żółkiewskiego*, #18.
17. We do not know the cossacks' precise grievances. One of the best Ukrainian historians surmises that the cossacks were not complaining about the killing of Kosinsky, but about Vishnevetsky's noncompliance with his promise to return cossack property. (See Hrushevsky, *Istoria Ukrainskavo Kozachestva*, 1:250.) Alexander Mikhailovich Vishnevetsky died in September and it is conceivable, too, that his successor reneged on the promises.
18. *Listy Żółkiewskiego*, loc. cit.
19. Kulish, *Otpadenie*, 1:63.
20. Ivan P. Novitsky, "Kniazia Ruzhinskie," pp. 60–70.
21. Letter of Vereshchinsky to Zolkiewski, 4 Oct. 1593, in *Listy Żółkiewskiego*, #18.
22. Ibid. See also Vereshchinsky to Zamojski, 29 Aug. 1593, and 20 Mar. 1596, in Storozhensko, *Stefan Batorii*, pp. 307–9, 314–16. About Vereshchinsky also see Storozhenko, "Vereshchinskii, Biskup Kievskii (1540–1598)."
23. *Listy Żółkiewskiego*, loc. cit.
24. Ibid.
25. Ibid.
26. We will examine their fighting style more closely in the story of the next rebellion, of which we have better military descriptions because of the presence of a crown army and its recorders.
27. *Listy Żółkiewskiego*, #17.
28. Certainly Moscow was well informed about events in the Polish Ukraine, and there is evidence of Muscovite–Ukrainian contacts. Tsar Fedor wrote to the Don cossacks in 1593 that they should assemble on the northern Donets where they would be joined by the Zaporozhians, "who by our order are coming to serve the Tsar on the Donets commanded by the Zaporozhian *cherkassy* hetman Krishto Kositsky [sic] . . " (Quoted in Bagalei, *Ocherki*, p. 151.) This, of course, proves nothing more than that Fedor was aware of their existence and claimed them as subjects, as he conceived all in Rus territory to be. Still, it is probable that the Tsar had communications with the Zaporozhians and that he had made them offers of employment. Vishnevetsky charged that Fedor had sent money and cloth to the sich early in 1593 and had promised them more. (*Listy Żółkiewskiego*, #17.) There is no evidence of a cossack–Tatar agreement.

13. COSSACK DIVISIONS AND CONFLICTS OF INTEREST

1. Hejdensztejn, 2:363; see also X. Franciszek Siarczyński, *Obraz Wieku Panowania Zygmunta III . . . Zawieraiący Opis Osób zyiących pod jego Panowaniem . . .*, 1:297–98.

2. Hrushevsky, "Materialy," ##5, 7, 11–12.

3. Ibid., pp. 11–21 passim; Kamanin, "Voprosu," p. 18; Kulish, *Istoria*, 2:431. During the rebellion Loboda had to fight to hang on to the wealth his marriage had brought him. As was customary, he had probably kidnapped his wife, and sometime later she escaped to her father's house. Loboda attacked Oborskoi, his father-in-law, with 700 men to take revenge for this desertion and to reclaim his wife. Oborskoi was saved by Zolkiewski and the royal army. See *Listy Żółkiewskiego*, #71.

4. Hrushevsky, "Materialy," #13.

5. *Archiwum Domu Sapiehów* (Ch), Lvov. p. 131.

6. Hrushevsky, "Materialy," p. 16, ##3, 9, 16; *Arkhiv Yugo-Zapadnoi Rossii*, pt. 7, vol. 1, 372; pt. 7, vol. 2, 365; and pt. 6, vol. 1, 170–74.

7. Hrushevsky, "Materialy," #13; *Listy Żółkiewskiego*, p. 60; *Arkheograficheskii Sbornik Dokumentov Severo-Zapadnovo Rusi* (D), 1:178–85.

8. *Archiwum Domu Radziwiłłów*, p. 152; *Listy Żółkiewskiego*, ##80, 74.

9. *Listy Żółkiewskiego*, #42.

10. Quoted in Hrushevsky, *Istoria Ukrainskavo Kozachestva*, 1:276.

14. MERCENARY DIPLOMACY

1. *Archiwum Sapiehów*, #109. Within Poland there was a strong pro-Austrian party, composed primarily of the followers of the Archduke Maximilian from his earlier candidacy for the Polish throne. They were, by and large, personal enemies of Zamojski as well as opponents of his foreign policy. Zamojski was determined to keep the peace with Turkey, but because of his domestic opposition within Poland he had to proceed with duplicity and discretion, trying above all to avoid a confrontation with the Austrians, the Pope, and the numerous foreign envoys who continually pressed him to join the war.

2. Kortepeter, *Ottoman Imperialism*, p. 129.

3. Furthermore, he was influenced by his Jesuit tutor and mentor toward an obsessive hatred for the Moslems. Denis Sinor, *History of Hungary*, pp. 174–75; Platon Nikolaevich Zhukovich, *Seimovaya Borba Pravoslavnavo Zapadno-russkavo Dvorianstva s Tserkovnoi Unii do 1609 g.*, pp. 177–79.

4. *Documents concerning Rumanian History (1427–1601)*, ed. E. D. Tappe (D), p. 77; Vaughan, pp. 180–85; Seton–Watson, p. 63.

5. Tappe, p. 63.

6. Tappe, pp. 63, 77–79; Seton–Watson, p. 63; Vaughan, pp. 180–85.

7. Bielski, pp. 225.

8. Hejdensztejn, 2:321–29; W. S. de Broel–Plater, ed., *Zbiór Pamiętnikow do Dziejów Polskich* (D), 2:214.

9. *Cambridge History of Poland*, 1:451–57.

10. *Pamiatniki Diplomaticheskikh Snoshenii Drevnei Rossii s Derzhavami Inostrannymi* (D), 1:1282.

11. Zbigniew Wójcik, introd. to *Eryka Lassoty i Wilhelma Beauplana Opisy Okrainy* (Warsaw: 1972), p. 19; Hrushevsky, *Istoria Ukrainy-Rusy* 7:196.

12. Hrushevsky, op. cit., p. 197; *Pamiatniki*, op. cit., pp. 1280–1310; Solovev.

13. Evhen Barvinsky, "Prychynky do Istorii Znosyn Tsesaria Rudolfa II i Papa Klement VIII do Kozakamy 1593–94," p. 22.

14. Lassota, from the old Moravian nobility, was born about 1550; he attended the universities of Leipzig and Padua, and became a soldier of fortune, fighting for Philip II of Spain during 1576–84. He then entered the service of the Emperor and the Archduke Maximilian, and was sent on numerous diplomatic and military commissions to Poland, Muscovy, and the Balkans; he was rewarded by being made lord high steward to the archduke. Straying into Sweden en route to Muscovy in 1590 he was kept in Swedish custody for three years. He died in 1616, still in the Habsburg service. In short, he was an unusually cosmopolitan man, well qualified as an observer of the cossacks. In sending Lassota, Rudolf II claimed to be responding to an unauthorized, but characteristic, offer from a free-lance cossack, Khlopitsky, whom we met before, to supply eight to ten thousand cossacks for imperial service. See F. Brun, introd. to Lassota's *Putevya Zapiski*. The entire story that follows is taken from Brun's translation of Lassota's diary.

15. Lassota, pp. 44–45.

16. Ludwik Boratyński, "Kozacy i Watykan," pp. 21–40.

17. Komulovich, or Komuleo in Rome, was a Croat educated in Rome and had already served Gregory XIII as an apostolic visitator in the Balkans.

18. Oscar Halecki, *From Florence to Brest*, pp. 255–65; Paul Pierling, S. J., *La Russie et le Saint-Siège, Études Diplomatiques*, 2:344–45.

19. Hejdensztejn, 2:326.

20. Halecki, pp. 263–64; Pierling, 2:344–45; Domanitsky, "Kozachchina," p. 32.

21. Quoted in Domanitsky, loc. cit.; see also Barvinsky, p. 18. Komulovich did not name the cossack leader he paid, but the fact that he promised to join him with the Dnieper or Zaporozhian cossacks suggests that the leader was not himself one of them, and could well have been Nalivaiko. Nalivaiko himself described an expedition he made to Kilia in a letter written a year later to the king. He did not mention encouragement or money from a papal envoy, but this is hardly surprising, since he would surely have known that dealings with the Vatican would not endear him to Zamojski. Nalivaiko and Komulovich do not agree on the date of this raid, but the former might have dated it later to imply that it took place after Poland was at war with Turkey, whereas the former might have dated it earlier to support his claim that he initiated it. See *Archiwum Sapiehów*, ##114–141; Broel–Plater, p. 215.

22. Yazlovetsky's background and earlier adventures were discussed in Part IV. One of many Polish nobles who lived out their fantasies on the steppe, playing cossack and seeking riches and power in the Balkans, he had been appointed chief of the 1590 Kremenchug fort that was never built, hetman of the registered cossacks, and a member of the royal commission sent to deal with Kosinsky.

23. Pierling, 2:348; Hejdensztejn, 2:326.

24. Bielski, p. 225; Heidenstein in *Rerum ab excessu*, quoted in Domanitsky, "Kozachchina," p. 54.

25. In Lubomyr R. Wynar's introduction to an English translation of Lassota's diary, he attributes the cossacks' desertion to their unwillingness to serve under a Polish official! There is no evidence for this, nor was Yazlovetsky more Polish than others the cossacks had served, and the judgment illustrates the tendency of some Ukrainian historians to attribute nationalist motives to the cossacks where they did not exist. See Wynar, ed., *Habsburgs and Zaporozhian Cossacks: The Diary of Erich Lassota von Steblau 1594*, p. 44.

26. Bielski, pp. 224–25; Tappe, p. 73.

27. Broel–Plater, 2:215.

28. Ibid.; Bielski, p. 225; Hejdensztejn, 2:327; Kulish, *Istoria*, 2:93–94 n.; Evarnitsky, 2:129.

29. Broel–Plater, loc. cit.

30. Tappe, p. 81.

31. Hejdensztejn, 2:340–41; Kulish, *Istoria*, 2:429–34; Tappe, pp. 72–73. Rozwan, the Moldavian commander, led a coup against his own ruler Aron; he was put up to this, probably, by Transylvanian Voevoda Batory, who considered Aron dangerously pro-Polish.

32. Seton–Watson, p. 63; Vaughan, pp. 183–85; Tappe, pp. 63, 77–79.

33. Bielski, pp. 212–13; Hejdensztejn, 2:321; *Archiwum Sapiehów*, #145.

34. *Archiwum Sapiehów*, #113.

35. Ibid., #126; *Cambridge History of Poland*, 1:458.

36. Hejdensztejn, 2:322–41; *Archiwum Sapiehów*, #96; Domanitsky, "Kozachchina," pp. 66–67.

37. *Archiwum Radziwiłłów*, p. 117.

38. Ibid.; Hejdensztejn, 2:342.

39. Bielski, pp. 232–39; Hejdensztejn, 2:344–45.

40. Bielski, pp. 241–50; Hejdensztejn, 2:343–54; Zhukovich, pp. 180–89.

41. Hejdensztejn, 2:353–54; Domanitsky, "Kozachchina," p. 68; *Cambridge History of Poland*, 1:458.

42. *Archiwum Radziwiłłów*, p117; Hejdensztejn, 2:350; Broel–Plater, 2:216.

43. Broel–Plater, 2:216.

44. Kulish, *Istoria*, 2:81. That the imperial army drove them out does not prove that they had not really been asked by the Habsburgs to serve in

the Balkans. Since the cossacks would almost certainly not have been paid, they would soon have turned to looting and thus forced their employers to get rid of them.

45. Domanitsky, "Kozachchina," pp. 71–72; Bielski, p. 253.

15. URBAN REVOLT

1. Kulish, *Materialy*, pp. 20–21.
2. Efimenko, p. 17; Baranovich, *Ukraina*, pp. 56–60.
3. *Arkhiv Yugo-Zapadnoi Rossii*, pt. 8, vol. 1, 290–92.
4. Tarnawski, pp. 333–50.
5. None of this is meant to imply that the Bratslav rebellion was *primarily* supported by burghers, or that burghers did not support the cossacks *elsewhere* in the Ukraine. Everywhere the cossacks received support from both burgher and peasant groups. We emphasize the role of townspeople here because (1) it was particularly visible in Bratslav, and (2) the cossack mode of operation in Bratslav involved using urban support by seizing control of towns.
6. Hejdensztejn, 2:327.
7. Bielski, p. 225; Broel–Plater, 2:215.
8. Domanitsky, "Kozachchina," p. 55.
9. Bielski, p. 225.
10. Bielski, p. 225; Broel–Plater, 2:215. Denying that he had wronged Nalivaiko, Kalinovsky claimed that another noble, Andrei Taranovsky, a long-time personal rival of Kalinovsky, had put Nalivaiko up to the attack; and some of the goods Nalivaiko took in the robbery were indeed sent to Taranovsky. See Domanitsky, "Prichinok do Istorii Nalivaika," pp. 4–6. There is no necessary contradiction between Nalivaiko's and Kalinovsky's stories. Individual cossack leaders frequently sought protection and sponsorship from the enemies of their enemies.
11. *Arkhiv Yugo-Zapadnoi Rossii*, pt. 3, vol. 1, #2, p. 2; Domanitsky, "Kozachchina," p. 55; Nikolaichik, p. 531.
12. *Arkhiv Yugo-Zapadnoi Rossii*, pt. 3, vol. 1, #22.
13. Hrushevsky, "Materialy," p. 10; Antonovych, "K Istorii Vozstania Nalivaiko," pp. 3–4.
14. Ibid.
15. Ibid.
16. Letter from Jakob Pretvich, sheriff of Terebovl, to Zolkiewski, 25 Nov. 1594, in *Listy Żółkiewskiego*, #37.
17. Ibid.
18. Hejdensztejn, 2:327.
19. Domanitsky, "Kozachchina," p. 61.
20. Kulish, *Istoria*, 2:434–35, writing to Zamojski.
21. Kulish, *Materialy*, pp. 20–21.

22. *Listy Żółkiewskiego*, #37.
23. In Kulish, *Istoria*, 2:429–36 passim.
24. Ibid., pp. 93–94.
25. Ibid., pp. 432–33.
26. Broel–Plater, 2:215–16; *Archiwum Radziwiłłów*, pp. 219–20.
27. *Archiwum Radziwiłłów*, pp. 219–20.
28. Antonovych, "K Istorii . . . Nalivaika," p. 4.

16. A HOLY WAR?

1. Uniate refers to the Brest Union of Catholic and Orthodox churches; see Part II. For the original Polish charges against Ostrozhsky, see *Archiwum Radziwiłłów*, pp. 43–44; Kulish, *Istoria*, 2:438; Oskar Halecki, "Jeszcze o Nowych Źródłach do Dziejów Unii Brzeskiej," pp. 117–40.

2. Baranovich, *Ukraina*, pp. 112–13.

3. Ibid., pp. 114–15.

4. Yuzefovich, pp. xi, xv ff.

5. *Cambridge History of Poland*, 1:459.

6. Bykov, pp. 25–26.

7. *Akty . . . Yuzhnoi i Zapadnoi Rossii*, 1:280–89.

8. Halecki, *From Florence to Brest*, pp. 342–62 passim.

9. V. Bodnov, *Pravoslavnaya Tserkov v Polshe i Litve*; T. Titov, *Russkaya Pravoslavnaya Tserkov v Polsko-Litovskom Gosudarstve*; Hrushevsky, *Kulturno-Natsionalyni Rukh na Ukraini v XVI-XVII vv.*; Zhukovich, *loc. cit.*

10. Halecki, *From Florence to Brest*, pp. 287 ff.

11. Ibid., pp. 342–62 passim; Bykov, pp. 32–33.

12. Baranovich, *Ukraina*, p. 118; Pompei Nikolaevich Batiushkov, *Volyn, Istoricheskie Sudby Yugo-Zapadnavo Kraya*, p. 126.

13. The pogrom of Lutsk was so severe that on Dec. 1 the king issued a special dispensation releasing its population from certain significant taxes until the next Diet. "Dnevnik Novgorodskavo Podsudka Fedora Evlashevskavo (1564–1604)," (Ch), *Kievskaya Starina*, 1 (Jan. 1886), 153; *Arkhiv Yugo-Zapadnoi Rossii*, pt. 3, vol. 1, #23.

14. "Dnevnik Evlashevskavo," *loc. cit.*

15. *Arkhiv Yugo-Zapadnoi Rossii*, pt. 1, vol. 1, pp. xlvi, lviii.

16. Yuzefovich, p. xv ff.

17. Allen, p. 84.

18. *Arkheograficheskii Sbornik*, 1, #64.

19. *Arkhiv Yugo-Zapadnoi Rossii*, pt. 3, vol. 1, #24.

20. *Sacrum Poloniae Millenium*, 4 (1957), pp. 132 ff.

21. Halecki, *From Florence to Brest*, p. 306.

22. Nalivaiko, Ostrozhsky's chief contact among the cossacks, did not participate in this attack; it is possible, however, that the leader of the assailants, Rostopich, was one of Nalivaiko's men.

23. Damian Nalivaiko was an educated man who did translations from the Russian; later he also served Otrozhsky by writing polemics against the Uniates. Domanitsky, "Kozachchina," pp. 24–25; *Kievskaya Starina*, 4 (1897), p. 382.

24. *Arkhiv Yugo-Zapadnoi Rossii*, pt. 3, vol. 1, #27, Kostomarov, "Yuzhnaya Rus," 265–66.

25. Yuzefovich, pp. xv ff.

26. *Arkhiv Yugo-Zapadnoi Rossii*, pt. 3, vol. 1, #27.

27. Ibid., #25.

28. Zhukovich, p. 191; ibid, 3, 1, ##25–26.

29. *Arkhiv Yugo-Zapadnoi Rossii*, pt. 3, vol. 1, #41, and pt. 1, vol. 6, pp. 124 ff.

30. Ibid, pt. 5, vol. 4, pp. 225–27.

31. Ibid., pt 3, vol. 1, #33.

32. Ibid., pt. 3, vol. 1, #34.

33. Ibid, pt. 3, vol. 1, #40.

34. Bykov, p. 3.

35. *Arkhiv Yugo-Zapadnoi Rossii*, pt. 3, vol. 1, #37.

36. There is sharp historiographical dispute on this point. Many historians, primarily the Great Russians, have been reluctant to concede that Ostrozhsky collaborated in these attacks, fearing that this concession would attribute a religious and national program to the cossacks. Domanitsky, Kostomarov, Zhukovich, Nikolaichik, and Holobutsky belong to this camp. On the other hand, those who argue for Ostrozhsky's complicity, such as Antonovych and Kulish, assume that his ties with the cossacks prove that they were partisans of orthodoxy against the Breast Union. See historiographical essay.

37. Halecki, *From Florence to Brest*, p. 350.

38. Ibid., p. 401.

39. Ibid.; Storozhenko, *Stefan Batorii*, pp. 314–19, Storozhenko, "Vereshchinskii," passim.

40. *Archiwum Sapiehów*, p. 541.

41. Domanitsky, "Kozachchina," p. 170.

17. PEASANT REBELLION

1. Belorussia was not a nation or even a term in the sixteenth century. Indeed, despite the claims of some Belorussian historians, it seems unlikely that anything like a Belorussian nation ever existed. The closest thing to it, perhaps was the appange of Vseslav, son of Isiaslav, in the eleventh century, often known as Polotskian Rus. (In the Middle Ages all the eastern Slav lands were known as "Rus," and more precise definitions were given by using the name of the principal town—thus, Polotskian Rus, Kievan Rus, Novgorodian Rus.) By the fifteenth century, "Belorussia" was politically a part of the Grand Duchy of Luthuania, but without definition as a nation.

Its people were Orthodox. Its language began to distinguish itself from Ukrainian and Russian only in the late sixteenth century; within the Grand Duchy only one language, Rus, was formally recognized, though it had numerous variants. Nor did Belorussians demonstrate any national consciousness as a minority under Lithuanian rule at this time. Yet this Rus–Lithuanian state, by breaking the ties uniting eastern Slavic peoples, had begun the separation of the future Belorussian and Ukrainian peoples of the Great Russians. The Krevo Union of 1385, which joined Lithuania to the Kingdom of Poland, still left most of the Rus peoples within the Grand Duchy. The political separations of Belorussians from Ukrainians began in mid-sixteenth century, when the Lublin Union transferred the Ukrainian provinces from Lithuania to Poland, subjecting the inhabitants of these districts to intensive Polonization. The future Belorussians were left under Lithuanian administration. See Nicholas P. Vakar, *Belorussia: The Making of a Nation*, p. 40; R. Ostrowski. *Fragments from the History of Byelorussia.*

2. V. K. Shcherbakov, "Krestianskoe Dvizhenie v Belorussii v XVI-XVII vv.," 4:7–17.

3. *Arkheograficheskii Sbornik*, 1, #60–61, & 2, Appendix, p. v.

4. Broel–Plater, 2:218–19.

5. Pokhylevich, passim.

6. *Arkheograficheskii Sbornik*, 7, #41; *Listy Żółkiewskiego*, #42.

7. *Archiwum Sapiehów*, #150, 8 Jan. 1596.

8. *Archiwum Radziwiłłów*, p. 44.

9. *Archiwum Sapiehów*, loc. cit.; *Archiwum Radziwiłłów*, p. 117; *Listy Żółkiewskiego*, #46.

10. *Listy Żółkiewskiego*, #42; Hejdensztejn, 2:363.

11. Letter from K. Radziwill to N. K. Radziwill, in T. N. Kopreev, ed., 'K Istorii Dvizhenia Nalivaiko," (Ch), pp. 149–51; *Arkheograficheskii Sbornik*, 7, #41.

12. *Arkheograficheskii Sbornik*, 7. #41; *Listy Żółkiewskiego*, #42.

13. *Listy Żółkiewskiego*, #42; Hejdensztejn, 2:363.

14. *Arkheograficheskii Sbornik*, 7, #39.

15. *Listy Żółkiewskiego*, #42.

16. *Arkheograficheskii Sbornik*, 7, #39.

17. Bielski, p. 254; letter from K. Radziwill to N. K. Radziwill, in Kopreev, p. 148.

18. *Archiwum Radziwiłłów*, pp. 42–44.

19. Hobsbawm, *Bandits* and *Primitive Rebels*; Kamen, pp. 331–32; Eric Wolf. *Peasant Wars of the Twentieth Century.*

20. Hobsbawm, *Primitive Rebels*, p. 22.

21. *Archiwum Radziwiłłów*. pp. 42–44.

22. Bielski, p. 254; Kopreev (Ch), p. 148.

23. *Archiwum Radziwiłłów*, p. 114.

24. "Dnevnik Evlashevskavo," pp. 153–54.

25. "Borkulabovskaya Khronika," p. 64.
26. Bielski, p. 254.
27. *Zherela*, 8, #54.
28. *Zherela*, 7, ##59, 61; "Borkulabovskaya Khronika," p. 64; *Arkhiv Yugo-Zapadnoi Rossii*, pt. 7, vol. 1, 221.
29. Broel–Plater, 2:216–17.
30. Ibid., p. 217.
31. *Archiwum Sapiehów*, p. 305; *Akty Otnosiashchiesie k Istorii Zapadnoi Rossii* (D), 4:173.
32. "Borkulabovskaya Khronika," p. 64; Bielski, p. 254; *Arkheografi-cheskii Sbornik*, 2:Appendix, p. v.
33. Bielski, p. 254; *Archiwum Sapiehów*, p. 126.
34. *Archiwum Sapiehów*, p. 305; *Akty . . . Zapadnoi Rossii*, 4:173.
35. Kulish, *Istoria*, 2:107–8; F. D. Nikolaichik, "Pervie Kozatskia Dvizhenia v Rechi Pospolitoi," pp. 536–37; Domanitsky, "Kozachchina," p. 77.
36. Mogilev had gained the Magdeburg privileges only in 1578; seven years later King Stefan Batory added concessions to the Mogilevians' autonomy by exempting them from certain taxes in return for the corvee, absolving their merchants from taxes for their use of the Dnieper River for fishing or trading, and allowing them to establish their own ferry and bridge across the Dnieper, thus permitting them to quit paying tolls to the nobles who had previously controlled those means of transportation. *Arkheografi-cheskii Sbornik*, 2:Appendix, pp. iv–v.
37. Vakar, p. 33
38. Hejdensztejn, 2:363.
39. Broel–Plater, 2:216–18. Some historians consider this letter a forgery, written in Nalivaiko's name but without his knowledge by a Lithuanian noble adventurer, Jan Meshkovsky, trying to aggrandize himself by mediating between king and cossacks. Like Khlopitsky, whom he resembled in many respects, Meshkovsky was a former royal courtier who had recently joined the cossacks (perhaps because he was out of favor in the capital.) He is suspected of writing this letter largely because he admitted having previously forged a letter from the king to Nalivaiko offering pardon in return for cessation of cossack hostilities. (When arrested in April 1596, he claimed to have written it at the instruction of Jan Firlei, vice-treasurer of the kingdom, and denied having written Nalivaiko's letter.) The content of Nalivaiko's letter has also seemed suspicious, since it assumed a more extensive authority over other cossacks than cossack hetmans ever had. See Domanitsky, "Kozachchina," pp. 79–81. The evidence of forgery is inconclusive, however. Furthermore, the document is significant no matter who wrote it. Even if Meshkovsky was the author, it represents cossack thinking and attitudes as Meshkovsky had absorbed them.
40. The "Conditions" displayed a remarkable inconsistency with the line taken in the letter itself, suggesting that the two parts of the communication might have been written separately, but hardly demonstrating this.

Such inconsistency—of the sort: "We didn't do it, and besides we were doing it in a good cause"—was typical of the cossacks. In the letter the cossacks denied any wrongdoing; in the Conditions they offered to cease their wrongdoing in return for concessions. The document handles this inconsistency with great delicacy. Its preamble said: "In order to restrain cossack insubordination, various hetmans previously have been estranged from the Crown . . . for which reason great harm, worse than that caused by the enemy, occurs in the Kingdom, loss to the treasury and great discredit to the Rzecz Pospolita and the Crown."

18. A ROYAL VICTORY?

1. *Arkhiv Yugo-Zapadnoi Rossii*, pt. 3, vol. 1, #38; *Listy Żółkiewskiego*, #55; Niemcewicz, 2:174; *Zherela*, 8, #67; "Dyaryusze Sejmowe 1597," in *Scriptores Rerum Polonicarum*, 20:334.

2. Tarnawski, pp. 333–50.

3. *Archiwum Radziwiłłów*, pp. 115–17.

4. Ibid., p. 115.

5. Sapieha was notable among those rejecting the commission and demanding mobilization. *Archiwum Sapiehów*, #153. Lithuanian nobles were generally more militant against the cossacks than Ukrainians.

6. Yuzefovich, pp. xv ff.

7. *Archiwum Sapiehów*, #154.

8. *Arkhiv Yugo-Zapadnoi Rossii*, pt. 3, vol. 1, #28.

9. *Listy Żółkiewskiego*, ##43–44; Kulish, *Otpadenie*, 1:90.

10. *Zherela*, 7, ##59, 61; "Borkulabovskaya Khronika," p. 64; *Arkhiv Yugo-Zapadnoi Rossii*, 7, 1, p. 221.

11. "Dnevnik . . . Evlashevskavo," 154; *Zherela*, 8, ##56–57, 59.

12. Domanitsky, "Kozachchina," pp. 85–86; Zhukovich, pp. 190–94.

13. *Arkheograficheskii Sbornik*, 7, #42; Kopreev, p. 151, letter of Kristof Radziwill to N. K. Radziwill.

14. Kopreev, loc. cit.

15. "Borkulabovskaya Khronika," pp. 64–65.

16. *Listy Żółkiewskiego*, #44.

17. Nalivaiko escaped because he was warned by a treacherous Polish soldier who defected to the cossacks. Defections and desertions by Polish soldiers were heavy throughout this campaign; the men were hungry, often nearly naked, and did not receive their salaries. *Listy Żółkiewskiego*, ##43–46.

18. Kulish, *Istoria*, 2:437–38, letter of Ostrozhsky to K. Radziwill, 2 Mar. 1596.

19. Ibid.; Bielski, p. 262; Hejdensztejn, 2:364.

20. Kulish, loc. cit.; Hejdensztejn, loc. cit.

21. Hejdensztejn, 2:365; Bielski, pp. 262–63.
22. *Listy Żółkiewskiego*, #46.
23. Hejdensztejn, 2:367; Domanitsky, "Kozachchina," p. 105.
24. Hejdensztejn, loc. cit.
25. Ibid. 2:368; Bielski, p. 263.
26. It would be valuable to have the exact text of what Nalivaiko offered, to compare it to the letter from Belorussia, and to see what his attitude here towards the peasant "irregular" cossacks was.
27. Hejdensztejn, 2:365–66; *Listy Żółkiewskiego*, #46.
28. Ibid.
29. Ibid. The cossack rank and file demanded absolute rejection of the offer. In fact, Loboda merely wrote Zolkiewski that he, Loboda, deserved a higher-ranking envoy, and neither accepted nor rejected the terms.
30. Storozhenko, "Vereshchinskii," p. 40; Storozhenko, "Iz Perepiski Zaporozhia XVI v.," pp. 68–69.
31. Hejdensztejn, 2:367. The figure of 8000 may well be an exaggeration.
32. From a speech of Zamojski to the 1597 Diet, in *Dyaryusze Siemowe z g. 1597*, in *Scriptores Rerum Polonicaru*, 20 (1907), pp. 80–81.
33. *Listy Żółkiewskiego*, pp. 74–75.
34. Kulish, *Otpadenie*, 1:98; Novitsky, pp. 60–73.
35. *Listy Żółkiewskiego*, #47; Hejdensztejn, 2:366.
36. *Listy Żółkiewskiego*, #48.
37. Ibid., #49. The cossack scheme did not go quite as planned, however, because, in their hatred for Ruzhinsky, the cossacks were foolish enough to trust another, equally treacherous, "friend" of theirs—Bishop Vereshchinsky. Asked to deliver the letter to Ruzhinsky, he also delivered the news that the cossacks were planning an attack, giving Ruzhinsky a warning.
38. Ibid., #49.
39. Hejdensztejn, 2:367.
40. Belotserkov was traditionally a pro-cossack town.
41. Hejdensztejn, 2:367–68; Bielski, p. 263; *Listy Żółkiewskiego*, ##47–49, 52.
42. Hejdensztejn, 2:368–69; *Listy Żółkiewskiego*, #52.
43. Ibid.; Bielski, pp. 263–64.
44. One addition to the cossacks' united forces was ambushed: Hetman Krempsky was leading another regiment north from Zaporozhe to aid his brothers; but, stopping in Kanev on Easter, he and several hundred of his men participated in an Easter celebration with the townspeople there. The Poles caught them unawares, and ambushed and massacred them; they also looted Kanev and the nearby towns thoroughly, and carried off the cossacks' stores of salt—a very severe blow in a salt-short land. Bielski, p. 264; *Listy Żółkiewskiego*, #54.
45. Hejdensztejn, 2:367.
46. Ibid., 2:370, *Pisma Żółkiewskiego*, pp. 148–52.

47. *Hejdensztejn*, 2:373.

48. *Ibid*, 2:370–74; *Bielski*, pp. 265–66; *Zherela*, 8, #63.

49. Hejdensztejn, 2:374–76; Bielski, pp. 275–77.

50. *Zherela*, 8:91.

51. Hejdensztejn, 2:376–77; Bielski, pp. 277-80.

52. Hejdensztejn, 2:377.

53. To the extent that the Solonitsa massacre was motivated by greed, the Polish soldiers were disappointed. Zolkiewski's sources told him that the total value of the booty they got there was at most 4000 zlotys. The same source thought that the massacre was stimulated by the soldiers' fear that if they did not take the valuables themselves, their officers would confiscate it all; and that Zolkiewski suppressed the soldiers' riot and punished many of them. *Listy Żółkiewskiego*, p. 82.

54. Bielski, p. 280.

55. The story of Nalivaiko's torture is not authoritative; the story is dubious because the alleged purpose of the torture was to make him talk about the cossacks' dealings with foreign powers, and one doubts that Nalivaiko would have been reluctant to confess on this subject. He was also, however, periodically questioned by nobles who wanted to find out the location of rumored buried treasure. *Archiwum Sapiehów*, #170; *Akty . . . Zapadnoi Rossii*, 4:173. Nalivaiko's treatment in general was reminiscent of Batory's execution of the cossack pirate Ivan Podkova twenty years earlier. Domanitsky, "Kozachchina," pp. 121–24; Bielski, p. 281.

56. Bielski, p. 280.

57. *Prawa*, pp. 1446–48; *Inventarz*, p. 258.

58. Hrushevsky, "Materialy," p. 16.

59. Ibid., ##5, 7, 11, 12; Kamanin, "Materialy," p. 18. Loboda had left his money and valuables, and possibly land titles, in the care of the monks of two different Orthodox monasteries, and when the crown bestowed them upon a Polish noble, the monks resisted; lengthy litigation was required before the noble got his prize. The litigation reflected the growing support of the Orthodox clergy for the cossacks in this period.

60. Hrushevsky, "Materialy," p. 16.

61. Domanitsky, "Kozachchina," pp. 83#n.

62. Hrushevsky, "Materialy," #6.

63. Ibid., p. 29, for example.

CONCLUSION

1. *Listy Żółkiewskiego, passim*, esp. p. 80.

2. *Archiwum Radziwiłłów*, p. 119; Hrushevsky, "Materialy," #13.

3. J. U. Niemcewicz, *Zbiór Pamiętników Historycznych o Dawnej Polszcze* (D), 2:169.

4. *Prawa*, pp. 1446–48; *Inventarz*, p. 258.

5. *Arkhiv Yugo-Zapadnoi Rossii*, pt. 3, vol. 1, #38.

6. Niemcewicz, 2, 174; *Listy Żółkiewskiego, #55*.

7. *Listy Żółkiewskiego, #55*.

8. *Arkhiv Yugo-Zapadnoi Rossii*, loc. cit.

9. *Prawa*, p. 1525; *Inventarz*, p. 258.

10. The following comments on seventeenth-century cossack history are based on a variety of different interpretations, notably: Allen, *The Ukraine;* I. F. Bykadorov, *Istoria Kazachestva* (Prague: 1930); D. I. Evarnitsky, *Istoria Zaporozhskikh Kozakov;* Holobutsky, *Zaporozhskoe Kazachestvo;* Hrushevsky, *Istoria Ukrainskavo Kozachestva;* I. Kamanin, "Esche o Drevnosti Bratstva i Shkoly v Kiev;" idem, "Voprosu o Kozaches- tive;" Kulish, *Istoria Vozsoedinenia Rusi;* idem, *Otpadenie Malorossii ot Polshi;* D. M. Odinets, *Prisoedinenie Ukrainy k Moskovskomu Gosu- darstvu;* F. Rawita-Gawroński, *Kozaczyzna Ukrainna w Rzeczypospolitej Polskiej do Końca XVIII-go Wieku;* I. I. Smirnov, *Vosstanie Boltonikova 1606–1607* (Leningrad: 1951); Stökl; G. Vernadsky, *Bohdan, Hetman of Ukraine.*

11. This analysis is widespread in the histories of the Khmelnitsky rebellion, argued well by Hrushevsky, op. cit.

12. Peter Bartl, "Der Kosakenstaat und das Osmanische Reich in 17 und in der Ersten Haelfte des 18 Jahrhunderts," 166–94.

13. For example, under the hetmanship of Sahaidachny; or in 1630 in the rebellion of the Zaporozhians *against* the registered cossacks.

14. For examples, the behavior of hetmans Sahaidachny and Doroshenko.

Historiographical Essay

All historiography has political underpinnings and implications, but none more so than cossack historiography. Cossacks have, as we have seen in this book, been symbols, positive and negative, of Ukrainian and Russian national (and sometimes imperial) aspirations for at least four centuries. Even those who took the position that the cossacks were nothing but bandits did so in a context in which their denial of the nationalist content of cossack activity was itself a political statement. Since cossack symbolism has been vivid in popular as well as scholarly literature, the historian must disentangle not only scholarly biases but also folkloric overlays of myth and romance.

For the Ukraine, virtually all aspects of its historiography could be and usually were in the service of establishing or disestablishing its right to national independence or autonomy. This national-intellectual campaign begins with the fundamental question of who the Ukrainians are, ethnically; of what their national-historical accomplishments were, in culture, state building, settlement, for example; of who their best allies and what their best form of social organization have been. With the cossacks, these controversies are equally fundamental and persistent. They begin with the controversy about whether the Zaporozhian cossacks are Ukrainian, i.e., Ruthenian, in nationality; and include questions of what they did, why they did it, and what they accomplished. A high proportion of the statements in this book are, therefore, controversial. It would be inappropriate and nonproductive to attempt to summarize here all the relevant controversies. However, enabling the reader to approach this work without complete gullibility requires a bit of orientation amidst the tangles of these arguments among historians. What follows is a brief narrative of cossack historiography.[1] In the interests of brevity and relevance, I will discuss only those historians whose works bear directly on the sixteenth-century cossacks.

249

The Birth of Romantic Ukrainian Nationalist History

The beginning of Ukrainian history writing was part of a Ukrainian cultural renascence and nationalist revival in the nineteenth century. It produced the first historian of the cossacks, Dmitri Bantysh-Kamensky (1788–1850). Russian, son of a noted archivist, he studied under the pioneering eighteenth-century historian G. F. Muller. He went to the Ukraine as secretary to its Russian governor-general, Nikolai Repnin, in 1816, and there wrote his *Istoria Maloi Rossii* . . ., which appeared in 1822. This work was still very like a chronicle, but it made critical use of documents, twenty of which were published in an appendix.

Bantysh-Kamensky applied to the Ukraine the imperial schema of Russian history as it had been set out first by the "founder" of Russian history, Karamzin. This conception assumed the national unity of the Eastern Slav peoples. Yet Bantysh-Kamensky's empirical judgments led him into at least one inconsistency: he identified the Ukrainians as the indigenous residents of the Ukraine, although the Great Russian imperial interpretation was that the bulk of the Kiev-Rus population had migrated north during the Tatar period, leaving the Kievan lands empty for several centuries. The significance of this question of the population history of the Kievan lands might easily be missed by a reader not familiar with the political context of this historiography. Great Russian historians claimed the Kievan state as part of the history of *Russia*, using a dynastic legend that the Romanovs were descended from the Rurikovichi. The argument that the Kievan lands were at one time totally empty reinforces the view that the Russians were as much its owners as the Ukrainians. By contrast, Ukrainian historians were later to challenge this interpretation; to insist that the Kievan state was specifically Ukrainian and not Russian; and to support this argument with evidence that many Ukrainians (Ruthenians) had never left the Kievan lands.

But this is getting ahead of the story. It took time for the lines to be formed so clearly. An earlier battle was led by Nikolai (Mykola) Kostomarov (1817–1885), himself a Russian, although his mother may have been a Ukrainian serf. Kostomarov went to school at Kharkov University, which had become, in the early nineteenth century, a kind of Ukrainian cultural center. Kostomarov's *Books of the Genesis of the Ukrainian People* grew out of his early period of activity with the radical, secret Ukrainian nationalist organization, the Brotherhood of Saints Cyril and Methodius—indeed, the book was treated by that organization as something of a catechism. The *Books of the Genesis* are rich with thoughts that were later to be the shared principles of Ukrainian historiography. For example:

> Ukraine loved neither the tsar nor the Polish lord and established a Cossack Host amongst themselves, i.e., a brotherhood in which each upon entering was a brother of the others—whether he had before been a master or a slave, provided that he was a Christian; and the Cossacks were all equal amongst themselves, and officials were elected at the assembly and they had to serve all according to the word of Christ, because they accepted duty as compulsory, as an obligation, and there was no sort of seignorial majesty and title among the Cossacks.
>
> And they resolved to preserve their purity, therefore the old chroniclers say of the Cossacks: thievery and fornication are never named among them.
>
> And the Cossack Host decided to guard the holy faith and free their neighbors from captivity. . . .
>
> And day after day the Cossack Host grew and multiplied and soon all people in Ukraine would have become Cossacks, i.e., free and equal, and there would have been neither a tsar not a Polish lord over Ukraine, but God alone, and as it would be in Ukraine, so it would also be in Poland and then also in other Slavic lands. . . .
>
> And when the popes and Jesuits wished to subordinate Ukraine forcibly to their authority in order that the Ukrainian Christians might believe that all that the pope says true and equitable, then in Ukraine there appeared brotherhoods such as there were among the first Christians; and each person on enrolling in the brotherhood, whether he had been a master or a slave was called a brother. And this was so that all might see that in Ukraine the ancient, true faith remained and that in Ukraine there were no idols and for this reason no types of heresies had appeared there. . . .
>
> And Ukraine was destroyed. But it only seems to be so.
>
> She was not destroyed; because she wished to know neither a tsar nor a master, and although a tsar was over her he was a foreigner and although there were nobles they were foreign, and although these degenerates were of Ukrainian blood they yet did not soil the Ukrainian language with their foul mouths and they did not call themselves Ukrainians; but the true

Ukrainian—whether of simple origin or noble—must love neither a tsar or master but he must love and be mindful of one God, Jesus Christ, the king and master of heaven and earth. Thus it was in the beginning, is now and ever shall be.

The great themes here are the independence of the Ukrainian nationality, the association of Ukrainian-ness with the instinctual love of equality and liberty, and some sort of Ukrainian messianism. The passages quoted make it clear how central the cossacks were to these conceptions. Indeed, in this work the cossacks themselves had become simply the highest expression of the Ukrainian people itself.

Kostomarov's early nationalism and populism were part of a pan-European romantic movement among intellectuals. In his later years Kostomarov became more scholarly and empirical in his work, and made political compromises with the imperial regime in an effort to protect his position. The legacy of his populism remained simultaneously a strength in his writing and a limitation on its reliability. He consistently romanticized the cossacks, and particularly the Zaporozhians. He was suspicious of the seventeenth-century rule of the hetmans and criticized its antidemocratic nature. But he did not see any of those tendencies in the period before 1654, when the Zaporozhians were gradually winning the enthusiasm of many Ukrainians. The very absence of any political program among the Zaporozhians he tended to interpret as evidence that they acted out of instinctive anti-authoritarianism.

Kostomarov's influence on Ukrainian historiography was great, particularly inasmuch as he practiced and taught the necessity of relying on original sources. His was among the influences that led to the first collective project for the publication of sources, the Kiev Vremennaya Komissia dlia Razbora Drevnikh Aktov, established in 1843. (Almost simultaneously a similar commission was founded in Vilno.) The Kiev commission published a number of different series of documents and chronicles: the *Pamiatniki*, in four volumes, between 1845 and 1859; a *Sbornik Letopisei . . . k Istorii Yuzhnoi i Zapadnoi Rossii*, in 1888; and, most important of all for this book, the *Arkhiv Yugo-Zapadnoi Rossii*, with a total of 35 volumes published between 1859 and 1914. The activities of the Kiev commission gained official government support for a time after the Polish rebellion of 1863, when St. Petersburg thought for a time to use Ukrainian nationalism to combat Polish influences in the right-bank Ukraine. In the 1870s, however, under Alexander II, came a repression of Ukrainian cultural activity, and specifically, of publishing in the Ukrainian language. This was followed, in the 1880s, by a rebirth of Ukrainian historical activity and the emergence of two new historical journals, *Kievskaya Starina* and the *Chtenia* of the Istoricheskoe Obshchestvo Nestora Letopistsa of Kiev University.

Among the strengths of these and numerous other journals and scholarly publications was that they were collective endeavors, pooling the labors of many fine scholars, preventing duplication of work and allowing healthy cross-fertilization of data and analyses. Still, behind these efforts, and behind the Kiev commission especially, the contributions of Volodymyr B. Antonovych stand out. Antonovych (1834–1908), the son of a small landowner, lived all his life in the Ukraine, primarily in Kiev, and played an important political role there for over 50 years, particularly as head of the Kiev "Stara Hromada." Influenced by Kostomarov, he was a populist: he spoke of his secession from his own class and of having cast his lot with democrats and abolitionists.

As a historian, however, Antonovych differed from Kostomarov. He was the veritable founder of scientific Ukrainian history; he was an archivist, and some of his best work was as editor of numerous publications of documents for the Kiev commission; and he was an administrator and teacher, and some of his greatest contributions were in instigating and organizing scholarly work and publication throughout the Ukraine and in Galicia. For this book, and possibly in general, Antonovych's most important work is his essay "O Proiskhozhdenii Kozachestva." Influenced here by Kostomarov's and Bantysh-Kamensky's ideas about the evolution of Ukrainian society out of Kievan Rus, he then went on to elaborate the specific hypothesis, which Hrushevsky has since shown to be quite improbable, that the cossack organization was a direct descendant of the old Kievan *veche*. Still, he showed conclusively that it was necessary to study the cossacks as a singularly Ukrainian phenomenon, even if the relative weights of tradition and environment were still to be debated for many decades.

Another important historian of this era was Panteleimon Kulish (1819–97). Himself of cossack descent, Kulish at the beginning of his career was as much a romantic populist as Kostomarov or Antonovych. Like Kostomarov, he was arrested and exiled for his membership in the Brotherhood of Saints Cyril and Methodius, and survived his punishment with his nationalism undiminished. Kulish's first writings, from the years 1847–1863, were largely ethnographic. He wrote studies of Ukrainian folklore, several historical novels, based on folk legends, and an epic poem, not without similarities to Kostomarov's *Books of the Genesis.*

In the 1860s and 70s, Kulish entered into a different intellectual mood, publishing several monographs distinctly critical of the cossacks. In some Ukrainian intellectual circles his views were considered heretical and even traitorous. In fact, Kulish's rejection of the Zaporozhians as heroes was not anti-Ukrainian, but rather directed toward the exploration of other parts of the Ukrainian heritage. For example, he emphasized the progressive role of the small Ukrainian bourgeoisie in fighting to defend their faith and nationality, as opposed to what he considered the reactionary role of the cossacks in weakening social order in the Ukraine. Kulish's best work, *Istoria Vozsoedinenia Rusi,* in three volumes, appeared in the 1870s as part of this period, accompanied by another volume, *Materialy,* of valuable source materials, largely taken from Polish archives and never before published. In this work Kulish criticized the leading "cossackophiles" such as Kostomarov and Shevchenko.

It now seems clear that Kulish's book—despite its bad press at the time—was the best, most reliable and most objective overall work on the fifteenth-to-seventeenth-century Ukraine and cossacks yet written; and that it remained the best until the work of Hrushevsky. But the merits of this work were harder to perceive because it was soon followed by an inferior book, *Otpadenie Malorossii ot Polshi* (1888–1889). Kulish now indulged an eccentric cossack hatred, entirely different from his earlier serious efforts at critical history. The *Otpadenie* showed no new research since the *Istoria,* and painted the cossack rebellion as mere piracy, vandalism, rapine, and murder. This work was doubly unfortunate, because it justified the more nationalistic historians in ignoring the value of Kulish's earlier work.

In the 1890s an old controversy about the origins of the cossacks was reopened in the scholarly circles of the Ukraine by Ivan Kamanin in his "K Voprosu o Kozachestve do Bogdana Khmelnitskavo." Kamanin (1859–1921), director of the central archives in Kiev, argued that the cossacks originated in part as the private retainers of Ruthenian princes and even Polish nobles. Kamanin was answered by a well-known Russian historian of Belorussian origin, Matvei Liubavsky (1860–1937). A pupil of Kluchevsky and a member of the Imperial Academy of Sciences, Liubavsky was in a delicate position: he was expected to be able to enunciate the imperial point of view, yet was himself dedicated to writing the history of Rus-in-Lithuania, i.e., arguing that those Kievan people who had fallen under Lithuanian rule were part of the Rus nation. Possibly as a means of handling this contradictory situation, Liubavsky hit upon the odd theory that cossacks were in fact of Tatar origins, which he advanced in his article "Nachalnaya Istoria Malorusskovo Kazachestva."

The belief that the cossacks were not of Slavic origin was old. The eighteenth-century chronicler Hrabianka, himself a cossack, argued that they were descendants of the Khazars! It was a theory uniquely important to imperial Russian cossack historiography: Karamzin, Muller, and Solovev all derived the cossacks from some Turkic group. It seems clear that they mainly wanted the cossacks *not* to be Ukrainian. The reopening of this controversy in the 1890s, after both Antonovych and Kulish had compellingly argued that cossackdom had been created by the conditions of the Ukraine rather than by any ethnic heredity, suggests that the Russian historiographical school was again feeling threatened by the role of Ukrainian historians in building national consciousness.

Liubavsky's "Turkish theory" was picked up by the Polish historian Aleksander Jabłonowski (1829–1911) in 1897 in a manner that suggests the cross-cutting interests of Polish historians. A Pole born in Kiev, Jabłonowski devoted most of his work to the Ukraine and was probably more sympathetic to its national strivings than most Poles of the time. Still, his ultimate conclusion (an inevitable one, since it follows from his assumptions) is that the Ukrainian lands never constituted an entity, nor the Ukrainian population a people. Rather, the Poles had been the civilizers of a barbaric and pagan land. In some ways this view is symmetrical with that of the Great Russians, but in other ways it is different. The Poles had to justify themselves as foreign rulers, and did not attempt to claim national or dynastic continuity with Old Rus. They therefore had a less ambivalent, and more consistently critical, view of the cossacks as representing an important part of, and surely a symptom of, the barbarity of the area. Prefiguring later Polish cossack history, Jabłonowski's work had the strength of some detachment in relation to Ukrainian–Russian differences in interpretation.

On the eve of the twentieth-century revolutionary period appeared a Russian work strongly influenced by the Polish historical style, Andrei Storozhenko's *Stefan Batorii* . . . (1904). Storozhenko valued scholarly caution and precision and veered away from romanticization of the cossacks, while respecting their accomplishments. He reproduced valuable documents taken from Polish sources, and challenged some previously unquestioned conventions about actual Polish treatment of the cossacks.

Hrushevsky

With the Russian revolution of 1905 the atmosphere in the Ukraine became a little freer toward the "national question," and in this context the works of the young Ukrainian historian Mykhailo Hrushevsky first gained widespread attention. Born in 1866, Hrushevsky had studied under Antonovych, who, in 1897, got him a chair at the University of Lvov. Here Hrushevsky became president of the newly organized Shevchenko Scientific Society, which position he held until 1913. Hrushevsky, like Antonovych, made important contributions both as an archivist and administrator and as a writer of history; and his breadth of conception made him still today the dominant influence in Ukrainian historiography.

More than any of the other Ukrainian "populist" historians, Hrushevsky dedicated himself to writing the history of a people, and rejected the state or dynasty as organizing principles for this project. He was so persevering about this goal that his scholarly career appears, in retrospect, remarkably integrated. His life's work, *Istoria Ukrainy-Rusy*, a virtually encyclopedic history and interpretation of the Ukrainians, was written and published slowly, volume by volume, between 1898 and 1922. But its conception was already evident in the article "Zvichaina Skhema 'Russkoi' Istorii . . .," published in 1904. Indeed, the *Istoria* is in a sense the filling out of the outline given in that article, while his history of the cossacks, published in Kiev in 1913–1914, is an elaboration on materials included in the great *Istoria*.

"I was brought up," wrote Hrushevsky, "in the strict tradition of Ukrainian radical Populism, which originated with the Brotherhood of Sts. Cyril and Methodius, and firmly believed that, in the conflict between the people and the government, blame attaches to the government since the interests of the working people are the highest good, and if they are flouted the people are free to change their social system."[2] Given this view, it is not surprising that Hrushevsky found in the peasant uprisings of the fifteenth and sixteenth centuries, and the cossack rebellions of the sixteenth and seventeenth centuries, the beginnings of "world-historical" upheavals which could be justified in the name of liberty, equality, Christianity, or any number of values. Hrushevsky approved of revolution, and his works about the Ukraine, more than any others, apprehended the potential revolutionary force that lay in the eastern European peasant communities.

Hrushevsky's sympathies with the oppressed should not, however, be misconstrued as Marxist. Nationality, not class, was his basic category. His work contains a rather sociological emphasis on social strata and societal rather than governmental organization. His liberalism, also, committed him to a struggle against his own subjectivity and a belief, rather Rankean, in the absolute truth to be found in history.

Hrushevsky's enduring sympathies for the "masses," and his sociological approach to history, help explain how it was possible for him to continue to live and work productively in Kiev for over a decade after the Bolshevik revolution. During the Civil War period, of course, the struggle for Ukrainian independence was a great stimulus to many of the nationalist historians. But it was in 1924, when independence seemed out of the question, that Hrushevsky returned from abroad to head the historical section of the All-Ukrainian Academy of Sciences. For the next six years he worked organizing a large series of publications, finished his *Istoria Ukrainy-Rusy*, began a history of Ukrainian literature, and published numerous monographs. Equally important were his activities as a teacher. Among his students were many exceptional historians—most of whom were Marxists, which suggests something about Hrushevsky's openness to other points of view. Of those students, one needs specific mention here: O. I. Baranovych, a Ukrainian publishing in that language in the 1930s and in Russian in the 1950s. His empirical studies of the social and economic history of the sixteenth-century Ukraine were indispensable for the analysis contained in this book.

The 1920s

Although Hrushevsky was the giant, so to speak, in the strongest decade of Ukrainian historical scholarship, he was by no means the only hegemonic influence. Indeed, the remarkable 1920s was characterized by energetic pluralism in historical work in the Ukraine. As Hrushevsky was the dominant influence in Kiev, D. I. Bahaliy (Bagalei), another pupil of Antonovych, was the mentor of historians at Kharkov. Starting in the 1880s, Bahaliy had conducted and supervised extensive empirical studies into Ukrainian socioeconomic history. Also at Kharkov, although less concerned with the cossacks, M. Vasylenko developed legal history. And even more striking, also in Kharkov, the leading Marxist historian, Matvei Yavorsky, produced remarkably critical, open-minded work based on Hrushevsky's paradigm of the autonomous history of the Ukrainian people. Even the leading Soviet historian Pokrovsky at this time accepted the necessity to study Ukrainian history separately from Russian, without forcing the former into the latter's categories. As Lowell Tillett argued, what is today hailed as Great Russian leadership was then condemned as Great Russian chauvinism.[3]

The rise of Stalin produced a complete rout of critical history about the Ukraine. Beginning with the prosecution of members of the secret Union of Liberation of the Ukraine in 1929–1930, the Stalinist fear of Ukrainian nationalism viewed its historical expressions as potent and requiring suppression. Not only was Hrushevsky condemned as a bourgeois nationalist and deported to Moscow in 1931 (where he died in 1934), but even Yavorsky, the protegé of Pokrovsky, was denounced and labeled a "nationalist-Kulakist." (His fall was a prefiguring of Pokrovsky's own loss of influence after his death in 1932.) Having lost their mentor Hrushevsky, and their "buffer", the Marxist Yavorsky, lesser historians were now helpless. Separate Ukrainian historical institutes were eliminated and archives were made inaccessible to any but approved historians. The efforts of the approved historians were directed not to primary research but to the writing of textbooks with the correct lines, and shifting subtle interpretations required that these be frequently rewritten. The Russification of Ukrainian history preached the essential unity of the Eastern slavs, and their destiny of political unity under Great Russian leadership. Lowell Tillett has assembled a set of quotations from Ukrainian history textbooks that vividly illustrate this shift in interpretation of Russian Imperialism:

> "They [the Ukrainians] did not know that a fate worse than that under the *szlachta* awaited them in the future at the hands of the Muscovite *dvorianstvo* and its autocrat—the 'white tsar.' " (The consequences of the annexation of the Ukraine, from a 1928 textbook, M Iavorskii, *Istoriia Ukrainy v styslomu narysi* [Kharkov, 1928], p. 58.)

> "The Ukraine's incorporation into the Russian state was for her a lesser evil than seizure by the Poland of the Pans or the

Turkey of the Sultans." (The 1940 view, from the textbook, *Istoriia SSSR*, ed. A. M. Pankratova [1st ed. Moscow, 1940], I, 189.)

"The Ukraine's incorporation into the Russian state signified a reunion of two great brotherly peoples which was to save the Ukraine from seizure by Poland and Turkey." (The same passage, as rewritten for the 1947 and subsequent editions).[4]

This gospel prohibited independent and critical investigation of cossack history, and the Polish–Lithuanian period of the Ukraine received little attention altogether.

Until the Soviet occupation of Poland in the Great War, the Shevchenko Scientific Society in Lvov, in Polish Galicia, maintained a group of Ukrainian active historians. With this group were associated several historians whose work contributed original findings to cossack history—for example, Barvinsky, Terletsky, Krypiakevych, Chubaty, and Pritsak. Other Ukrainian historians continued work, particularly in Prague, where a Ukrainian free university was set up, its history section headed by Dmytro I. Doroshenko, and in Warsaw and Berlin.

Post–World-War-II Ukrainian Historiography

Briefly, after the Twentieth Party Congress, de-Stalinization seemed to promise a loosening of the dogmatic reins on Soviet historiography. Symbolic of the promise was the establishment of the *Ukrainskyi Istorichnyi Zhurnal* in 1957. In a 1959 monograph, Shevchenko, editor of that journal, discussing political and economic links between the Ukraine and Russia, used concepts alien to the Stalinist orthodoxy: for example, he called the acquisition of the Ukraine by Russia "annexation" instead of "reunification," and wrote "national liberation war" instead of "people's liberation war." But he was soon sharply criticized by a Ukrainian party organ, and the signs of flexibility quickly disappeared. The attacks on Kulish, Antonovych, and Hrushevsky continued. Empirical and archival work is proceeding once again, but on questions of class, nationality, religion, and culture the Stalinist historical dogmas seem to remain in place. The experience of World War II may even have intensified some of these dogmas: certainly the general experience of the near-destruction of the Soviet Union by encircling anticommunist powers, and the specific experience of a degree of Ukrainian–Nazi collaboration, exacerbated fears of any potentially secessionist nationalism.

Soviet Ukrainian historiography still pays the least attention to the Ukraine in the Polish–Lithuanian period, and most work touching on the sixteenth century emerges from the study of cossacks in the later centuries. Still, as an official 1970 survey of Ukrainian historical science put it, it was necessary to provide a scientific point of view on cossack history to rescue it from falsifications by "modern European bourgeois-nationalistic authors."[5] The leading Soviet historian of the cossacks is V. O. Holobutsky (Golobutsky, when he publishes in Russian), who has been studying the cossacks since the 1930s. His best work is on the eighteenth century, but in 1957 he published a survey of the Zaporozhians. Like many competent Soviet historians, he tries to avoid the worst effects of doctrinaire party requirements by separating his avowals of that ideology as much as possible from the substance of his historical narratives and evidence. Still, his class interpretations tend to be crude and thus inadequate to explain the intricate phenomena that the cossack rebellions presented. He concentrates, for example, on the struggle within the cossack host between registered and nonregistered cossacks, which he identifies as a class struggle. But in emphasizing intracossack dissension so exclusively, Holobutsky leaves unexplained the rebellions themselves, which, after all, were fought against Poles and landlords, not against other cossacks. A rigorous Marxist analysis of the cossack rebellions would lead to an examination of the social content of Ukrainian demands for national self-determination; by contrast, Soviet Marxism is committed to the ultimate consonance of class warfare and Great Russian–Ukrainian political unity.

The period after the "Great Patriotic War" has seen the reintegration of nationalist interpretations into Soviet Ukrainian writing about the cossacks. It is a subtle and complex nationalism, for it allows simultaneously a recognition of autonomous Ukrainian nationality and an assumption of the national unity of Ukrainians and Russians. These interpretations are most explicitly stated in some of the official summary pronouncements on cossack history. For example, an official encyclopedia of the Ukraine blames "foreign" domination of the Ukraine for the deteriorating condition of the peasants in the fifteenth and sixteenth centuries, and includes Poles and Lithuanians but not Russians among the foreigners.[6] Further, "The existence of a Russian centralized state was a major factor in the struggle of the Ukrainian and Byelorussian peoples against foreign [sic] enslavement. From the moment of its origin at the close of the 15th century, it supported the Cossacks' fight for Ukrainian freedom and independence . . ."[7] There is emphasis also on the cossacks' struggle against Catholicism and the Union. In other words, cultural factors, nationality and religion, are entertained in explaining the cossacks' motivations when those factors united them with the Russians and divided them from the Polish–Lithuanian state.

Ukrainians in exile have continued a different nationalist Ukrainian historiographical tradition, strongly anti-Russian as well as anti-Soviet. The dominant influence has been that of Dmytro Doroshenko (1882–1951). Born into an old cossack family, which had produced two seventeenth-century hetmans, Doroshenko served as foreign minister of the Ukrainian government in 1918. In 1919 he emigrated and taught in Vienna, Prague, and finally Munich until his death. Continuing the political tradition of many Ukrainian historians, a position thrust upon them by the Ukraine's nationally subordinate position, Doroshenko was influential both as a political spokesman and organizer of scholarly activity and as a scholar.

Ukrainian exile historians' work has been limited by lack of access to sources, and by the simplifying influence of contemporary national-political partisanship equal and opposite to that of the Soviets (although, understandably, more passionate). The work of such historians has taken on a polemical character, not only in terms of historical controversies but in being tied to a captive–nations ideology and to a demand for Western diplomatic, economic, and sometimes even military action against the Soviet Union. On the other hand, Ukrainian emigré historians have benefited from access to foreign archives and, perhaps above all, from contacts with Western scholarship. One of the problems faced by Ukrainians in the West is the fact that most Western historians, particularly Americans, have adopted the Russian view of the Ukraine in their writing and teaching. That is, they see Kiev Rus as the source of the Russian, not the autonomous Ukrainian, nation; they are skeptical of Ukrainian claims to political nationhood and are sympathetic to a kind of "manifest destiny" approach to the Russian conquest of the Ukraine. Thus the bias of Western scholarship itself has further strengthened the political and polemical tendencies of Ukrainian historical scholarship in exile.

About the cossacks, the general line of emigré Ukrainian history has been to emphasize their politicization and self-conscious national leadership. As the Soviets have reduced or at best assimilated cultural struggle to class struggle, so the emigrés have ignored or deemphasized conflicts within the cossack groups, among Ukrainians, and between cossacks and other Ukrainians. They have projected nineteenth-century populist Ukrainian nationalism backwards in time, ahistorically, and have often failed to examine aspects of cossack aspirations that did not fit this model.

Furthermore, the anti-Soviet convictions of the Ukrainian emigré historians have led to a too-exclusive focus on the history and historiography of the lands east of the Dniester. Important and potentially useful new history has been neglected because it does not touch directly on the Ukraine or directly challenge Soviet Russian interpretations: for example, the new Polish economic history, the world-systems-theory writings of Wallerstein and his followers, and the work of Braudel and the *Annales* school. Non-Soviet Marxist scholarship beyond the Russian-nationalist and vulgar-Marxist premises of Soviet Marxist work has also been ignored: here one thinks of the history writing of Rodney Hilton, Eric Hobsbawm, and Witold Kula, among others, and the sociological and economic studies of underdevelopment by Andre Gunder Frank, Samir Amin, and many others. These are but a few suggestions of sources of insight that would illuminate new aspects of Ukrainian history.

On the other hand, the Ukrainian emigré historians have made an important and unique contribution to the study of Eastern Europe today. Without their integrity, the intellectual disagreements they keep alive, and their reminder of the power, even in the West, of Soviet hegemony over Russian history, our knowledge and understanding would be developing even more slowly than it is.

Notes to Historiographical Essay

1. In this essay I have been aided by several useful works of historiographical scholarship, particularly by Doroshenko, Horak, Hrushevsky, Myhul, Ohloblyn, Pelenski, Polonska-Vasylenko, Tillett, and Wynar. All are listed in the bibliography. They will not be further noted here except when specific references were taken from them. Similarly, the original histories mentioned here are listed in the bibliography and will not be noted here unless they are quoted from.

2. Dmytro Doroshenko, *Ukrainian Historiography: Annals of the*

Ukrainian Academy of Arts and Sciences in the United States (New York: 1957; trans. of 1923 Ukrainian ed.), p. 270.

3. Lowell Tillett, *The Great Friendship: Soviet Historians on the Non-Russian Nationalities* (Chapel Hill, N.C.: 1969), p. 37.

4. Ibid., p. 35.

5. V. A. Dyadichenko, *Development of Historical Science in the Ukrainian SSR* (Kiev: Institute of History of the Academy of Sciences of the Ukrainian SSR, 1970), p. 59.

6. *Soviet Ukraine,* ed. M. P. Bazhan et al. (Kiev: Academy of Sciences of the Ukrainian SSR, 1969), p. 74.

7. Ibid., p. 76.

Bibliography

Contemporary Chronicles and Letters

I. Two chronicles are basic to this study, both Polish, and both by commoners who became royal servitors. The first, Joachim Bielski's *Dalszy Ciąg Kroniki Polskiej*, introduction by F. M. Sobieszczański (Warsaw, 1851), is a continuation of the *Kronika Polska* of his father, Marcin Bielski, covering the period from the death of King Stefan Batory to 1597. Marcin was the nephew of a cossack elder, and thus the family had a particular interest in cossack affairs. Marcin was a Protestant, but his son Joachim, no doubt due to the pressures of the Counter-Reformation, was a Catholic again. Joachim served both under Batory and Sigismund III as a secretary, and although literate and well-educated, his talents as a chronicler were less than his father's. In addition to having the expected bias—anti-Orthodox and anti-cossack—Joachim Bielski's work lacks the breadth and analysis of the earlier chronicle.

A second chronicle important to this study is Rajnold Hejdensztejn's *Dzieje Polski od Śmierci Zygmunta Augusta do Roku 1594* (St. Petersburg; 1857). Heidenstein (as the name is usually given in English) also served both Batory and Sigismund III, but did so primarily as a result of his position as a retainer and, reportedly, an intimate of Jan Zamojski. He is often described as a translator, putting Zamojski's and the royal correspondence in and out of Latin; but he was also used as a roving ambassador and an expert on German affairs. He had less special interest in the cossacks than Bielski; but his chronicle is more accurate and level-headed, if less discursive, than Bielski's.

II. Heidenstein and Bielski worked from letters and other reports that came into their hands, rather than from personal experience or observation. Some of these chronicles still in existence and used here, were direct, eyewitness reports of particular aspects of the early history of the cossacks.

Beauplan, Guillaume le Vasseur, le Sieur de, "A Description of Ukraine . . .," trans. from French in Churchill, Awnsham and John, *A Collection of Voyages & Travels* (London: 1732), 1:515–51.

———, *Description de l'Ukranie* . . . (Paris: 1861). Beauplan was a French engineer engaged by Polish Crown Hetman Koniecpolski in the 1630s to design and construct a fort on the Dnieper to keep the cossacks out of the Ukraine. While there, Beauplan wrote a description of the cossacks' organization, mores, and facilities with a precision perhaps appropriate to his profession. Beauplan's work was first published in 1660.

265

"Borkulabovskaya Khronika," in Kulish, *Materialy*, q.v. This was written by an Orthodox clergyman from Belorussia around the end of the sixteenth century. Although it describes the Orthodox brotherhoods, it represents the point of view of the szlachta as opposed to that of the burghers. It is valuable for information about the beginnings of the Brest Union and about the Zaporozhians' invasion of Belorussia in 1595.

Bronevsky, Martin, "Opisanie Kryma," trans. from Latin in *Zapiski*, Odessa Obshchestvo Istorii i Drevnostei, 1867, 6. Bronevsky was a Polish noble sent by Batory as an emissary to Crimea.

Chevalier, Pierre, *Discourse of the Original, Countrey, Manners, Government and Religion of the Cossacks, with another of the Precopian Tartars, and the History of the Wars of the Cossacks Against Poland*, trans. Edward Brown (London: 1672).

———, *Histoire de la Guerre des Cosaques contre la Pologne* (Paris: 1859). Another French visitor to the Ukraine, Chevalier, whose work was first published in 1663, was particularly interested in cossack military style.

Evlashevsky, Fedor, "Dnevnik," ed. and introd. Antonovych, in *Kievskaya Starina*, #14 (Jan. 1886). Evlashevsky was a Ruthenian noble, whose diary covers events from 1564 to 1604 in Novgorod, Minsk and Slutsk environs. He was an advocate in both royal and diet courts; he was Orthodox until 1555 when he became Protestant.

Guagnini, Alessandro, "O Kozakach Nizowych które Pospolicie Zaporozkimi Zowiemy," in *Kronika Sarmacyey Europskiey*, ed. Turowski (1611). Guagnini was an Italian who served in the Polish army; his chronicle, however, is largely a retelling of Bielski's.

Lassota von Steblau, Erich, *Putevya Zapiski*, trans. F. Brun (St. Petersburg: 1873). This edition is a translation of those parts of Lassota's long *Tagebuch* which deal with his trip to the Ukraine in 1594, as an emissary of Emperor Rudolf II. Lassota's journal is detailed and objective, if not overly perspicacious. On Lassota himself, see pt. 5, ch. 2.

Maszkiewicz, Samuel, "Dyaryusz," in Niemcewicz, *Zbiór*, q.v., 2:243–304. Maskiewicz, or Mashkovich, was a Lithuanian, probably of Ruthenian origin, a servitor of Lithuanian Hetman Radziwill at the end of the century. His diary is useful primarily for information about the situation in Lithuania at the time of the cossack uprisings.

de Vigener, Blaise, *La Description du Royaume de Poloigne, et Pays adjacens: avec les Statuts, Constitutions, Moeurs, et Façons de Faire d'Iceux* (Paris: 1573). Another French traveller, not very reliable.

Vereshchinsky (Wereszczyński, Józef), Bishop of Kiev, "Vernaya Doroga k . . . Zaseleniu . . . v Ruskikh Oblastiakh Polskavo Korolevstva . . .," in *Kievskaya Starina*, q.v., #48 (1895). In this small proposal, the bishop lays out a plan for hiring cossacks as frontier guards.

Zamojski, Jan, *La Deffaicte des Tartares et Turcs faicte par le Seigneur Jean Zamoisky* (Paris: 1859). Originally published in Lyon in 1590, this is basically a speech given by Zamojski in the Diet, issued abroad for propaganda purposes.

III. Also basic to the early history of the cossacks are letters of some of the principals in these events.

Archiwum Domu Radziwiłłów. Listy Ks. M. K. Radziwiłła Sierotki, Jana Zamoyskiego, Lwa Sapiehy, ed. and introd. August Sokolowski, vol. 8 of *Scriptores Rerum Polonicarum* (1885).

Archiwum Domu Sapiehów, ed. A. Prochaska (Lvov: 1892). Letters 1575–1606.

Kopreev, T. N., ed., "K Istorii Dvizhenia Nalivaika," in *Istoricheskii Arkhiv*, #2 (1956). This reprints newly discovered letters to N. K. Radziwill from his brother, the Lithuanian hetman, regarding Nalivaiko's Belorussian attacks.

Sinan Bassa, letter to Queen Elizabeth I, June 12, 1590, in Hakluyt, *The Principal Navigations, Voiages, Traffiques and Discoveries of the English Nation* . . . (London: 1599), vol. 2 pt. 2.

Zamojski, Jan, *Archiwum* (Warsaw: 1904–1913, and Cracow: 1948), 4 vols.

Zborowski, Krzysztof & Samuel, *Pamiętniki do Życia i Sprawy Samuela i Krzysztofa Zborowskich* (Lvov: 1846).

Żółkiewski, Stanisława, *Listy Stanisława Żółkiewskiego 1584–1623*, ed. Jan Tadeusz Lubomirski (Cracow: 1868).

———, *Pisma*, ed. August Bielowski (Lvov: 1861). The last two publications do not overlap in contents, but contain different letters.

The three most often cited of the chronicles of the Zaporozhian cossacks—by Hrabianka, Velychko, and Samovydets—relate seventeenth-century events, primarily. They are not listed, since they were not used in the preparation of this essay.

Collections of Documents

The available documents relevant to the history of the cossacks are, unfortunately, scattered throughout many different publications, issued in many different languages. Of the more well-known documents, it is not uncommon to find three different publications, often in three different versions and three different languages. But these are the exceptions, and most of the sixteenth-century materials were published in one arbitrarily chosen periodical. In the case of the cossack documents it is sometimes even unclear what the original language was. Listed here are only those collections of documents containing material directly relevant to this work. Some of the listed collections are filled with relevant material; others may contain one stray relevant letter. Some are scholarly periodicals, which publish both original and secondary materials. The reader should understand, then, that this part of the bibliography provides no guide for further study in this area. It is included merely to make it easier to find the documents that support the conclusions of this study.

Acta Historica Res Gestas Poloniae Illustrantia 1507–1795 (Cracow: Akademija Umiejetności, Komisya Historyczna, 1878–1909. 13 vols.

Akty Istoricheskie 1334–1700 (St. Petersburg: Arkheograficheskaya Komissia, 1841–1842). 5 vols. plus 12-vol. supplement.

Akty Otnosiashchiesia k Istorii Yuzhnoi i Zapadnoi Rossii (St. Petersburg: Arkheograficheskaya Komissia, 1865). 15 vols.

Akty, Otnosiashchiesia k Istorii Zapadnoi Rossii (St. Petersburg: Arkheograficheskaya Komissia, 1846–1853). 5 vols.

Arkheograficheskii Sbornik Dokumentov Severo-Zapadnovo Rusi (Vilna: Vilenskii Uchebnyi Okrug, 1905). 14 vols.

Arkhiv Yugo-Zapadnoi Rossii (Kiev: Komissia dlia Razbora Drevnikh Aktov, 1859–1914). Periodical.

Barvinsky, Evhen, "Prychynky do Istorii Znosyn Tsesaria Rudolfa II i Papa Klementa VIII z Kozakamy 1593-94," in *Zapysky*, Naukove Tovarystvo Imeni Shevchenka, (10) (1896).

Broel–Plater, Wlodzimierz Stanisław de, ed., *Zbiór Pamiętnikow do Dziejów Polskich* (Warsaw: 1858–1859). 4 vols.

Chtenia v Imperatorskom Obshchestve Istorii i Drevnostei Rossiiskikh pri Moskovskom Universitete (Moscow, 1815–1888). Periodical.

Chtenia v Istoricheskom Obshchestve Nestora Letopistsa (Kiev: 1879 ff.). Periodical.

Constitucie, Státutá i Przywileie ná Wálnych Seymiech Koron. 1550-1609. (Cracow: 1603–1609).

Dnevnik Liublinskavo Seima 1569 Goda (St. Petersburg: Arkheograficheskaya Komissia, 1869).

Documenta Pontificum Romanorum Historiam Ucrainae Illustrantia, ed. Fr. I. Nazarko (Rome, 1953-54), 2 V. Vol. I: 1075-1700.

Dokumenty Obiasniaiushchie Istoriu Zapadno-Russkavo Kraya i evo Otnoshenia k Rossii i k Polshe (St. Petersburg: Arkheograficheskaya Komissia, 1865).

Dyaryusze i Akta Sejmowe, various years including especially 1548, 1553, 1570, 1585, 1587, 1591-92, and 1597, in *Scriptores Rerum Polonicarum,* various volumes.

Hrushevsky, Mykhailo, ed., "Materialy do Istorii Kozatskykh Rukhiv 1590-kh rr.," in *Zapysky,* Naukove Tovarystvo Imeni Shevchenka, vol. 31 (1899).

Inventarz Nowy Praw, Statutow, Konstytucyi Koronnych, y W. X. Litew: Znayduiących się w Sześciu Tomach Voluminis Legum, ed. Zeglicki (Warsaw: Piarum Scholarum, 1754). Covers the years 1550–1683.

Kamanin, Ivan M., ed., "Materialy po Istorii Kozatskovo Zemlevladenia, 1494-1668," *Chtenia v Obshchestve Nestora Letopistsa* 8 (1894), pt. 3, pp. 3–28.

Kievskaya Starina, Ezhemesiachnyi Istoricheskii Zhurnal (Kiev, 1882–1907). Periodical.

Kulish, Panteleimon Alexandrovich, *Materialy dlia Istorii Vozsoedinenia Rusi* (Moscow: 1877).

Lashkov, F., ed., *Pamiatniki Diplomaticheskikh Snoshenii Krymskavo Khanstva s Moskovskim Gosudarstvom v XVI i XVII vv.* (Simferopol: 1891).

"Litovskii Statut, 1566," in *Vremennik, Imperatorskoe Obshchestvo Istorii i Drevnostei Rossiiskikh pri Moskovskom Universitete* (1855), bk. 23.

"Litovskii Statut, 1588," in ibid. (1854), bk. 19.

Malinovskii, A. F., ed. and trans., "Istoricheskoe i Diplomaticheskoe Sobranie Del . . . Kryma," in *Zapiski Odesskavo Obshchestva Istorii i Drevnostei*, 5, (1863).

Niemcewicz, J. U., *Zbiór Pamiętnikow Historycznych o Dawnej Polszcze*, ed. Jan Bobrowicz (Lipsk, 1838–1840). 5 vols.

Nikolaichik, F. D., ed., "Materialy po Istorii Zemlevladanie Kniazei Vishnevetskikh v Levoberezhnoi Ukraine," in *Chtenia v Obshchestve Nestora Letopistsa*, q.v., 14 (1900), pt. 3, pp. 84–90.

Pamiatniki (Kiev: Komissia dlia Razbora Drevnikh Aktov, 1898). 3 vols.

Pamiatniki (Kiev: Vremennaya Komissia dlia Razbora Drevnikh Aktov, 1845–1856). 4 vols.

Pamiatniki Diplomatycheskykh Snoshenii Drevnei Rossii s Derzhavami Inostrannymi (St. Petersburg: 1852), vol. 1.

Prawa Konstytucye y Przywileie; Krolestwá Polskiego, y Wielkiego Xięstwa Litewskiego, y wszystkich Prowincyi należacych: ná Wálnych Seymiech Koronnych (Warsaw: Piarum Scholarum, 1733), Vol. 2, covering 1588–1609.

Russkaya Istoricheskaya Biblioteka (St. Petersburg: Arkheograficheskaya Komissia, 1872–1827). Periodical.

Sacrum Poloniae Millenium. Rozprawy-Szkice-Materialy Historyczne (Rome: 1954 ff.). Periodical.

Sbornik (St. Petersburg: Imperatorskoe Russkoe Istoricheskoe Obshchestvo). Periodical.

Sbornik Letopisei, Otnosiashchikhsia k Istorii Yuzhnoi i Zapadnoi Rusi (Kiev: Komissia dlia Razbora Drevnikh Aktov, Sostoiashchei pri Kievskom, Podolskom i Volynskom General-Gubernatore, 1888).

Scriptores Rerum Polonicarum (Cracow: Komisya Historyczna, Akademija Umiejętności). Periodical.

Sobranie Gosudarstvennykh i Chastnykh Aktov Kasaiushchikhsia Istorii Litvy i Soedinennykh s nei Vladenii (Vilna: Vilenskaya Arkheologicheskaya Komissia, 1858).

Soderzhanie Aktov o Kozakakh 1500–1648, Part 3, vol. 1 of *Arkhiv Yugo-Zapadnoi Rossii*, q.v.

Sotsialna Borotba v Misti Lvovi v XVI-XVII st.: Zbirnyk Dokumentiv (Lvov: Lvov University, 1961).

Sprawy Wojenne Króla Stefana Batorego, vol. 1. of *Acta Historica Res Gestas Poloniae Illustrantia*, ed. X. I. Polkowski (Cracow: 1887).

Tappe, E. D., ed., *Documents concerning Rumanian History (1427-1601)* (The Hague: Mouton & Co., 1964).

Tyszkiewicz, Le Comte Michel, ed., *Documents Historique sur l'Ukraine et ses Relations Avec la Pologne, la Russie et la Suede (1569-1761)* (Lausanne: 1919).

Zapysky (Lvov: Naukove Tovarystvo Imeny Shevchenka). Periodical.

Zherela do Istorii Ukrainy-Rusy (Lvov: Naukove Tovarystvo Imeni Shevchenka, 1895-1919).

Żródła Dźiejowe. (Warsaw: Komisja Historyczna, Towarzystwo Naukowe, 1876-   ).

Secondary Works

Allen, W.E.D., *Problems of Turkish Power in the Sixteenth Century* (London: Central Asian Research Centre, 1963).

———, *The Ukraine: A History* (New York: Russell & Russell, 1963).

Anderson, Perry, *Lineages of the Absolutist State* (London: New Left Books, 1974).

———, *Passages from Antiquity to Feudalism* (London: New Left Books, 1974).

Antonovych, V. B., *Besidy pro Chasy Kozatski na Ukraini* (Chernivtsi, 1897).

———, "K Istorii Vozstania Nalivaika", *Kievskaya Starina*, #55, sec. 2 (1896): 2–5.

———, "O Proiskhozhdenii Shliakhetskikh Rodov v Yugo-Zapadnoi Rossii," introd. to pt. 4, vol. 1, *Arkhiv Yugo-Zapadnoi Rossii*, 1867.

———, *Tvory* (Kiev: Vseukrainska Akademia Nauk, Sotsialno-Ekonomichnyi Viddil, 1932).

Apanovych, O.M., "Natsionalno-vyzvolni viiny v epokhu feodalizmu," *Ukrainskyi Istorychnyi Zhurnal*, #12 (1965).

———, "Peredumovy ta Naslidky Likvidatsii Zaporizkoi Sichi," *Ukrainskyi Istorychnyi Zhurnal*, #9 (1970).

Arnold, Stanislaw, and Marian Żychowski, *Outline History of Poland* (Warsaw: Polonia Pub., 1962).

Aston, Trevor, ed., *Crisis in Europe 1560–1660* (London: Routledge & Kegan Paul, 1965).

Backus, O.P., *Motives of West Russian Nobles in Deserting Lithuania for Moscow, 1377–1514* (Lawrence: Univ. of Kansas, 1957).

Bahaliy, D.I., ed., *Materialy dlia Istorii Kolonizatsii i Byta Stepnoi Okrainy Moskovskavo Gosudarstva (Kharkovskoi i Otchasti Kurskoi i Voronezhskoi Gub.) v XVI-XVIII Stoletii*. Vols. 1-2 of *Sbornik* (Kharkov: Istoriko-Filologicheskavo Obshchestva Kharkovskavo Univ., 1886-90).

———, *Narys Istorii Ukrainy na Sotsialno-Ekonomichnomu Grunti* (Kharkov, 1928).

———, "Ocherki iz Istorii Kolonizatsii Stepnoi Okrainy Moskovskavo Gosundarstva," *Chtenia v Imperatorskom Obshchestve Istorii i Drev-*

nostei Rossiiskikh pri Moskovskom Universitete, ##2,4 (1886; ##1,3 (1887).

Bantysh-Kamensky, D.N., Istoria Maloi Rossii, 4th ed., 3 pts. (Kiev: 1903).

Baranovich, A.I. (or O.I.), Magnatskoe Khoziaistvo na Yuge Volyni v XVIII v. (Moscow: Akademia Nauk SSSR, 1955).

————, "Naselenie Predstepnoi Ukrainy v XVI v.," Istoricheskie Zapiski (Moscow: Akademia Nauk SSSR, Institut Istorii), #32 (1950).

————, Ukraina Nakanune Osvoboditelnoi Voiny Serediny XVII v. (Moscow: Akademia Nauk SSSR, 1959).

————, Zaliudnennia Volinskoho Voevodstva v Pershii Polovyni XVII St. (Kiev: Vseukrainska Akademia Nauk, 1930).

Baranowski, Bohdan, Chłop Polski w Walce z Tatarami (Warsaw: Ludowa Spółdzielnia, 1952).

————, Najazdy Ludów Stepowych (Warsaw: 1947).

————, Położenie i walka klasowa chłopów w królewszczyznach województwa łęczyckiego w XVI-XVIII w. (Warsaw: Książka: Wiedza, 1956).

————, Powstania Chłopskie na Ziemiach Dawnej Rzeczypospolitej (Warsaw: Ministerstwo Obrony Narodowej, 1952).

Baron, Salo Wittmayer, A Social and Religious History of the Jews, 16 vols. (New York: Columbia Univ. Press, 1952).

Bartl, Peter, "Der Kosakenstaat und das Osmanische Reich im 17 und in der Ersten Haelfte des 18 Jahrhunderts," Südostforschungen, (1974) 33: 166–94.

Barvinsky, Evhen, "Prychynky do Istorii Znosyn Tsesaria Rudolfa II i Papa Klementa VIII z Kozakamy 1593-94," Zapysky, 10 (Naukove Tovarystvo Imeni Shevchenka: 1896).

Batiushkov, P.N., Podolia, Istoricheskoe Opisanie (St. Petersburg: 1891).

————, Volyn, Istoricheskie Sudby Yugo-Zapadnavo Kraya (St. Petersburg: 1888).

Bazhan, M.P., et al., eds., Soviet Ukraine (Kiev: Academy of Sciences of the Ukrainian SSR, 1969).

Beliaev, D.Ch.I., "O Storozhevoi, Stanichnoi i Polevoi Sluzhbe na Polskoi Ukraine Moskovskavo Gosudarstva do Tsaria Alekseia Mikhailovicha," Chtenia v Imperatorskom Obshchestve Istorii i Drevnostei Rossiiskikh pri Moskovskom Universitete, #4 (1846).

Białkowski, Leon, Podole w XVI Wieku, Rysy Spoleczne i Gospodarcze (Warsaw: 1920).

Blok, Antoine, "The Peasant and the Brigand: Social Banditry Reconsidered," Comparative Studies in Society and History, 14 (Sept. 1972).

Blum, Jerome, "The Rise of Serfdom in Eastern Europe," American Historical Review, 62 (1957).

Bodnov, Vasili, Pravoslavnaya Tserkov v Polshe i Litve (Ekaterinoslav: 1908).

Bogucka, Maria, "Towns in Poland and the Reformation," Acta Poloniae Historica, 40 (1979).

Bohomolec, Franciszek, Życie Jana Zamoyskiego, vol. 21 of Wybór Pisarzów Polskich, ed. Mostowski (Warsaw: 1805).

Boiko, I.D. "Do Pytannia pro Derzhavnist Ukrainskoho Narodu v Period Feodalizmu," *Ukrainskyi Istorychnyi Zhurnal,* #8 (1968).

———, *Selianstvo Ukrainy v Druhii Polovyni XVI-Pershii Polovyni XVII St.* (Kiev: Akademia Nauk Ukrainskoi RSR, 1963).

———, "Shche raz pro kharakter natsionalno–vyzvolnykh voien v epokhu feodalizmu," *Ukrainskyi Istorychnyi Zhurnal,* #2, 1965.

Boratyński, Ludwik, "Kozacy i Watykan," *Przegląd Polski* (Cracow), #484, 162, (1906).

Borschak, Elie, *La Légende Historique de l'Ukraine* (Paris: Institut d'Études Slaves, 1949).

———, *L'Ukraine dans la Littérature de l'Europe Occidentale* (Dijon: 1935).

Brenner, Robert, "Agrarian Class Structure and Economic Development in Pre-Industrial Europe," *Past and Present,* #70 (Feb. 1976).

Bykov, N.P., *Kniazia Ostrozhskie i Volyn* (Petrograd: 1915).

Chirot, Daniel, *Social Change in a Peripheral Society: The Creation of a Balkan Colony* (New York: Academic Press, 1976).

Chodynicki, K., *Kościół Prawoslawny a Rzecz Pospolita Polska, 1370-1632* (Warsaw: 1934).

Chowaniec, Czesław, "Sprawa Solonicka z 1596 r. (Przyczynek do Genezy Problemu Kozackiego Rz. P.)," *Teki Historyczne* (London: Polskie Towarzystwo Historyczne w Wielkiej Brytanii), 7 (1955).

Chubaty, Mykola, "The Ukrainian and Russian Conceptions of the History of Eastern Europe," *Proceedings: Naukove Tovarystvo Imeni Shevchenka,* 1 (1952), pp. 10-25.

Clawson, Mary Ann, "Early Modern Fraternalism and the Patriarchal Family," *Feminist Studies,* 6, #2 (Summer 1980).

Cohen, Israel, *History of the Jews in Vilna* (Philadelphia: Jewish Publication Society of America, 1943).

Collins, L.J.D., "The Military Organization and Tactics of the Crimean Tatars during the Sixteenth and Seventeenth Centuries," *War, Technology and Society in the Middle East,* ed. V.J. Parry and M.E. Yapp (London: Oxford, 1975).

Coulbourn, Rushton, ed., *Feudalism in History* (Princeton, N.J.: Princeton Univ. Press, 1956).

Czarnowski, Jan Nepomucen, *Ukraina i Zaporoże czyli Historya Kozaków od Pojawienia sie ich w Dziejach, do Czasu Ostatecznego Przyłaczenia do Rossyi Według Najlepszych Źródel Napisana,* 2 vols. (Warsaw, 1854).

Des Cosaques, ou Détails Historiques sur Les Moeurs, Coutumes, Vêtemens, Armes; et sur la Manière dont ce Peuple fait la Guerre, trans. L.-T. Karr (Paris: 1814).

Dobrowolska, Wanda *Książęta Zbarascy w Walce z Hetmanem Żołkiewskim* (Cracow: 1930).

———, *Młodość Jerzego i Krzysztofa Zbaraskich. Z wstępem o rodzie Zbaraskich i życiorysem Janusza Zbaraskiego* (Cracow: 1926).

Domanytsky, Vasyl, "Kozachchyna na Perelomi XVI-XVII Stolit (1591–1603)," *Zapysky,* 60–64 (Naukove Tovarystvo Imeni Shevchenka, 1904).

————, "Prychynok do Istorii Nalivaika," *Zapysky*, 40 (Naukove Tovarystvo Imeni Shevchenka, 1901).

Doroshenko, Dmytro, *History of the Ukraine*, trans. and abridged Chikalenko-Keller, ed. and introd. G.W. Simpson (Alberta, Canada: 1939).

————, *Pravoslavna Tserkva v Mynulomu i Suchasnomu Zhytti Ukrainskoho Narodu* (Berlin: 1940).

————, *A Survey of Ukrainian Historiography*. Special issue of *Annals; Ukrainian Academy of Arts and Sciences in the U.S.*, trans. from Ukrainian, 1st ed. 1923 (New York, 1957).

Dovnar-Zapolsky, M.V., "Ukrainskia Starostva v Pervoi Polovine XVI v.," introd. to pt. 8, vol. 5, *Arkhiv Yugo-Zapadnoi Rossii* (Kiev: 1907).

Dubnow, S.M., *History of the Jews in Russia and Poland*, trans. I. Friedlaender, 3 vols. (Philadelphia: Jewish Publication Society of America, 1916).

Dvornik, Frances, *The Slavs in European History and Civilization* (New Brunswick, N.J.: Rutgers Univ. Press, 1962).

Diadichenko, V.A., et al., *Development of Historical Science in the Ukrainian S.S.R.* (Kiev: Institute of History, Academy of Sciences, Ukrainian S.S.R, 1970).

Efimenko, A. Ya. (Stavrovskaya), *Istoria Ukrainskavo Naroda*, 2 vols. (St. Petersburg: 1906).

————, *Ocherki Istorii Pravoberezhnoi Ukrainy* (Kiev: 1895). Originally published in *Kievskaya Starina*, ##6, 8–11 (1894); ##4–5 (1895).

————, *Yuzhnaya Rus: Ocherki, Izsledovania i Zametki Alexandry Efimenka* (St. Petersburg: Obshchestvo Imeny Shevchenka, 1905).

Evarnitsky, D.I., *Istoria Zaporozhskikh Kozakov*, 3 vols. (St. Petersburg: 1892–97).

————, *Ocherki po Istorii Zaporozhskikh Kozakov i Novorossiiskavo Kraya* (St. Petersburg: 1889).

————, *Zaporozhe v Ostatkakh Stariny i Predaniakh Naroda* (St. Petersburg: 1888).

Franko, Ivan, "Nalyvajko v Midjanim Byci," *Naukovyi Zbirnik Prysviashenyi Prof. M. Hrushevskomu* (Lvov: 1906).

Freischyn-Chirovsky, Nicholas L., *Old Ukraine: Its Socio-Economic History prior to 1781* (Madison, N.J.: 1963).

Friedlaender, Israel, *The Jews of Russia and Poland* (New York: 1915).

Gerhard, Dietrich, "The Frontier in Comparative View," *Comparative Studies in Society and History*, 1 (1959).

Gieysztor, Aleksander, et al., *History of Poland*. (Warsaw: 1969).

Górski, Konstanty Marian, *Historya Artyleryi Polskiej*, ed. T. Korzon (Warsaw: 1902).

————, *Historya Piechoty Polskiej* (Cracow: 1893).

Halecki, Oscar, *Borderlands of Western Civilization: A History of East Central Europe* (New York: 1952).

————, *From Florence to Brest (1439–1596)*, Sacrum Poloniae Millennium (Rome), 5 (1958).

————, "Jeszcze o Nowych Źródłach do Dziejów Unii Brzeskiej," *Sacrum Poloniae Millennium* (Rome), 4 (1957).

Hammer-Purgstall, Joseph von, *Histoire de L'Empire Ottoman depuis son Origine jusqu'a nos Jours*, vol. 7, trans. J.-J. Hellert (Paris: 1837).

Hilton, Rodney H., "Peasant Society, Peasant Movements and Feudalism in Medieval Europe," in *Rural Protest: Peasant Movements and Social Change*, ed. Henry A. Landsberger (New York: International Institute for Labour Studies, 1973).

Hobsbawm, Eric J., *Primitive Rebels: Studies in Archaic Forms of Social Movement in the 19th and 20th Centuries* (New York: Norton, 1965).

————, *Bandits*, (New York: Dell, 1969).

Holobutsky, V.O. *Chernomorskoe Kazachestvo* (Kiev, 1956).

————, *Zaporizka Sich v Ostanni Chasy Svoho Isnuvannia 1734-75* (Kiev, 1961).

————, *Zaporozhskoe Kazachestvo* (Kiev: 1957).

Horak, Stephan M., "Periodization and Terminology of the History of Eastern Slavs: Observations and Analyses," *Slavic Review*, 31, #4 (Dec. 1972).

————, "Problems of Periodization and Terminology in Ukrainian Historiography," *Ukrainian Review*, 22, #3 (1976).

————, "Ukrainian Historiography 1953–1963," *Slavic Review*, 24, #2 (June 1965).

Horn, Maurycy, "Żydowski Ruch Osadniczy w Miastach Rusi Czerwonej do 1648 R.," *Biuletyn Żydowskiego Instytutu Historycznego w Polsce*, 90 (1974).

Hoszowski, Stanisław, "The Polish Baltic Trade in the 15th–18th Centuries," in *Poland at the XIth International Congress of Historical Sciences in Stockholm* (Warsaw: 1960).

————, "The Revolution of Prices in Poland in the 16th and 17th Centuries," *Acta Poloniae Historica*, 2 (1959).

Hrushevsky, Mykhailo, *Barskoe Starostvo* (Kiev, 1894).

————, *A History of Ukraine*, ed. O.J. Frederiksen (New Haven: Yale Univ. Press, 2d ed., 10 vols. 1941).

————, *Istoria Ukrainskavo Kozachestva*, 2 vols. (Kiev, 1913–14).

————, *Istoria Ukrainy-Rusy*, 2d ed., 10 vols. (New York, 1954–58).

————, *Kulturno-Natsionalnyi Rukh na Ukraini v XVI-XVII v.*, 2d ed. (Vienna, 1920).

————, "Zvichaina Skhema 'Russkoi' Istorii i Sprava Ratsionalnovo Ukladu Istorii Skhidnovo Slovianstva," *Stati po Slovianovedeniu*, 1 (St. Petersburg: Imperatorskaya Akademia Nauk, 1904).

Inglot, Stefan, ed., *Historia Chłopów Polskich* (Częstochowa, 1970).

Iorga, Nicolae, *A History of Roumania*, trans. Joseph McCabe (London, 1925).

Ivanishev, N.D., *O Drevnikh Selskikh Obshchinakh v Yugo-Zapadnoi Rossii* (Kiev: Vremennaya Komissia dlia Razbora Drevnikh Aktov, 1863).

Jabłonowski, Aleksander, *Historya Rusi Południowej do Upadku Rzeczy Pospolitej Polskiej* (Cracow: 1912).

————, "Trechtymirow," *Kwartalnik Historyczny*, 18 (1904).

————, "Ukraina," in *Źródła Dziejowe*, (D), q.v., 22 (1897).

"Jewrei-Kozacki w Naczale XVII Wieka," *Kievskaya Starina*, 1895, V.

Kamanin, Ivan, "Eshche o Drevnosti Bratstva i Shkoly v Kieve," *Chtenia v Istoricheskom Obshchestve Nestora Letopistsa*, 9, pt. 2 (1895).

———, "K Voprosu o Kozachestve do Bogdana Khmelnitskavo," *Chtenia v Istoricheskom Obshchestve Nestora Letopistsa*, 8, pt. 2, (1894). pp. 57-115.

Kamen, Henry, *The Iron Century* (London: Weidenfeld & Nicolson, 1971).

Kamiński, Andrzej, "Neo-Serfdom in Poland-Lithuania," *Slavic Review*, 34, #2 (June 1975).

Keep, J.L.H., "Bandits and the Law in Muscovy," *Slavonic and East European Review*, 35, #84 (1956).

Kerner, Robert Joseph, *The Urge to the Sea: The Course of Russian History* (Berkeley: Univ. of California Press, 1942).

Kliuchevsky, V.O. *Kurs Russkoi Istorii*, 5 vols. (Moscow, 1904–21).

Kocowski, Bronislaw, *Wyprawa Tatarów na Węgry Przez Polskį w 1594 r.* (Lublin: Towarzystwō Naukowe Katolickiego Uniwersytetu Lubelskiego, 1948).

Komarenko, N.V., "Utvorennia ta dialnist istorychnykh kafedr na Ukraini v 20-kh rokakh," *Istoriohrafichni Doslidzhennia v Ukrainskii RSR* (Kiev, 1970), Naukova Dumka, vol. 4.

Kortepeter, C.M., "Gazi Giray II, Khan of the Crimea, and Ottoman Policy in Eastern Europe and the Caucasus, 1588–94," *Slavonic and East European Review*, 44, #102 (Jan. 1966), pp. 139–67.

———, *Ottoman Imperialism during the Reformation: Europe and the Causasus* 2 (New York: New York Univ. Press, 1972).

Kostomarov, N.I., *Books of Genesis of the Ukrainian People*, commentary B. Yanivskyi. Mimeographed series, #60. (New York: Research Program on the USSR, 1954).

———, *Istoricheskie Monografii i Izsledovania*, 2d ed., 21 vols. D.E. Kozhanchikov (St. Petersburg: Imperatorskaya Akademia Nauk, 1867 ff.).

Krasinski, Count Henry, *The Cossacks of the Ukraine, Comprising Biographical Notices of the Most Celebrated Cossack Chiefs or Attamas [sic] . . . and a Description of the Ukraine . . .* (London, 1848).

———, *Polish Aristocracy, and Titles* (London, 1843).

Krupnytsky, Borys, "Trends in Modern Ukrainian Historiography," *Ukrainian Quarterly*, 6, #4 (1950).

Krypiakevych, I.P., "Do pytannia pro natsionalnu samosvidomist ukrainskoho narodu v kinets XVI-ho pochatok XVIII st.," *Ukrainskyi Istorychnyi Zhurnal*, #2 (1965):82–84.

———, "Sotsialno-politychni pohliady Bohdana Khmelnytskoho," *Ukrainskyi Istorychnyi Zhurnal*, #1 (1957).

Kula, Witold, *An Economic Theory of the Feudal System: Towards a Model of the Polish Economy 1500-1800*, trans. Lawrence Garner, (London: New Left Books, 1976; orig. Polish ed. 1962).

Kulish, P.A., *Istoria Vozsoedinenia Rusi*, 3 vols. (St. Petersburg, 1874; Moscow, 1877).

———, *Materialy dlia Istorii Vozsoedinenia Rusi;* vol. 4 of *Istoria Vozsoedinenia Rusi* (Moscow, 1877).

———, *Otpadenie Malorossii ot Polshi (1340-1654),* 3 vols. (Moscow, 1888–89).

Kuntze, Edouard, "Les Rapports de la Pologne avec le Saint-Siége à l'Epoque d'Etienne Batory," in *Etienna Bátory, Roi de Pologne, Prince de Transylvanie* (Cracow: Polska Akademia Umiejętności & Académie des Sciences Hongroises, 1935).

La Bizardière, Michael David de, *Historie des Dietes de la Pologne pour les Elections des Rois* (Amsterdam, 1697).

Lappo, I.I., *Velikoe Kniazhestvo Litovskoe,* 2 vols. (St. Petersburg, 1901; Yurev, 1911).

Lazarevsky, A.M., "Eremii Vishnevetsky," *Chtenia v Istoricheskom Obshchestve Nestora Letopistsa,* 11, 1 (1896).

———, *Opisanie Staroi Malorossii,* (Kiev, 1888–1902).

Lempicki, Stanisław, "Jan Zamoyski, Statesman, Soldier, Educator, 1542-1605," in *Great Men and Women of Poland,* ed. S.P. Mizwa (New York, 1942).

Lesur, Charles Louis, *Historie des Kosaques* (Paris, 1813).

Lewicki, Kazimierz, *Książę Konstanty Ostrogski a Unja Brzeska, 1596 r.* (Lvov: Tovarzystwo Naukowe, 1933).

Liaskoronskii, V., *Gilom Levasser-de-Boplan i evo Istoriko-Geograficheskie Trudy Otnositelno Yuzhnoi Rossii* (Kiev, 1901).

Linage de Vauciennes, P., *L'Origine Veritable du Soulevement des Cosaques Contre La Pologne* (Paris, 1674; 1st ed. 1673).

Lipiński, Wacław, ed., *Z Dziejów Ukrainy: Księga Pamiątkowa Kijowa* (Cracow, 1912).

———, *Szlachta na Ukrainie i Udział jej w Życiu Narodu Ukraińskiego na Tle jego Dziejów* (Cracow, 1909).

Liubavich, N., untitled article on cossack reporting on Tatar threats to Polish borders, in *Kievskaya Starina,* #43 (1893).

Liubavsky, M.K. *Litovsko-Russkii Seim* (Moscow: Imperatorskoe Obshchestvo Istorii i Drevnostei Rossiiskikh pri Moskovskom Universitete, 1900).

———, "Nachalnaya Istoria Malorusskovo Kazachestva," *Zhurnal Ministerstva Narodnovo Prosveshchenia* (July 1895).

———, *Ocherk Istorii Litovsko-Russkavo Gosudarstva do Liublinskoi Unii Vkliuchitelno* (Moscow, 1910).

Longworth, Philip, *The Cossacks* (New York: Holt, Rinehart & Winston, 1969).

Łowmianski, Henryk, "The Russian Peasantry," *Past and Present,* #26 (Nov. 1963).

Luckyj, George, S.N., *Between Gogol' and Ševčenko: Polarity in the Literary Ukraine: 1798–1847* (Munich: Harvard Series in Ukrainian Studies, 1971).

Lyashchenko, Peter I., *History of the National Economy of Russia,* trans.

L.M. Herman (New York: Macmillan, 1949).

Lybyer, Albert Howe, *The Government of the Ottoman Empire in the time of Suleiman the Magnificent* (Cambridge: Harvard Univ. Press, 1913).

McNeill, William H., *Europe's Steppe Frontier 1500–1800* (Chicago: Univ. of Chicago Press, 1964).

Mączak, Antoni, "The Social Distribution of Landed Property in Poland from the Sixteenth to the Eighteenth Century," *Third International Conference of Economic History* (Paris, 1968).

Maksimovich, A., "Istoricheskie Pisma o Kozakakh Zaporozhskikh," *Sobranie Sochinenii*, vol. 1 (Kiev, 1876–80).

————, "O Mnimon Zapustenii Ukrainy v Nashestvie Batya," in *Sobranie Sochinenii*, ibid.

————, "Pisma o Kniaziakh Ostrozhskikh (K Grafine A.D. Bludovoi)," ibid.

Małowist, Marian, "Le commerce de la Baltique et le probleme des luttes sociales en Pologne aux XVᵉ et XVIᵉ siècles," *La Pologne au Xᵉ Congrés International des Sciences Historiques a Rome* (Warsaw, 1955).

————, "The Economic and Social Development of the Baltic Countries from the Fifteenth to the Seventeenth Centuries," *Economic History Review*, 2d ser., vol. 12, (1959).

————, "Poland, Russia and Western Trade in the 15th and 16th Centuries," *Past and Present*, #13 (1958).

————, "Problem Genezy Podziału Gospodarczego Europe w XV-XVII w.," *Historia Polski do Połowy XV Wieku*, vol. 2 of *VIII Powszechny Zjazd Historyków Polskich* (Warsaw: 1958).

————, "The Problem of the Inequality of Economic Development in Europe in the Late Middle Ages," *Economic History Review*, 2d ser., vol. 19, #1 (1966).

Marx, Francis, *The Serf and the Cossack: A Sketch of the Condition of the Russian People* (London, 1854).

Medynsky, E.N., *Bratskie Shkoly Ukrainy i Belorussii v XVI-XVII vv. i ikh Rol v Vossoedinenii Ukrainy s Rossiei* (Moscow: Akademia Pedagog. Nauk RSFSR, 1954).

Mérilys, Jean, *Les Grand Adventuriers de L'Est Européen* (Paris, 1943).

Miakotin, V., "La Fixation des Paysans Ukrainiens a la glebe aux XVIIᵐᵉ et XVIIIᵐᵉ Siècles," *Le Monde Slave*, 10–11 (1932).

Milner, Rev. Thos., *The Crimea, Its Ancient and Modern History: The Khans, the Sultans and the Czars, with Notices of Its Scenery and Population* (London, 1855).

Mirtchuk, J., "The Ukrainian Uniat Church," in *Slavonic Review*, 10, #29 (1931).

Motyl, Alexander J., *The Turn to the Right: The Ideological Origins and Development of Ukrainian Nationalism 1919–1929.* (Boulder: East European Monographs, 1980).

Müller, Gerhard Friedrich, "Istoricheskia Sochinenia o Malorossii i Malorossianakh," *Chtenia v Imperatorskom Obshchestve Istorii i Drevnostei Rossiiskikh pri Moskovskom Universitete*, ##3–4 (1846); #6 (1847).

————, "O Nachale i Proiskhozhdenii Kozakov," *Sochinenia k Polze i Uveseleniu Sluzhashchia*, 4 (St. Petersburg, 1760).

Myhul, I.M., "Politics and History in the Soviet Ukraine: A Study of Soviet Ukrainian Historiography: 1956-1970," unpub. (Copy in Widener Library, Harvard Univ.)

Myshetsky, Prince S., "Istoria o Kozakakh Zaporozhskikh," in *Zapiski Odesskovo Obshchestva Istorii i Drevnostei* (Odessa, 1851).

Myshko, D.I., *Severyn Nalyvaiko* (Kiev, 1962).

————, *Sotsialno-Ekonomichni Umovy Formuvannia Ukrainskoi Narodnosti* (Kiev: Akademia Nauk Ukrainskoi RSR, 1963).

————, *Ukrainsko-Rosiiski Zviazky v XIV-XVI St.* (Kiev: Akademia Nauk Ukrainskoi RSR, 1959).

Nahayewski, Rev. Isidore, *History of Ukraine* (Philadelphia: "Providence" Association of Ukrainian Catholics in America, 1962).

Nikolaichik, F.D., "Pervye Kozatskia Dvizhenia v Rechi Pospolitoi," *Kievskaya Starina*, ##3, 4 (1884).

Novitsky, Ivan P., "Kniazia Ruzhinskie," *Kievskaya Starina*, #2 (1882).

————, "Ocherki Istorii Krestianskavo Soslovia v. Yugo-Zapadnoi Rossii v XV-XVIII v.," in *Arkhiv Yugo-Zapadnoi Rossii*, pt. 6, vol. 1.

Nowak, Frank, "The Foreign Policy of Poland under King Stephen Batory," Ph.D. diss., Harvard Univ., Cambridge, Mass., 1924.

O'Brien, C. Bickford, *Muscovy and the Ukraine: From the Pereiaslav Agreement to the Truce of Andrusovo, 1654–1667* (Berkeley: Univ. of California Publications in History), vol. 74.

Ochmański, Jerzy, "La grande réforme agraire en Lituanie et en Ruthénie Blanche au XVIe siècle," *Ergon*, appendix to *Kwartalnik Historyczny Materialnej*, vol. 2 (1960).

Odinets, D. M., *Prisoedinenie Ukrainy k Moskovskomu Gosudarstvu* (Paris, 1936).

————, *Vozniknovenie Russkoi Gosudarstvennosti i Ideia Russkovo Edinstva* (Paris, 1939).

Ohloblyn, Olexander, "Ukrainian Historiography 1917–1956," *Annals; Ukrainian Academy of Arts and Sciences in the U.S.*, 5, 6 (New York, 1957).

Ostrowski, R., *Fragments from the History of Byelorussia (to 1700)* (London: Byelorussian Central Council, 1961).

Otamanovsky, V. D., "Razvitie Gorodskovo Stroya na Ukraine v XIV-XVIII vv. i Magdeburgskoe Pravo," *Voprosi Istorii*, 3 (1958).

Pamiętnik Kijowski: Nakładem Kola Kijowian, ed. Z. Andrzejowski et al. (London, 1959).

Pashuk, A. I., *Sud i Sudochynstvo na Livoberezhnii Ukraini v XVII–XVIII St.* (Lvov: Lvivskyi Derzhavnyi Universytet, 1967).

Pelenski, J., "Soviet Ukrainian Historiography after World War II," *Jahrbucher für Geschichte Osteuropas*, N. F. Bild 12 (1964).

Picheta, V. I., *Agrarnaya Reforma Sigizmunda-Avgusta v Litovsko-Russkom Gosudarstve*, 2nd ed. (Moscow: Akademia Nauk SSSR, 1959).

———, *Belorussia i Litva XV-XVI vv.* (Moscow: Akademia Nauk SSSR, 1961).

Pierling, Paul, S. J., *La Russie et le Saint-Siège, Études Diplomatiques,* 3 vols. (Paris, 1897).

Pissot, Noel-Laurent, *Precis Historique sur les Cosaques, Nation sous la Domination des Russes: Leur Origine, Etablissement et Accroissement; Leur Grandeur et Abaissement; Leur Moeurs et Usages* (Paris, 1812).

Podhorodecki, Leszek, *Sicz Zaporoska* (Warsaw, 1960).

Pokhylevich, D. L., *Krestiane Belorussii i Litvy v XVI-XVII vv.* (Lvov, 1957).

Polonska-Vasylenko, N. D., *Les Relations de l'Ukraine avec les Etats Européens aux Xe-XIIIe siècles.* (Paris, 1967).

———, "The Settlement of the Southern Ukraine (1750–1775)," in *Annals; Ukrainian Academy of Arts and Sciences in the U.S.* (New York; Summer-Fall, 1955).

———, *Two Conceptions of the History of Ukraine and Russia* (London, 1968).

Polska Akademia Nauk, Instytut Historii, *Bibliografia Historii Polski,* vol. 1, ed. Helena Madurowicz-Ubańska et al. (Warsaw, 1965).

———, *Historia Polski,* ed. T. Manteuffl et al. (Warsaw, 1955).

Powidaj, Ludwik, *Kozacy Zaporożcy na Ukrainie* (Lvov: Nakładem Karola Wilda, 1862).

Pritsak, O., "Etymolohia ta zmist nazvy Kozak," *Ukrainskyi Istoryk,* ##3–4 (1965).

Pritsak, O., and Reshetar, J. S., *Kievan Rus' Is Not Identical with Russia!* (Cambridge: Harvard University Ukrainian Studies, 1973).

Prochaska, Antoni, *Hetman Stanisław Żołkiewski* (Warsaw: J. Mianowski, 1927).

Pułaski, Kazimierz, *Szkice i Poszukiwania Historyczne* (Cracow: J. K. Żupanski & K. J. Heumann, 1887).

———, "Wojewodowie Kijowscy w XV-XVI w.," *Przewodnik Naukowy i Literacki,* 2 (1876).

Rawita-Gawroński, Franciszek, *Geneza i Rozwój Idei Kozactwa i Kozaczyzny w XVI Wieku* (Warsaw: J. Czernecki, 1924).

———, *Kozaczyzna Ukrainna w Rzeczypospolitej Polskiej do Końca XVIII-go Wieku* (Warsaw: Gebethner & Wolff, n.d., prob. 1922).

Reddaway, W. F., et al., ed., *The Cambridge History of Poland to 1696* (Cambridge: Cambridge Univ. Press, 1950).

Roberts, Michael, *The Early Vasas, A History of Sweden, 1523–1611* (Cambridge: Cambridge Univ. Press, 1968).

Rolle, Józef (pseud. Dr. Antoni J.), "Semen Naliwajko, Opowiadanie z Końca XVI Stulecia," *Przewodnik Naukowy i Literacki,* 7 (1879).

Rozhdestvensky, S. V., *Sluzhiloe Zemlevladenie v Moskovskom Gosudarstve XVI Veka* (St. Petersburg: V. Demakov, 1897).

Rozhkov, N. A., *Obzor Russkoi Istorii s Sotsiologicheskoi Tochki Zrenia,* pt. 2, vol. 2 (Moscow: I. K. Shamov, 1905).

Rozner, I. G., *Severin Nalivaiko, Rukovoditel Krestiansko Kazatskovo Vosstaniia 1594–1595 gg. na Ukraine* (Moscow, 1961).

Rudnytsky, I. L., "Study of Cossack History," *Slavic Review*, #31 (Dec. 1972).

Savant, Jean, *Les Cosaques* (Paris, 1944).

Sbornik Statei i Materialov po Istorii Yugo-Zapadnoi Rossii, 2 vols. (Kiev: Komissia dlia Razbora Drevnikh Aktov, 1911).

Scherer, Jean Benoit, *Annales de la Petite-Russie, ou Histoire des Cosaques-Saporogues et des Cosaques de l'Ukraine*, 2 vols. (Paris, 1788).

Seeley, Frank Friedeberg, "Russia and the Slave Trade," *Slavonic and East European Review*, 23 #62 (Jan. 1945), pp. 126–36.

Sementovsky, N. M., *Starina Malorossiiskaya, Zaporozhskaya i Donskaya* (St. Petersburg, 1846).

Serczyk, W. A., *Historia Ukrainy* (Warsaw, 1979).

Seton-Watson, Robert William, *A History of the Roumanians from Roman Times to the Completion of Unity* (Cambridge: Cambridge Univ. Press, 1934).

Shcherbakov, V. K., "Krestianskoe Dvizhenie v Belorussii v XVI-XVII vv.," *Istoricheskii Sbornik*, vol. 4 (Moscow: Akademia Nauk SSSR, 1935).

Shevchenko, F. P., "Period Feodalizmu," in *Leninska Teoretychna Spadshchyna v Ukrainskii Radianskii Istoriohrafii*, ed. F. P. Shevchenko et al. (Kiev: Naukova Dumka, 1969).

———, *Politychni ta Ekonomichni Zviazky Ukrainy z Rosiieiu v Seredyni XVIII St.* (Kiev: Akademiia Nauk Ukrainskoi RSR, 1959).

Siarczyński, X. Franciszek, *Obraz Wieku Panowania Zygmunta III . . ., czyli Obraz Stanu, Narodu i Kraju . . .*, 2 vols. (Poznan, 1843).

———, *Obraz Wieku Panowania Zygmunta III . . ., Zawieraiący Opis Osób Żyiących pod jego Panowaniem, Znamienitych . . .*, 2 vols. (Lvov, 1828).

Siemieński, J., "Constitutional Conditions in the Fifteenth and Sixteenth Centuries," *The Cambridge History of Poland to 1696*, ed. W. F. Reddaway et al. (Cambridge: Cambridge Univ. Press, 1950).

Simpson, George W., "The Names 'Rus', 'Russia', 'Ukraine', and Their Historical Background," in *Slavistica* (Winnipeg, Manitoba: Institute of Slavistics of the Ukrainian Free Academy of Sciences), #10 (1951).

Sinor, Denis, *History of Hungary* (London: Allen & Unwin, 1959).

Skocpol, Theda, "Wallerstein's World Capitalist System: A Theoretical and Historical Critique," *American Journal of Sociology*, 82, #5, (March 1977).

Skwarczynski, P., "The Constitution of Poland before the Partitions," *Cambridge History of Poland*, ed. W. F. Reddaway et al., vol. 2 (Cambridge: Cambridge Univ. Press, 1950).

———, "Poland and Lithuania," chap. 12 in *New Cambridge Modern History*, vol. 3, ed. R. B. Wernham (Cambridge: Cambridge Univ. Press, 1968).

———, "The Problem of Feudalism in Poland up to the Beginning of the 16th Century," *Slavonic and East European Review*, 34, #83 (June 1956).

Słownik Geograficzny Królestwa Polskiego i Innych Krajów Słowiańskich, ed. Chlebowski & Walewski (Warsaw, 1880–90).

Smith, R. E. F., *The Enserfment of the Russian Peasantry* (Cambridge: Cambridge Univ. Press, 1968).

Sokolovsky, P. A., *Ekonomicheskii Byt Zemledelcheskavo Naselenia Rossii u Kolonizatsii Yugo-Vostochnykh Stepei Pred Krepostnym Pravom* (St. Petersburg, 1878).

Solovev, S. M., *Istoria Rossii s Drevneishikh Vremen*, 29 vols. (St. Petersburg, 1896).

Śreniowski, Stanisław, *Zbiegostwo Chłopów w Dawnej Polsce* (Warsaw: Spółdzielnia Wydawnicza Ksiazka, 1948).

Stavrianos, L. S., *The Balkans since 1453* (New York: Rinehart, 1958).

Stökl, Gunther, *Die Entstehung des Kosakentums* (Munich: Osteurope-Institut, 1953).

Storozhenko, A. V., "Iz Perepiski Zaporozhia XVI v.," *Chtenia v Istoricheskom Obshchestve Nestora Letopistsa*, 19, pt. 3 (1906).

———, "Jan Orishovsky," *Chtenia v Istoricheskom Obshchestve Nestora Letopistsa*, 11, pt. 1 (1896).

———, *Ocherki Pereyaslavskoi Stariny. Izsledovania, Dokumenty i Zametki* (Kiev: G. L. Frontskevich, 1900).

———, *Stefan Batorii i Dneprovskie Kozaki. Izsledovania, Pamiatniki, Dokumenty i Zametki* (Kiev: G.L. Frontskevich, 1904).

———, *Sbornik Statei i Materialov. . .* , s.v. vol. 1 "Vereshchinsky, Biskup Kievskii (1540–1598)."

Storozhenko, N. V., *Zapadno-Russkie Provintsialnye Seimiki vo Vtoroi Polovine XVII Veka* (Kiev: K.N. Milevsky, 1888).

Stroński, Zdzisław, "Swawola Ukrainna u Schyłku XVI w.," *Kwartalnik Historyczny*, 38 (1924)

Świecki, Tomasz, *Historyczne Pamiątki Znamienitych Rodzin i Osób Dawnej Polski*, 2 vols. (Warsaw, 1858–59).

Szczesniak, Boleslaw, "The Ostrog Estates and the End of the Knights of Malta in the Commonwealth of Poland (1609–1795)," *Études Slaves et Est-Européenes*, vol. 6 (Montreal: Univ. of Montreal)

Tarnawski, Aleksander, *Działalność Gospodarcza Jana Zamoyskiego* (Lvov: Instytut Popierania Polskiej Twórczości Naukowej, 1935).

Tawney, R.H., *The Agrarian Problem in the Sixteenth Century* (London, 1912).

Tazbir, Janusz, *Reformacja a Problem Chłopski w Polsce* (Wrocław: Polska Akademia Nauk, 1953).

Tikhomirov, Mikhail, *Rossia v XVI Stoletii* (Moscow: Akademia Nauk SSSR, 1962).

———, *The Towns of Ancient Rus* (Moscow: Foreign Languages Publishing House, 1959).

Tillett, Lowell, *The Great Friendship: Soviet Historians on the Non-Russian Nationalities* (Chapel Hill: Univ. of North Carolina, 1969).

Titov, Fedor, *Russkaya Pravoslavnaya Tserkov v Polsko-Litovskom Gosudarstve XVII-XVIII vv.*, 3 vols. (Kiev, 1905–16).

Tolstoi, Yuri, *Pervya Sorok Let Snoshenii Mezhdu Rossieiu i Anglieiu 1553–1593* (St. Petersburg, 1875).

Tolybekov, S.E., "O Patriarkhalno-Feodalnykh Otnosheniakh u Kochevykh Narodov," *Voprosy Istorii*, #1 (Jan. 1955).

Tomkiewicz, Władysław, "O Składzie Społecznym i Etnicznym Kozaczyzny Ukrainnej na Przełomie XVI i XVII wieku," *Przegląd Historyczny*, 37 (1948).

Topolski, Jerzy, "La Regression Économique en Pologne du XVIᵉ au XVIIIᵉ Siècle," *Acta Poloniae Historica*, 7 (1962).

Topolsk, J., and Jerzy Wiśniewski, *Lustracje Województwa Podlaskiego 1570 i 1576* (Wroclaw & Warsaw: Polska Akademia Nauk, Instytut Historii, 1959).

Turtsevich, A. O., *Russkie Krestiane pod Vladychestvom Litvy i Polshi* (Vilna: A.G. Syrkin, 1911).

Tymieniecki, Kazimierz, "W Sprawie powstania zaostrzonego poddaństwa w Polsce i Europie Środkowej," *Roczniki Historyczne*, 24 (1958).

Upham, Edward, *History of the Ottoman Empire, from its Establishment, till the year 1829*, vol. 2 (Edinburgh: Constable & Co., 1829).

Urban, Waclaw, *Chłopi Wobec Reformacji w Małopolsce w Drugiej Połowie XVI w.* (Cracow: Polska Akademia Nauk, 1959).

Vakar, Nicholas P., *Belorussia: The Making of a Nation* (Cambridge: Harvard Russian Research Center, 1956).

Vasenko, P., "Zametki k Istorii Sluzhilovo Klassa v Moskovskom Gosudarstve: Atamany Sluzhilye-Pomestnye," *Dela i Dni* (St. Petersburg), 1 (1920).

Vaughan, Dorothy M., *Europe and the Turk: A Pattern of Alliances, 1350–1700* (Liverpool: Liverpool Univ. Press, 1954).

Velychenko, Stefan, "The Origins of the Ukrainian Revolution of 1648," *Journal of Ukrainian Graduate Studies* (Toronto), 1, #1 (Fall 1976).

Vernadsky, George, *Bohdan: Hetman of Ukraine* (New Haven: Yale Univ. Press, 1941).

———, *The Mongols and Russia* (New Haven: Yale Univ. Press, 1953).

———, *Russia at the Dawn of the Modern Age* (New Haven: Yale Univ. Press, 1959).

Vladimirsky-Budanov, M.F., "Krestianskoe Zemlevladenie v Zapadnoi Rossii do Poloviny XVI v.," *Chtenia v Istoricheskom Obshchestve Nestora Letopistsa*, vol. 7, pt. 2 (1893).

———, "Naselenie Yugo-Zapadnoi Rossii ot Poloviny XIII do Poloviny XV Veka," *Arkhiv Yugo-Zapadnoi Rossii*, p. 7, vol. 1.

von Loewe, Karl, "Commerce and Agriculture in Lithuania, 1400–1600," *Economic History Review*, 2d ser., vol. 26, #1 (Feb. 1973).

Wallerstein, Immanuel, *The Modern World-System: Capitalist Agriculture and the Origins of the European World-Economy in the Sixteenth Century* (New York: Academic Press, 1974).

Weinryb, Bernard Dov, *The Jews of Poland: A Social and Economic History of the Jewish Community in Poland from 1100–1800* (Philadelphia: Jewish Publication Society of America, 1973).

Wielewicki, Jan, S.J., Prince, "Dziennik Spraw Domu Zakonnego OO. Jezuitów u ś. Barbary w Krakowie, 1579–1599," *Scriptores Rerum Poloni-*

carum, 7 (1881).

Wójcik, Zbigniew, *Dzikie Pola w Ogniu* (Warsaw, 1960).

Wojskowy Instytut Historyczny, *Zarys Dziejów Wojskowości Polskiej do Roku 1864*, 2 vols. (Warsaw, 1965–66).

Wolf, Eric R., *Peasant Wars of the Twentieth Century* (N.Y.: Harper & Row, 1969).

Wyczański, Andrzej, *Studia nad Folwarkiem Szlacheckim w Polsce w Latach 1500-1580* (Warsaw, 1960).

——, *Studia nad Konsumpcja, Żywności w Polsce w XVI i Pierwszej Polowie XVII w.* (Warsaw, 1969).

——, "Tentative Estimate of Polish Rye Trade in the Sixteenth Century," trans. Jerzy Eysymontt, *Acta Poloniae Historica*, 4 (1961).

Wynar, Lubonyr R., "Birth of Democracy on the Dnieper River: The Zaporozhian Kozakdom in the XVIth Century," *Ukrainian Quarterly*, 33, #1, 2 (1977).

——, ed., *Habsburgs and Zaporozhian Cossacks: The Diary of Erich Lassota von Steblau*, trans. Orest Subtelny (Littleton, Col.: Ukrainian Academic Press, 1975).

——, *Kniaz Dmytro Vyshnevetsky* (Munich, 1964).

——, "Ukrainian-Russian Confrontation in Historiography," *Ukrainian Quarterly*, 30, #1 (1974).

Yakovlev, A.I., *Kholopstvo i Kholopi v Moskovskom Gosudarstve* (Moscow: Akademia Nauk SSSR, 1943).

Yuzefovich, M., "Predislovie," in *Arkhiv Yugo-Zapadnoi Rossii*, p. 4, vol. 1.

Zaklinsky, K., "Znoshenia Tsesaria Rudolfa II z Kozakami i ikh Uchast v Voine Ugorsko-Turetskoi v g. 1594 i 1595," *Sprawozdnik* (Lvov: Akademia Gimnaz., 1881–81).

Zhukovich, P.N., *Seimovaya Borba Pravoslavnavo Zapadnorusskavo Dvorianstva s Tserkovnoi Unii do 1609 g.* (St. Petersburg, 1901).

Zotov, R.M., *Voennaya Istoria Rossiiskavo Gosudarstva*, vol. 1 (St. Petersburg: A. Smirdin, 1839).

Żytkowicz, Leonid, "Grain Yields in Poland, Bohemia, Hungary, and Slovakia in the 16th to 18th Centuries," *Acta Poloniae Historica*, 24 (1971).

——, "The Peasant's Farm and the Landlord's Farm in Poland from the 16th to the Middle of the 18th Century," *Journal of European Economic History*, 1, #1 (Spring 1972).

Index